THE
MOBILIZATION
OF SHAME

The Mobilization of Shame

A WORLD VIEW OF HUMAN RIGHTS

ROBERT F. DRINAN, S.J.

YALE UNIVERSITY PRESS *New Haven & London*

Set in Carter-Cone Galliard type by Keystone Typesetting, Inc.
Printed in the United States of America by R. R. Donnelley &
Sons, Harrisonburg, Virginia.

Library of Congress Cataloging-in-Publication Data
Drinan, Robert F.
The mobilization of shame : a world view of human rights /
Robert F. Drinan.
    p.   cm.
Includes bibliographical references and index.
ISBN 0-300-08825-6 (cloth : alk. paper)
ISBN 0-300-09319-5 (pbk. : alk. paper)
1. Human rights. I. Title.
JC571 .D84 2001
314.4'81—dc21   00-011312

A catalogue record for this book is available from the
British Library.

The paper in this book meets the guidelines for permanence and
durability of the Committee on Production Guidelines for Book
Longevity of the Council on Library Resources.

10   9   8   7   6   5   4   3   2

Governments should understand that the international *mobilization of shame* is not limited to governments which violate human rights directly, but also extends to those which refuse to take effective action in the IGO context. [emphasis added]

— Turkey campaign documents,

Amnesty International

CONTENTS

PREFACE

The chaos in Europe during World War II prompted a dream by the victorious powers — the United States, Russia, and Great Britain. That dream was the concept of internationally recognized human rights to be implemented by several international entities, most of which would be attached to the United Nations.

For fifty-five years that dream has developed in a wide variety of ways, some encouraging and many disappointing. Hardly any nation or multinational entity has rejected the dream or vision of internationally recognized human rights. But the question recurs: can a world of 191 very different countries be induced to comply with rulings handed down by courts that have worldwide jurisdiction over some of the most basic actions of all nations?

The simplest reply would be to say that the question is too cosmic, too vast, too imponderable to yield any single answer. What is certain is that the international community, in seeking to manage some 6 billion people, has to endure and to accelerate its efforts to bring some form of the rule of law to the world.

The broader, amazing story of how the family of nations has struggled to develop and inculcate human rights in the past three generations deserves to be told. It is a sprawling story with few spectacular victories and with many tales of neglect and defiance by nations dominated by dictators or generals.

The establishment of a catalog of internationally recognized human rights for the first time in the history of the world is a monumental achievement in itself, apart from the enforceability of such rights. But the creation of such a catalog engenders scores of other questions. Could the lack of enforcement of these rights lead to a cynicism among people everywhere as to the availability of the most basic justice? Could the weakness — even the impotence — of international machinery to guarantee human rights encourage the advent of military rulers who will seek to utilize arms in order to achieve what legislators and courts are unable to produce?

Other hard questions abound. But the rise and the worldwide acceptance of a growing list of human rights is a fact of primordial importance. Its impact is dramatically visible in the proclamation subscribed to by 171 nations at the June 1993 U.N. World Conference on Human Rights in Vienna (the Vienna declaration is reprinted in the appendix to this book). That conference was called together by the United Nations after the Soviet empire collapsed in 1990. The leadership of the United Nations knew that the end of the Cold War had made it possible and necessary to revisit the extraordinary work on human rights that had been carried out by the United Nations and its agencies since 1945.

The eight-day conference in Vienna, in which I participated as a delegate of the American Bar Association, resulted in an astonishing proclamation of the rights of humanity. Because the statement was agreed to by virtually every nation on earth, the document constitutes customary international law. This form of law develops when nations generally agree that a certain form of conduct is forbidden. Although an international tribunal or instrument may not be in place to prevent or punish the forbidden conduct, that activity is still deemed a violation of customary international law or, better, global law.

It is safe to say that the conclusions set forth in the Vienna declaration will continue to be accepted as binding on governments everywhere. The conclusions reached in Vienna will be cited by legislatures, by courts, and by scholars as edicts binding on everyone.

The Vienna statement is cited and explained in this book as the synthesis and epitome of all the proclamations made by the United Nations and its instrumentalities in the past fifty-five years. Indeed, the Vienna declaration contains some visionary and idealistic conclusions which have not yet entered into the public consciousness of the world — or even into the consciousness of some of its human rights activists. Nevertheless, these conclusions can still be regarded as customary international law because they have been agreed to by the vast majority of countries.

Some will feel that the thrust of the Vienna declaration should not be exaggerated or overinterpreted. After all, it is only an agreement by the representatives of nations that represent some 85 percent of the world's inhabitants. These observers are partially correct. The dreams of Vienna are not self-enforcing. But the extent of the consensus in the Vienna proclamation continues to be remarkable. For the first time in some fifty years — since the proclamation of the 1945 Charter of the United Nations in San Francisco by forty-eight nations — the world came together and after solemn deliberation boldly reaffirmed every human right agreed to by the United Nations and its agencies.

But has Vienna made a difference? Have all the pronouncements on human rights since 1945 really elevated the status of freedom and equality around the world? This book seeks to explain that question with dispassion and analysis. The basic assumption is that the acceptance and enforcement of basic moral norms elevates the standards of public morality and thereby enhances the dignity of all human beings. The law teaches and deters. Law may be a feeble instrument, but sometimes it works and the human family becomes less barbarous and more civilized.

The official declaration at the end of the conference in Vienna is the centerpiece of this book. This volume comments on economic and political rights, on the rights of women and children and on other topics, some familiar and some relatively new. All the declarations of human rights made in countless ways by world bodies prior to Vienna are not neglected here. They are summed up and incorporated in the final product of the unprecedented Vienna meeting.

At the opening of the Vienna conference China protested that human rights are a western construct and that cultural relativity should excuse Asian nations from some of the mandates of the human rights law built up by the United Nations and its ancillary bodies. But during the conference in Vienna this contention faded and was withdrawn. The Vienna declaration made it clear that human rights — civil, cultural, economic, and political — are interrelated, interdependent, and indivisible.

Similarly, the Vienna declaration gave a new and elevated acceptance to human rights as a product of international or world law. No longer could any leader scoff at the prescriptions of international human rights law as inconsistent with a nation's sovereignty. Indeed, the Vienna declaration ushered in a new era in the recognition of those human rights binding on all countries.

Vienna also signaled the beginning of a time when the quarrel was no longer about the content of individual human rights law, but rather about methods for their enforceability.

The 100 short paragraphs of the 8,500-word declaration of the Vienna conference echo, amplify, and clarify some of the key concepts in the U.N. charter. But the declaration adds to the charter. The Vienna statement insists, for example, that the right to development is an "integral part of fundamental human rights." A special place is secured for the least developed countries, "many of which are in Africa" (Article 9).

Other specific items are added. A plea is made to all nations, for example, to implement existing conventions "relating to the dumping of toxic and dangerous products and waste and to cooperate in the prevention of illicit dumping" (Article 11).

There is no priority given in the Vienna declaration to political over economic rights. Article 14 says, "The existence of widespread extreme poverty inhibits the full and effective enjoyment of human rights; its immediate alleviation and eventual elimination must remain a high priority for the international community."

The rights of women, migrant workers, persons belonging to ethnic or racial minorities, and the indigenous are given special attention. The document states, for example, that "gender-based violence and all forms of sexual harassment and exploitation . . . are incompatible with the dignity and worth of the human person" (Article 18).

The panoramic view taken of international human rights by the Vienna conference owes a great deal to the thousands of nongovernmental organizations (NGOs) who were present in Vienna and who had carefully worked to make sure that the major issues related to world law and human rights were taken up in the final document.

The conference in Vienna, which included all but a handful of the world's nations, was impressive (indeed, overwhelming), yet the question persists: Does the existence of ever more clear international norms on human rights have an effect on a world that has seen the massacres in Cambodia, Rwanda, and the former Yugoslavia? Despite the existence since the 1950s of global bans on genocide and the violation of internationally acknowledged human rights, the second half of the twentieth century may have been almost as bloody and violent as the first half, with its two world wars. One has, of course, the consoling thought that the crimes against humanity might have been even more barbarous if international law had not proclaimed the sanctity of human rights and made their violation an offense against world law.

It is not always possible to predict the effect of a law on human behavior. It can be assumed that society criminalized murder after Cain killed Abel, but murders have occurred ever since. The Kellogg-Briand pact in the 1920s outlawed war, yet World War II, with 30 million persons killed, was the worst conflict in human history. But in 1945 the nations of the earth pledged as never before to initiate a worldwide crusade to protect human rights. The document that contained that pledge is the U.N. charter. It was updated in the Vienna declaration in 1993. Can these norms be accepted and enforced? Can the protection of human rights be the public morality of the global village?

Part I

THE
UNITED NATIONS
AND
HUMAN RIGHTS

1

THE
U.N. CHARTER:
A BLOW
TO NATIONAL
SOVEREIGNTY

The paradox of the formation of the United Nations is that the original 48 nations and the 152 countries who have joined them since 1945 voted for the erosion of their own national sovereignty. It is indeed astonishing that the United Nations, which entered into force on October 24, 1945, was the beginning of the decline of a view taken of the state since the days of Grotius. The major presumption of the nations that signed and ratified the Charter of the United Nations was the conviction that world wars would continue unless nations pledged to transfer the power to make war to the Security Council of the United Nations.

The theory that war could be controlled by the United Nations — the very essence of the U.N. charter — was coupled with the co-equal idea that the United Nations would have to declare, implement, and oversee the observance of human rights on which there was world agreement.

The dream and vision of the United Nations were made real and concrete to the signatories because each of them learned in Article I(3) that by being a member of the United Nations that country agreed to become a partner in the task of achieving "international cooperation in solving international problems of an economic, social, cultural or humanitarian character." That objective was paired with the goal of "prompting and encouraging respect for human rights and for fundamental freedom for all without distinction as to race, sex, language or religion."

That sweeping language is still breathtaking. The obligations of the nations which joined the United Nations was made clear to them in Article II(2), which requires all member-nations to "fulfill in good faith obligations assumed by them in accordance with the present charter." The term "good faith" is a well-known concept in law which makes clear that nations must be willing and ready to comply with the duties they have agreed to perform.

The new vision of the United Nations and the solemn duty of nations to fulfill their obligations as members of the United Nations are even clearer in Article 55. This article asserts that the United Nations desires to create "conditions of civility and well being which are essential for peaceful and friendly relations among nations." This is an amazing goal and commitment; it is based, the charter reads, on the "principle of equal rights and self-determination of peoples."

It seems impossible to overstate the revolutionary nature of Article 55. It is in essence a pledge by the rich nations to create an economic system which would bring "conditions of civility and well being" to all countries. The drafters who wrote those noble words probably had little real understanding that in the next few years well over 100 nations would declare independence from the colonial powers that had conquered them and that consequently these new nations would ask for economic "conditions of stability."

It is clear, however, that the authors of Article 55 knew what they were demanding of countries joining the United Nations. These nations would be partners in an enterprise that would "promote higher standards of living, full employment and conditions of economic and social progress and development." If this part of Article 55 sounded like a utopian fantasy the nations, both rich and poor, which joined the United Nations did not protest. Article 55 promised even more: the new world organization would promote "solutions of international economic, social, health and related problems." In addition, it would advance "international cultural and educational cooperation."

All this is combined with the promotion of "universal respect for, and observance of human rights and fundamental freedoms for all without distinction as to race, sex, language or religion."

It is clear that the allied powers in the depths of World War II had a blueprint for the post-war period which can only be described as extensive, unlimited, and comprehensive. It is notable that the concept of human rights was not really mentioned in the charter of the League of Nations. Somehow that idea was born before and during World War II and became one of the seminal concepts in the U.N. charter.

The architects of the U.N. charter wanted signatories to fully comprehend their new obligations. Article 56 requires the countries to pledge "to take joint and separate action in cooperation with the United Nations for the achievement of the purposes set forth in Article 55." Each nation consequently agreed and indeed solemnly pledged as an oath or vow to act individually as a country but also in joint action with other nations and with the United Nations itself.

It is very difficult to come to some judgment as to the world's level of compliance with the solemn pledges they made pursuant to Articles 55 and 56 of the U.N. charter. In one sense the burdens of complying with Articles 55 and 56 are not very stringent. But if a nation took its obligations as a member of the United Nations seriously it would change its attitudes and actions in almost drastic ways. After all, a nation upon becoming a member of the United Nations agrees to participate individually and collectively in the remaking of the world because that is precisely what the United Nations set out to achieve. The charter affirms that for the first time in the history of the world all nations are equal and that all will pledge and promise to share their resources so that basic economic rights can be obtained by all the citizens of all countries.

The U.N. charter has been compared to the Articles of Confederation adopted by the thirteen American colonies. The states promised confederation, but it turned out that the federal government which they established was too weak to unite them. The Constitutional Convention in 1787 consequently did that by writing a Constitution with a strong federal government capable of compelling the states to subject their sovereignty to national standards.

The present U.N. charter shares the weaknesses in the Articles of

Confederation. It seems unlikely that those weaknesses can be corrected in the immediate future. But even without such a strengthening, the members of the United Nations have still pledged to work on their own and, through the United Nations, to promote basic economic and political equality among all the countries in the world.

The attitudes and actions of the United States toward the fulfillment of the objectives of the United Nations have always been central to the future of that organization. After all, it was the United States which was the principal architect of the United Nations. President Roosevelt undertook the principal initiative. President Truman signed the U.N. charter in San Francisco in the presence of representatives of forty-eight other nations. In addition, the United States agreed and even insisted that the United Nations be located in the United States.

This prime sponsorship of the United Nations by the United States has been a blessing and a curse for that organization. It has been a blessing that the United Nations has the prestige which it might not have had if it had been located in Geneva or The Hague. But it has been a curse because the United Nations can be victimized by the vicissitudes of American politics. The power of the United Nations indeed has been sharply curtailed in carrying out its basic responsibilities by the intensity of the decades-long east-west struggles between the United States and the U.S.S.R. Many of the United Nations' aspirations have been overshadowed by the Kremlin–White House tensions.

One of the basic ways in which the fundamental purposes of the United Nations has been frustrated is the separation of economic rights from political rights. The right to economic equality was basic to the U.N. charter and to the Universal Declaration of Human Rights. It was not separated from political rights. All the world's nations agreed to this. But when it came to implementing economic and political rights, the United States and the U.S.S.R. divided. The U.S.S.R. declined to sign on to guaranteeing freedom of speech or the right to demand elections, while the United States was reluctant to guarantee economic rights, which arguably were to some extent inconsistent with the principles of capitalism.

This struggle between the superpowers in the early 1950s is, unfortunately, underdocumented. It was and still is an invisible but enormously important struggle, resulting in 1966 in the creation of two separate covenants—one for political rights and the other for economic and social rights. These two covenants were agreed to by the requisite number of countries and hence entered into force in 1976.

If this split had not occurred, the enforcement of human rights might well have developed in essentially different ways. The u.s.s.r. and the Communist bloc would have been under the pressure of international law to allow elections, grant freedom to the press, and release captive nations from their colonial status. Americans and other capitalistic nations would have been under pressure to give health insurance and economic equality to millions of workers.

That was a part of the original dream of the U.N. charter and the Universal Declaration of Human Rights. It was made inoperative in part by the division between east and west and by the obduracy of the divided nations.

The United States finally ratified the Covenant on Civil and Political Rights in 1994. But, as mentioned above, the United States has never ratified the International Covenant on Economic, Social, and Cultural Rights, although President Carter signed it in 1978. In 1999, 141 nations had become parties to the Covenant on Civil and Political Rights and 144 parties to the International Covenant on Economic, Social, and Cultural Rights.

It is significant that the Vienna declaration made no distinction between political and economic rights. The "schism" between the east and the west was over in 1993. But the harm had been done: the split between economic and political rights had entered into the world's psyche. For the west—or at least for the United States—the lasting impression had been given that although world law guaranteed political rights like religious liberty and freedom of the press, economic rights such as entitlement to a living wage and health insurance were in a second tier.

It is not entirely clear how important this division is. But it needs to be stressed that there is no historic, legal, or international reason for any distinction between political and economic rights. It should, however, also be noted that the economic demands made by the International Covenant on Economic, Social, and Cultural Rights need not be guaranteed by any nation immediately but only as resources become available. But this concession does not mean that economic rights are less important or urgent than are political rights.

The vast explosion in the past fifty years in judicial rulings and academic literature concerning human rights inevitably raises questions about the ultimate definition of what is a human right. The question has been around since the Biblical question "Am I my brother's keeper?" The plea for human rights is as old as the demand made by Moses of Pharaoh, "Let my people go."

The remarkable and unprecedented consensus on the definition of human rights came together in the words of the U.N. charter and the very specific guarantees of the Universal Declaration of Human Rights. Although those documents make no direct reference to a supreme being as the ultimate origin of the inalienable rights of every human being, the language of both documents reflects a deep agreement on fundamental values.

The preamble of the U.N. charter speaks of the "dignity and worth of the human person." It insists that all nations must practice "tolerance" and "live together in peace with one another as good neighbors."

These values are very familiar to all Americans and to some extent to the peoples who live in democracies. But in 1945 and even more today these values are universally accepted. They are totally consistent with the values spelled out in the U.N. charter. They are the philosophical basis for the rights set forth in Article 55 describing "higher standards of living, full employment and conditions of economic and social progress and development."

One has to wonder whether the success of the United Nations as an organization would have been assured if the moral and spiritual values underlying the charter had been spelled out more clearly. One also must ponder on a continuous basis whether the assertion of human moral values has in fact influenced individuals and nations. The assumption must be made that the violent civil wars have had some impact, because the adoption of the U.N. charter addresses the question concerning what ideals should be followed on a global basis.

The Universal Declaration of Human Rights also reflects a broader agreement on some of the fundamental questions about the nature and origin of human rights. This document repeats the basic concept that "all human beings are born free and equal in dignity and rights," proclaiming boldly that all peoples should "act toward one another in a spirit of brotherhood," and that all human beings "are endowed with reason and conscience."

Nations have not protested over the past fifty years the inclusion of that profoundly meaningful word "conscience." It seems clear that the Universal Declaration of Human Rights has been the most important legal document in the history of the world. Scores of constitutions and thousands of laws at the national level have been modeled after pronouncements of the Universal Declaration.

In 1992 the Scandinavian University Press issued a volume entitled *The Universal Declaration of Human Rights: A Commentary*. It was edited by Asbjorn Elde and Theresa Swinehart, academics in Scandinavia. The volume, which includes thirty essays on each of the articles in the Universal Declaration, reminds us of the immense range of rights in the declaration and their potential impact.

A reader of the book from Scandinavia as well as anyone who peruses the ocean of literature on the Universal Declaration has to wonder how a document of such moral strength with such compelling consensus underlying it could have been so neglected by so many nations over the past fifty years. Undeniably, the very existence of all these moral standards and proposed rights has had a salutary effect on the enjoyment of human rights throughout the world. Indeed, the moral decrees of the Universal Declaration have become to an astonishing extent the law of almost all the nations that have become independent countries after their decades as colonies of the capitalistic world.

It undoubtedly would be worthwhile to explore further the premises and presuppositions of the authors of the U.N. charter and the Universal Declaration of Human Rights. But the nations present at the Vienna conference in 1993, after an initial raising of the question of the universality of human rights, have seemed satisfied to accept the suppositions of the writers of these two documents.

While a discussion or a debate about the moral or metaphysical assumptions of the Charter of the United Nations and the Declaration of Human Rights might be useful, there appears to be a relatively settled feeling that the broad acceptance of the idea of human rights as universal is adequate to continue to make human rights enforceable. But some academics and observers, dismayed at the appalling failure of many nations to guarantee human rights, feel that a clarification of the morally compelling reasons for compliance might be a useful task in encouraging countries to comply. These advocates of human rights, however, bump up against the imponderable — and perhaps almost the insolvable — question of why some rulers shamelessly violate human rights and defy international law. Can laws, penalties, or threats deter rulers who are prone to such conduct?

Because answers to these questions are so difficult, it follows that we need more exploration of the psychological, moral, and historical reasons tyrants resist law. Often these tyrants are supported by the military under their command. The U.N. charter is strong on promoting and protecting human rights. But it is also emphatic in promoting new worldwide checks on military power. It is therefore a mistake to separate the human rights aspect of the charter from its demands for a new international order based not on military force but on the rule of law.

The United Nations, to be sure, has sought to control arms and curb military dictators. Again, the United States has an imperfect record. During the Cold War, for example, it formed its own military alliances, often supporting anti-Soviet dictators with bad records on human rights. Even after the plain need for such alliances ceased with the collapse of the u.s.s.r., the United States has continued to sell arms to countries without an adequate evaluation of their record on human rights. Indeed, the United States in the period following the Cold War has become the world's top supplier of weapons of war. To point out that these weapons do or can lead to a denial of human rights is to state the obvious.

The dream and the drive for international human rights for everyone sometimes seems impossible to implement. There are too many impediments. It almost seems that the underdeveloped capacity for democracy in former colonial nations has to be reversed before the idea of human rights can be said to be succeeding. It also appears at times that multinational corporations are imposing such heavy debts on Latin America and in Africa that goals such as universal education and the right to health care cannot be achieved in the foreseeable future.

All these problems were known to the groups at the World Conference on Human Rights in Vienna in 1993. Some individuals within these groups appeared in ways to be dreamers and idealists who tended to overlook the harsh realities of living in poor or recently liberated countries. But if that charge can be made by the enthusiasts for human rights in Vienna it can also be leveled at the forty-eight nations who were the original sponsors of the United Nations in San Francisco in 1948 and the countries that signed the U.N. Declaration of Human Rights in Paris on December 10, 1948.

It is probably true that all these persons were dreamers of a higher order than were the authors of the Magna Carta, the Declaration of Independence, or other proclamations created for the citizens of any nation. The authors of the U.N. charter and the Universal Declaration of Human Rights wrote for a whole world — a universe never before linked by an international law binding on all countries.

If there is discouragement at the results after fifty-five years of the existence of the United Nations, it could be countered that the progress and advancement in the area of human rights since 1945 has actually been more spectacular than might have been expected or even imagined.

Those achievements could have been more substantial, however, if the United States had not expressed a disinterest in economic rights. This disinterest is clear from the fact that it has never even attempted to ratify the Covenant on Economic Rights. If the United States had not distinguished between political and economic rights, the principal areas of contention in the world today might well have been the rights of poor people to food, shelter, and medical care.

The third world nations made constant appeals to these rights in repeated calls for the right to development. For forty years, underdeveloped nations had little official support in this area from the United States. The dismal statistics today on poverty, hunger, and illiteracy in sub-Saharan Africa and Asia might be radically different if the attitudes of the United States had been different.

It is apparent that the global struggle for human rights for the whole world that began in 1945, as world movements go, is very young. In addition, the population of the earth has practically doubled since 1945. Much of this increased population resides in newly liberated, desperately poor countries. Their number increases by almost 100 million persons each year. Even in more stable situations it would be difficult to bring them the economic and political rights proclaimed by world law that ought to be their heritage and their legacy.

But world law proudly and openly proclaims that the majestic rights declared to be the valid claims of every human being cannot be compromised away or denied or overlooked. The assertion of those rights is emphasized again and again by diplomats, jurists, human rights activists, and politicians.

Will those assertions be agreed to and implemented in the twenty-first century? That probably is the central question facing the human family. But its answer does not depend alone on the enforcement of the international law on human rights. Even if the enforcement were vigorous, law cannot prevail unless there is an acceptance of it at a deep level. The passions and violence that could arise in the twenty-first century are almost totally beyond prediction. Terrorists, new nations, millions of refugees, and violent hordes seizing land and property are all possible. These frightening prospects emphasize once again the need to reassure the poor and dispossessed of the truth that their internationally recognized human rights to economic equality are in the process of being fulfilled. If the 2 billion poor people of the world have no reasonable assurance that they will have a decent life for their families, they will do what desperate groups have often done in human history.

The virtual certainty of mass uprisings if the world does not move toward some type of economic justice for all is one more reason the economic rights promised by world law have such primordial importance.

The chapters that follow chronicle how the world in the past fifty years has moved to carry out the solemn promises made in 1945 and 1948, and in dozens of covenants on human rights made by the United Nations and its affiliated agencies. But the fulfillment of these rights will not bring stability and justice to the human family unless the startling disparity between the economic status of rich and poor nations is diminished.

2

THE U.N.

COMMISSION ON

HUMAN RIGHTS

The original dream of some of the founders of the United Nations was to place a mechanism to implement human rights in the charter itself. But this concept died somewhere in the process. The Charter of the United Nations did, however, specify that there should be a commission on human rights. This is the only agency specifically authorized by the charter.

It may be that in 1945 the actual authorization of any unit designed to activate human rights was unusual, even amazing. The concept of human rights has developed so unbelievably in the past fifty years that it is easy to forget how obscure, even threatening, that idea was in 1945. The colonial powers of the several European nations seemed to be intact. Even the United States would not liberate the Philippines until July 4, 1946. The idea that some 100 nations colonized by England, France, Spain, and other nations would be liberated in the name of self-determination and human rights was almost unthinkable to the framers of the charter of the United Nations. The authorities of those countries who signed the U.N. charter in San Francisco probably had little idea of the consequences of the establishment of the U.N. Commission on Human Rights.

Indeed, even the persons appointed to represent the original members of the U.N. Commission on Human Rights seemed unclear about whatever mission the United Nations intended to give them, or at least they did not follow that mission during the first twenty years of its existence. To be sure, it had helped draft the twin covenants concerning political and economic rights. But every attempt to have the commission receive petitions about violations was rejected until 1966.

This is difficult to condone or even explain because in all those years, the western bloc of nations had a comfortable majority in the United Nations. And there was certainly an abundance of complaints to be heard from the Soviet Union and the "captive nations" in Eastern Europe.

The United States resisted any attempt by the U.N. Commission on Human Rights to hear individual complaints. As early as 1947 petitions on behalf of the 13 million Americans of African ancestry came to the commission. It seemed clear that the United Kingdom, France, Belgium, Portugal, and the other colonial powers shared America's fears and prevented the commission from receiving petitions concerning the denial of rights clearly contained in the Universal Declaration of Human Rights.

The best explanation of the silence and inaction of the U.N. Commission on Human Rights is set forth by Philip Alston in *The United Nations and Human Rights: A Critical Appraisal,* published by Oxford University Press in 1992. Professor Alston, an Australian who is now the chairman of the U.N. Committee on Economic, Social, and Cultural Rights, pulls together virtually everything known about the evolution of the U.N. Commission on Human Rights. But even the magisterial account of Professor Alston leaves the reader with the question of why the major powers of the world could permit the United Nations' top agency for human rights to remain on the sidelines for so long.

In 1967, the U.N. Commission on Human Rights ended its hands-off policy and authorized action to identify specific human rights violations. An expansion of this policy adopted in 1972 brought some 200,000 to 300,000 petitions each year. Typically, they were generated by nongovernmental organizations and concerned some very difficult and notorious situations. An excellent book by Professor Howard Tolly, Jr., *The United Nations Commission on Human Rights* (Westview, 1987), records the struggles over the jurisdiction of the commission. Yet, despite the attempts of the commission to designate specific violations of human rights, its record has to be described as disappointing.

But the resistance of the U.N. Commission on Human Rights to becoming a judge and an arbitrator on human rights complaints demonstrates graphically that until very recently, nations have assumed that their sovereignty is inviolate and that no international concept like human rights can in any manner alter the way they conceive of their rights and privileges. Indeed the way countries cherish, magnify, and idolize their sovereignty is probably the major reason the idea of internationally recognized human rights is still widely perceived by politicians and diplomats as the enemy of their power.

The United States added significantly to this excessive nationalism in an announcement by Secretary of State John Foster Dulles in April 1953. He stated that the Eisenhower administration would not seek the ratification of the U.N. covenants on human rights. Dulles was motivated to take this position in order to defeat an amendment to the U.S. Constitution by Senator John Bricker, the Republican from Ohio, which would have amended the Constitution in order to prevent any U.N. covenant on human rights from becoming the "supreme law of the land" (as set forth in the Constitution) after being ratified by two-thirds of the Senate.

By this and other actions the Eisenhower administration reversed the momentum toward an enforceable international bill of rights that had taken hold of the world since the acceptance of the U.N. charter in 1945. It is arguable that the United States has never completely reversed the Eisenhower position on human rights. Virtually all treaties, for example, proposed by any administration for ratification are not self-executing and do not become the law of the land until they are passed by both houses and signed by the president.

But since its period of abdication (1946–1966), the U.N. Commission on Human Rights has become a responsive and important forum for the development of human rights. Provisions were eventually authorized for hearing complaints on a public or a confidential basis.

In fairness to the Commission on Human Rights, however, the world half expected it to be an international criminal commission, a court that could award damages and an agency that could bring the attention of the world to the hideous violations of human rights that were occurring almost everywhere. The U.N. commission was ill equipped to accomplish any of these laudable goals.

In his book, Professor Alston urges several reforms on the procedures followed by the Commission on Human Rights. They are all commendable, but the massive political will needed to transform the commission is not apparent. Crippled and inhibited by its own history and machinery, it seeks to accommodate the needs and aspirations of its members, whose number is now up to fifty-three. It is now overshadowed a bit by the visibility of the U.N. High Commissioner for Human Rights, a post finally established in 1995 after years of debate and postponement.

The U.N. Commission on Human Rights acted creatively in the 1980s by establishing a task force to focus on such issues as disappearances, systematic torture, and mass executions. Reports multiplied, presumably some dictators were deterred, and standards for government conduct were elevated.

Other initiatives by the commission are ongoing, and some are successful. They include seminars, advisory services, monitoring, fellowships in Geneva, and the dissemination of public information. Obviously the most important of these initiatives is education.

Every examination of the activities of the U.N. Commission on Human Rights over the past fifty years indicates that its activities have been spasmodic, uneven, and heavily reliant on the political events and currents in the world.

But it can also be argued that in the past few years, since the collapse of the Soviet empire, the U.N. Commission on Human Rights has taken on a new life. Suddenly everything looks different in the world of human rights. The commission has been freed of the necessity to denounce the U.S.S.R. on every occasion. Free also of the urgency to denounce apartheid in South Africa, the commission is aiming at new horizons.

The new energy and the renewed vision of the Commission on Human Rights were evident at the U.N. World Conference on Human Rights in Vienna in 1993. The ambassadors of the newly inaugurated Clinton administration were there as well as delegates from the newly liberated countries in central and eastern Europe. Indeed participants in the Vienna conference wanted to feel that the first fifty years of the intellectual human rights movement had been superseded by an entirely new era in the development of democracy and human equality.

One of the central reasons for the collapse of the Warsaw Pact and the surge in the development of human rights had been the amazing increase in the number of nongovernmental organizations devoted to human rights. The U.N. charter was among the first of all international organizations to accredit NGOs. Although the machinery to grant consultant status to NGOs is cumbersome and slow, the number of groups with consultant status is constantly growing. Their impact and their importance could and should be the basis for a definitive study. To be sure, some of the NGOs lobby for causes that are nationalist, even extremist in some cases, but the overall work and thrust of NGOs is the advancement of human rights and democracy. These groups are active in Geneva and have a significant impact on the deliberations and the votes of the U.N. Commission on Human Rights.

The Commission on Human Rights was the first world organization devoted to human rights. It has been replicated in part by the European Court on Human Rights in Strasbourg and the Inter-American Commission and Court in Costa Rica. But the commission has no juridical powers, nor can it fine or penalize nations — except in the realm of public opinion.

The new changes and improvements in the procedures of the U.N. Commission on Human Rights are self-evident. But like other sprawling entities within the structure of the United Nations, it is not easily susceptible to change. It does not have a powerful executive in charge, and its mission and mandate are not as precise as they could be. Yet, the amazing fact remains that an agency which had virtually abdicated its principal duties for the first twenty years of its existence is now an articulate advocate for the defense and enhancement of economic and political rights. More poor nations will be seeking to become members of the U.N. commission, and more private organizations will be asking to have the commission direct its attention to the rights of the disabled, the indigenous, children, and all groups not receiving those rights which international law and the Vienna convention have promised them.

No one can accurately predict what newly perceived rights will gain the attention of the world. In the United States, for example, the newly decreed rights of the disabled as guaranteed in the Americans with Disabilities Act have, ideally in large part, been accepted. The rights of all persons including children to be free from sexual harassment has been recognized. These rights have suddenly attained a status close to the rights of the blind or of visually impaired persons, which were universally recognized decades ago.

Because of the unpredictability of how certain rights suddenly flower, it may well be that the U.N. Commission on Human Rights has achieved far more than is visible at the moment. The commission began its work for the disappeared and the tortured at a time when the world was unaware of or not sensitive to these groups of victims. In thousands of reports and press releases the commission made known its work, and scores of rapporteurs sensitized millions of people to the evils of unjust dictators or governments that were deaf and blind to violations of human rights.

The Vienna conference appears to have finally created the momentum and international will to establish the office of the U.N. High Commissioner on Human Rights. This long-pending institution, recommended by virtually every nation including the United States, was implemented in the mid-1990s. How it coordinates with other U.N. agencies is not clear. The articulate presence of Mary Robinson, the former president of Ireland, as the high commissioner gives prominence to the importance of human rights, but her statements have no binding juridical power. Some human rights specialists hope or dream that the high commissioner could be the "czar" of human rights. But the sprawling and frequently changing international human rights scene is not amenable to neat juridical boundaries.

The U.N. Commission on Human Rights is less well known than other U.N. agencies, like the World Health Organization, UNESCO, UNICEF, and the Food and Agricultural Organization. The missions of these groups are tangible and concrete. In contrast, the act of voting on the abuse of human rights is unpleasant, controversial, and unattractive to most audiences. In judging the record of the commission, moreover, it must be noted that the world's attitude toward the abuse of human rights has recently become much more sensitive to reports on such abuses. Some of that sensitivity is due to reporting and education and the relentless energy of the commission itself. It has been in the forefront of the human rights movement. In the coming decades, as the world becomes more aware of the preciousness of human rights, the role of U.N. Commission on Human Rights may expand its decrees and its findings have an importance in public opinion that is hard to even imagine.

3

ECONOMIC
EQUALITY
FOR ALL

The 1945 Charter of the United Nations, the Universal Declaration of Human Rights, and the International Covenant on Economic, Social, and Cultural Rights (CESCR) contain the astonishing dream and declaration that everyone in the world should have basic equality and economic rights. That dream has been endemic in human history. But it had never before been acclaimed in a document promulgated to be accepted by every nation on earth.

The brutality of World War II and the inhumanity of the treatment inflicted by the colonial powers on the nations they occupied combined at the end of the war to prompt the world community to compose and promulgate the CESCR. It is an amazing document. Is it naive? Is it a Socialist concoction? Is it a manifestation of guilt over the conquest and occupation of over 100 nations by the European colonial powers?

The document on economic rights, now ratified by 150 nations (but not the United States), is amazing. It guarantees the right to work, the right to join unions, and a qualified right to strike. Fair wages are assumed, and periodic holidays with pay are mandatory. Mothers are guaranteed "special protection" before and after childbirth including "paid leave." Signatories to the treaty are required to guarantee "adequate food, clothing and housing." Even more demanding is the requirement that governments offer a "continuous improvement of living conditions."

To be sure, the covenant requires governments to fulfill their obligations only in ways which are consistent with the "maximum of a nation's available resources." But every government is urged—even commanded—to adopt "legislative measures" which carry out the objectives of the CESCR. It is astonishing to see how the more than 150 signatories of the CESCR, put in force only in 1976, have undertaken responsibility for the compelling duties imposed on them by international law and are presumably seeking to carry out the promises they made to the world and to their own citizens.

Some observers—especially in the United States—have treated the CESCR with scorn and derision. Some anti-Communist hardliners suggested that the dreams and demands of the CESCR are Socialist manifestos. The implication is that the attainment of economic equality, however desirable, imposes no duty on governments to bring it about.

The thrust of the economic covenant is directly the opposite. It clearly requires the governments which ratify the CESCR to live up to their solemn obligations. Apparently, the framers of the CESCR do not approve of unregulated capitalism and are very serious and determined to compel governments to redistribute a nation's resources in ways that maximize the potential for real economic equality.

One of the most difficult problems in assessing the intended effect of the CESCR is the speed of compliance expected of poor nations. The treaty makes it clear that it does not expect the impossible of nations with limited resources. Similarly, it does not demand that governments require banks or private companies to challenge their traditional ways of operation. The treaty is hortatory, not mandatory.

The vast, almost impossible task of supervising compliance with the CESCR has been given to the Committee on Economic, Social, and Cultural Rights. Established in 1979, the committee regularly receives reports from the signatory nations. Many countries try to report as completely as possible. But the problem of compliance depends upon the basic philosophy of the nations' rulers in charge of the economy. Does a poor agricultural country seek to attract foreign corporations in order to manufacture consumer goods and thereby generate revenue for the government? Or does that nation seek to capitalize farming so that crops for export are generated? The central question, of course, is whether the committee has a right to direct and advise nations to proceed in specific ways in order to maximize their compliance with the objectives that they promised to uphold when they signed the CESCR.

Philip J. Alston is now the chairman of the U.N. Committee on Economic Rights. His essay of thirty-five pages contained in the volume *The United Nations and Human Rights* is one of the best descriptions of the committee, which has awesome but also amorphous responsibilities.

A reading of all the reports of the committee that supervises the implementation of the Covenant on Economic Rights conveys the overwhelming impression that a relatively small committee has the almost unmanageable task of assisting nations as they seek to fulfill the promises they made when they ratified the treaty, which requires them to provide their citizens with the basic rights of a modern welfare state. The members of the committee do not have the expertise or mandate to change economic policies of a small nation like El Salvador. If the committee feels or even knows with some degree of certainty that El Salvador has adopted a policy which enriches the bankers but impoverishes the farmers, the most that it can do is offer recommendations to the authorities in the responding nation assessing the potential or future impact of the policy issue on the overall objectives of the CESCR.

It may be that the Committee on Economic, Social, and Cultural Rights will become bolder in its objectives in the same way that the U.N. Commission on Human Rights developed. It is clear to everyone associated with the U.N. agencies that seek the implementation of human rights that additional cooperation and collaboration among all the agencies is essential. Nations are now required to fill out extensive forms in order to comply with the demands of several U.N. bodies. There is clearly overlap among these units. The Committee on Economic, Social, and Cultural Rights, one of the youngest of all U.N. bodies, regularly asks for information already furnished by countries to other U.N. bodies. In addition, it is not clear how the committee will treat copious statistics on the economy, the labor force, and the literacy rate of a particular country.

If the task is so vast and so complicated, the question arises about the usefulness of the Committee on Economic, Social, and Cultural Rights. The world struggled over that question from 1945 to 1966, when the two treaties on political and economic rights were finally agreed to by the United Nations. That debate continued during the ten years before the covenants in 1976 entered into force with the required number of ratifications.

In the years to come, it will almost certainly be the less developed nations that will seek to obtain rulings from the Committee on Economic, Social, and Cultural Rights that will be favorable to the economy of these nations. The forty years of struggle waged by the underdeveloped nations for the vindication and fulfillment of the right to development, then, will be reenacted in that committee.

The expandable concepts in the CESCR can suggest that the rich nations have a duty to share their resources with poorer nations. In other words, the logic would go, all nations are fellow signatories in a noble enterprise to give basic economic equality to every person. As a result, nations with more resources have some duty to assist the less endowed nations that have promised to make the objectives of economic equality attainable.

This concept is to some extent implicit in the philosophy and structure of the World Trade Organization. That unit seeks to maximize and equalize trade among all nations. The most powerful nations have some obligation of sharing their expertise with all countries, rich and poor. At least indirectly, the ultimate purpose of the World Trade Organization is the same as that of the CESCR — the elevation of the tragic living standards of the 6 billion people in the global village.

In a certain sense, the Covenant on Economic, Social, and Cultural Rights is the least successful of all of the endeavors of the United Nations. But paradoxically it may be the most meaningful and potentially successful of all of the aspirations of the United Nations. The goals of the CESCR are what humanity needs most. Political rights such as freedom of the press and religion are important, but over 3 billion people are in desperate need of food, work, medicine, and education.

For the first time in the history of the world a global body has responded to the cry for basic economic equality. Some 80 percent of the world's population have ratified that treaty and have solemnly promised to work for the objectives of a covenant that is truly sweeping in its aspirations and demands.

The fact that the United States remains outside that global effort can only be detrimental to the reputation of the United States and to the potential of the U.N. committee that supervises the implementation of the CESCR.

Fifty or one hundred years from now, will the demands of the Covenant on Economic, Social, and Cultural Rights be routinely accepted by lawmakers as binding obligations under international law? Will the rights to food, medicine, and education be as accepted as the duty of every nation to punish pirates and ban slavery? That is the hope of the visionaries who came together to write the CESCR. The vision of that group was restated and re-ratified in the final declaration of the World Conference on Human Rights held in Vienna in 1993.

The same nations that agreed to accept the CESCR in 1966 and 1976 once again proclaimed their promise to work for economic equality. When Vienna is added to previous declarations, it seems safe to say that the promises and commitments of the economic covenant are customary international law.

A treaty is a contract between nations. In addition, a treaty is a promise by each signatory that it will faithfully carry out the objectives of the covenant.

For centuries the human race has aspired to eliminate hunger and famine and to control deadly diseases. For the first time in the history of the world those objectives have become attainable.

The Covenant on Economic, Social, and Cultural Rights is a noble expression of the age-old dream — along with the basic steps which nations must follow — to eliminate hunger and conquer disease.

The dream is noble. Its attainment will depend upon the level of moral energy the world's leaders will extend to it. Participation of the United States through ratification of the CESCR would be enormously beneficial. The absence of the United States can only be foreboding.

4

THE
UNITED NATIONS
AND POLITICAL
AND CIVIL RIGHTS

If you want to see the dimensions of the global earthquake contemplated by the U.N. International Covenant on Civil and Political Rights (ICCPR), imagine a world of 185 nations that adhere to and follow the directives of the same document on civil and political rights now ratified by these countries.

The legislative history of the adoption of the Covenant on Civil and Political Rights has not been researched. The covenant is the result of the deep grief and guilt of the victims of World War II, as well as the anxieties of the colonial powers as they saw their empires dissolve in the 1950s and 1960s. Article 1 reflects that anxiety by proclaiming that "all peoples have the right of self-determination."

The Covenant on Civil and Political Rights also recognizes that, despite the separation of the covenants on political and economic rights, they are linked and inseparable.

If most nations had begun to enact the prescriptions set out in the ICCPR on March 23, 1976, the date the covenant had entered into force, the world situation today would be very different. First of all, there would be elections. Article 25 makes it clear that there must be universal and equal suffrage, "genuine and periodic elections" conducted by "secret ballot." There would also be a universal ban on all discrimination on "any grounds such as race, color, sex, language, religion, political or other opinion, national or social origin, property, birth or other status." Clearly, this covenant outlaws any inherited social system, such as in India with its caste system.

It is significant that the outline which was finalized in 1966 did not ban discrimination based on age, physical or mental disability, or sexual orientation. One likes to think that the concept of equal protection which is at the core of the ICCPR has developed and expanded in the view and the conscience of the human race.

Careful analysis of the words of the Covenant on Political Rights is especially important because the United States ratified the ICCPR on June 8, 1992, and the covenant entered into force in the United States on September 8, 1992. Even though the Senate's reservations, understandings, and declarations are lamentable, the fact that the United States has finally ratified the visions of the ICCPR is surely one of the most significant events in the story of the international human rights revolution, which began in 1945 with the adoption of the Charter of the United Nations.

The ICCPR, like the Universal Declaration of Human Rights, asserts forcefully in Article 23 that the "family is the natural and fundamental unit of society and is entitled to protection by society and the state." No marriage, furthermore, "shall be entered into without the free and full consent of the intending spouses."

But the covenant does not include the directive in Article 26(3) of the Universal Declaration of Human Rights that "parents have a prior right to choose the kind of education that shall be given to their children." This clause was inserted on behalf of Catholic parents in Europe, Muslims in Islamic countries, and minorities everywhere in order to protest "l'ecole unique," which tended to be the rule in France and elsewhere prior to the onset of the twentieth century.

For some years the advocates of pluralism in elementary and secondary education in the United States have employed Article 26 as a part of their argument. To date it has not been successful. But the differences between the view of the 150 nations that have ratified the political covenant and the prevailing view in the United States on aid to church-related schools of less than collegiate rank demonstrate dramatically the need for (or the fear of) a world standard that in some cases could be different from the norm established by legislative or judicial measures in the United States.

A graphic example of such a disparity can be imagined on the issue of abortion. The views on abortion reached by the majority of nations that subscribe to the Covenant on Civil and Political Rights could well be different from the arrangements set forth in 1973 in *Roe v. Wade*.

The majority of countries could reach the conclusion that women should not be allowed to have an abortion except for serious medical reasons in the first three or four months of pregnancy. Theoretically the United States should be prepared to accept and adopt the collective decision of the vast majority of countries. Such a decision by most nations would be termed "customary international law." Obviously there would be dissenters in the United States and elsewhere. Those individuals would be protected by the reservations made by the U.S. Senate in its ratification of the ICCPR.

But the issue is broad, complicated, and difficult. Are nations expected to yield some part of their sovereignty when they ratify an international treaty on human rights? On some sensitive point, are they required to yield their view because the world has reached a different conclusion?

That is the issue that will not go away. But the ICCPR tends to finesse that problem. It sets out those legal and moral truths on which there appears to be a consensus around the world. But it is not always clear whether the Covenant on Civil and Political Rights is expressing a new consensus or whether some nations or some nongovernmental organizations have persuaded U.N. officials to adopt a policy that does not yet constitute a world consensus.

That may be the case in the covenant's approach to the death penalty. The document in Article 6 does not ban capital punishment but it certainly discourages it. The document states firmly that "nothing in this article shall be invoked to delay or prevent the abolition of capital punishment." The covenant stipulates that the death penalty can be rendered only by a competent court pursuant to a clear pre-existing law; it cannot be imposed for crimes "committed by persons below 18 years of age and shall not be carried out on pregnant women."

On some issues, the ICCPR appears to be more progressive than American public opinion or even world opinion. Echoing the U.N. document of 1955 entitled "Standard Minimum Rules for the Treatment of Prisoners," the Covenant on Civil and Political Rights (Article 10) asserts very forcefully that the "penitentiary system shall comprise treatment of prisoners the essential aim of which shall be their reformation and social rehabilitation." That philosophy appears to be really at odds with the dominant approach of federal and most state officials in the past several years in the United States; their aim is to penalize and punish prisoners rather than to reform or rehabilitate them.

The Covenant on Civil and Political Rights is overall very modern and progressive in its orientation. It includes the presumption of innocence, the right not to testify against one's self, the right to counsel of one's own choosing, and the right to compensation by those who have been victims of a miscarriage of justice.

Privileges associated with the right to speak, to practice religion, and to hold opinions without interference are strongly protected under the ICCPR. Indeed, the nations which have publicly pledged their allegiance to the treaty have had few quarrels with its provisions.

The framers of the Covenant on Civil and Political Rights propose two methods of enforcement: the optional protocol, and the U.N. Committee on Human Rights.

A total of 95 nations have agreed to the optional protocol. This gives the citizens of these nations the right to file a protest against their own government. The petitioners must first exhaust their local remedies, obtain supporting documentation, and expect a long process before any adjudication is finalized. Theoretically the concept of the optional protocol is attractive. It is contrary to the outdated policy that no subject can sue the king. A world tribunal is now in place under which any person can have a day in court and prevail against any local government official in any faraway land.

The plan sounds wonderful. It has great potential. A century from now it might be a routine way for citizens with legitimate complaints to obtain a just result — or at least they could be heard.

The fact that the millions of citizens in Germany during World War II had no place to complain haunts the west. How could this have happened? On a continent with a highly developed court system, the inhabitants of a large and sophisticated nation had no access to world public opinion or to tribunals anywhere! The mechanism of the optional protocol was designed to prevent the impotence imposed on German citizens and all the millions of other persons victimized by dictators who had immunized themselves by banning the press and closing domestic courts to all complaining prospective plaintiffs.

The entity designed by the Covenant on Civil and Political Rights to hear the petitions alleging violation of the rights protected under the covenant is the U.N. Committee on Human Rights. Unfortunately, the work of this group is little known. Its sessions are not covered by the press, and its responses and reports to the signatory countries receive little publicity.

Currently, seven human rights treaties are in effect, and the states or nations that have ratified them have agreed to submit periodic reports on their compliance. It is encouraging to think that each of these monitoring units is a sleeping giant and that its reports will soon, ideally, become items of worldwide discussion. After all, these supervisory entities evaluate the performance of countries in explosive topics like the rights of women, the ways children are protected, the extent of racial discrimination, and the global ban on torture. Unfortunately, little is known about the first submission by the United States to the U.N. Committee on Human Rights after the U.S. Senate ratified the Covenant on Civil and Political Rights.

The committee that monitors compliance with the ICCPR is made up of members chosen by individual countries because of their competence in the field of human rights. Since the ratification of this covenant by the U.S. Senate, the United States for the first time has a representative on the committee that monitors the ICCPR. He is Professor Thomas Buergenthal, a survivor of the Holocaust, a human rights expert, and a former member of the Inter-American Commission on Human Rights, which convenes in Costa Rica.

The first report submitted by the United States pursuant to its duties under the Covenant on Civil and Political Rights was carefully crafted by the State Department and affiliated agencies. It is a 250-page document, filed in July 1994, that acknowledges America's problems but offers a candid and honest appraisal of how the United States is striving to cope with its new responsibilities. Drafted by John Shattuck, assistant secretary of human rights in the Clinton administration, the report openly admits to the "bitter legacy of slavery" but seeks to vindicate the efforts of the United States to eliminate segregation and prevent discrimination. The report does concede, nonetheless, that while 11.6 percent of the white population is living below the poverty line, 33.3 percent of African Americans and 29.3 percent of Hispanics fall below the poverty level.

The Shattuck report is possibly the most comprehensive and candid document on the state of civil rights and civil liberties ever to have originated from a high level of the American government. But it refrained from rejecting views issued by the Supreme Court and the executive branch. It is, as a result, hedged and cautious in some of its conclusions.

Even though the human rights community has the highest regard for John Shattuck, who was active in the American Civil Liberties Union and in Amnesty International prior to his appointment, human rights activists in the United States before and after the Shattuck report continue to be critical. In a joint statement by Human Rights Watch and the ACLU it was pointed out that the ICCPR mandates that each signatory to the covenant provide an effective remedy for violations of covenant rights and that these remedies be enforced. In the view of Human Rights Watch and the ACLU, the United States has not corrected those conditions in the area of education, housing, and race relations which are not in compliance with the demands of the ICCPR.

The NGOs are also critical of the Shattuck report. Native American rights groups complain that they are still plagued by abuse and discrimination. Amnesty International, women's groups, labor unions, and the advocates of children's rights have also entered statements to the effect that governments in the United States have not complied with the new obligations it assumed when it ratified the International Covenant on Civil and Political Rights.

In reaction to America's first submission on its compliance with the ICCPR, the comments by the U.N. Commission on Human Rights were also blunt and, on some points, harsh. Although the actual response of the commission was routine (every country receives a standard reply), in this case the response expressed the regret that America's first submissions contained too "few references to the implementation of covenant rights at the state level." The commission, in rebuking the United States for the extent of its declared "reservations, declarations and understandings," added, almost brutally, that it believed "the United States has accepted what is already the law of the United States." This is precisely what critics in the United States agree on. The White House, first of all, constructed a treaty that is *not* self-executing, which means that its promises are not effectively the law of the land unless they have been passed by both houses of Congress and have been signed by the president. In addition, the reservations, understandings, and declarations make it clear that despite America's acceptance of the covenant, its final obligations do not go beyond what American courts have already held to be the meaning of civil and political rights. The U.N. Commission on Human Rights is therefore correct when it points out that the United States, despite the ratification and its report on compliance, has not agreed to do anything not already required by U.S. law.

The U.N. commission has had other sharp criticisms of the United States. It has lamented "the large number of persons killed or wounded or subjected to ill treatment by members of the police force" and the "easy availability of firearms to the public." It has criticized laws that have criminalized "sexual relations between adult consenting partners." It also has openly urged the adoption of "affirmative action" and flatly stated that in connection with disputes over affirmative action for minorities and women the "obligation to provide covenant's rights in fact as well as law be borne in mind." The commission concluded its long series of recommendations by urging greater public awareness of the provisions of the covenant, adding that the legal profession should be particularly aware of the guarantees of the covenant "in order to insure their effective application."

The encounter between the United States and the U.N. Commission on Human Rights is almost unique in the evolving history of international human rights. The United States has not ratified the Convention on the Elimination of All Forms of Discrimination Against Women or the Convention on the Rights of the Child, and it has not agreed to the Inter-American Convention on Human Rights, which applies exclusively to the area of Latin America. Consequently, it cannot be criticized by the commission or court in Costa Rica.

When federal officials and the U.S. Senate address the question of ratifying these treaties, they will remember that the United States received a strong rebuke when it filed its first submission on its compliance with the Covenant on Civil and Political Rights.

All the nations that have ratified the ICCPR are expected to report periodically — usually every five to eight years. When the United States is expected to report again, officials will obviously want to rebut some of the charges of the NGOs and, more important, the blunt assessments in the rebuke by the monitors of the Covenant on Civil and Political Rights.

The process is, lamentably, somewhat political. The State Department does not want to publicize the dialogue between it and a generally unknown unit in Geneva which does not have the funds or the desire to make known its findings. In addition, there are no credible reasons the White House or the State Department desires to limit the obligations of the United States to meet only those requirements that are specifically spelled out in federal or state laws or regulations. Moreover, all kinds of political reasons exist for restricting legal requirements on human rights to national and not international obligations.

In addition, the whole process is severely flawed in that every administration will insist that no treaty be self-executing. Consequently, the United States can be criticized by nations abroad because of its apparently adamant refusal to accept any obligations from an international entity which are not already binding on the United States.

Some have suggested that the Constitution should be amended to permit the president to enter into treaties with foreign nations, with only a majority vote required by the Senate. But such a proposal would probably be dead on arrival even though a two-thirds vote is very difficult to obtain.

It is difficult to explain to foreign observers of the American political processes why the United States, the powerful architect and author of the United Nations, is now such a reluctant partner. An oversimplified explanation is the isolationist attitude of Senator Jesse Helms, the Republican chairman of the Senate Foreign Relations Committee. But America's reluctance to enter into treaties and to be judged by commissions and tribunals is deep-seated among Americans and, indeed, may be growing.

The experience the United States has had in ratifying the Covenant on Civil and Political Rights is not likely to induce future administrations to enter into the thicket of international politics and human rights. The political disincentives make active participation by the NGOs indispensable if the United States is, in turn, to participate actively in the development of a world in which the enforcement of internationally recognized human rights is the essential basis of international comity and peace.

Amnesty International, founded in 1961 and now perceived as one of the strongest of the founders of the international human rights movement, has deemed that the "mobilization of shame" is one of its principal purposes. This captivating phrase assumes that nations, like individuals, experience "shame" when its conduct is perceived to be degrading, unworthy, humiliating, in essence, shameful. The feeling of "shame" which citizens have for the conduct of their country can, Amnesty assumes, be "mobilized."

It is difficult to isolate and gather hard empirical evidence of why or how nations become "ashamed" of their conduct. But it has been done — and perhaps will be done more and more frequently. Nations like South Africa, Argentina, and Brazil have created truth and reconciliation commissions. These groups seek to publish all the awful truths about what their governments have done and thereby produce shame and guilt, but also reconciliation. Little is known about the subtle and serious ways by which individuals and nations discover their guilt and make peace by accepting it. But we do know there is "shame" and that its presence can prompt citizens and governments to change their attitudes.

The remedies of the optional protocol and the reporting system set up by the Covenant on Civil and Political Rights were designed to reveal wrongdoing and thereby induce governments to regret their misconduct and feel ashamed.

The process inaugurated by the U.N. Civil Rights Committee is not legal or juridical. It seeks to persuade governments to confess in public that they have made mistakes and violated the law in their failure to live up to the promises they made when they ratified the Covenant on Civil and Political Rights. The response of the U.N. Commission on Human Rights to a nation's report can be a teachable moment for many nations. Criticism of its human rights record has to be a negative event for a small nation seeking to create a reputation as a law-abiding country which could be a valuable ally in banking or business to a wealthier nation.

Private agencies of all kinds collect information about human rights in every country seeking to attract business or investment. If this information can be supplemented by reports from the U.N. Commission on

Human Rights, a nation's reputation as a safe and favorable place can be strengthened. On the other hand, if the commission has disseminated one or more negative reports, a nation can be damaged.

Why should the United States be concerned with this process, which might have a negative impact on struggling nations in Africa or Asia but cannot have an adverse impact on America? The answer to this question is both moral and jurisprudential. The United States in ratifying the U.N. Covenant on Civil and Political Rights made a statement. It declared that it was making solemn promises that it intended to keep. It was in essence entering into a contract with the United Nations and its agencies. The decision to ratify a treaty is not unlike a new state joining the United States. Some years ago Alaska and Hawaii became states; they undertook all the obligations of a state that subscribes to federalism, with all the duties this places on states.

Articles 55 and 56 of the U.N. charter stipulate that nations who join the United Nations not merely promise but "pledge" that they will carry out their duties as members of the United States. The same understanding carries over when a nation ratifies a treaty. That country "pledges" to fulfill its new obligations.

That is what the United States did when it ratified the Covenant on Civil and Political Rights. Even the unfortunate reservations do not cancel out the fact that the White House and the Congress solemnly undertook obligations under international law. Even though there may not be any precise procedures to force compliance, the United States nonetheless made solemn promises to do certain things which otherwise it would not have done. An old and venerated adage in international law is *pacta sunt servanda* — promises must be kept.

The first exchange between the United States and the U.N. Commission on Human Rights did not end in glory for the United States. But the dialogue or debate in which the two entities engaged was the first major exchange the United States, along with 185 other members, was required to have with the commission. A growing body of literature concerns how nations view human rights vis-à-vis the worldview advanced by U.N. officials.

In a generation or two we will know which nations faithfully seek to comply with their obligations under the Covenant on Civil and Political

Rights and which nations evade or avoid their obligations. We will also know which nations have listened to the importunate views of NGOs and have complied with international law.

The United States has many lessons to learn and a long way to go. But at least it has fulfilled its obligations to report. Perhaps it will in the future make available to American citizens their rights under the optional protocol. It may be that eventually the United States will decide that it should listen to and heed the international voice of those who plead and argue for the millions of citizens who are entitled by world law to the rights guaranteed them by the Covenant on Civil and Political Rights.

If America listens to the voice and conscience of other nations, it will be heeding the words in the Declaration of Independence — that we should have "a decent respect for the opinions of mankind."

5

WOMEN'S WORLDWIDE PLEA FOR EQUALITY

On December 18, 1979, the U.N. General Assembly adopted the Convention on the Elimination of All Forms of Discrimination Against Women (also known as the Covenant on Women's Rights or CEDAW). It was clearly a historic occasion. The acceptance of CEDAW may have been one of the most important decisions in world history.

President Carter signed the CEDAW on July 18, 1980, and submitted it to the Senate for ratification. It was in all probability the support and encouragement of the Carter administration that brought about the adoption of the covenant in the United Nations. The treaty entered into force on September 3, 1981.

Subsequently, neither the Reagan nor the Bush administration took any action on the CEDAW. No Senate action occurred until 1993, when sixty-eight senators asked President Clinton to take the steps necessary for ratification. In October 1994, the Senate Foreign Relations Committee voted 13–4 in favor of sending the covenant to the full Senate. But no action has been taken by the Senate since that time.

I testified at the hearings in the Senate in 1994 on behalf of the American Bar Association, which in the 1980s had endorsed the CEDAW. The committee seemed receptive. The witnesses against the covenant seemed to reflect an attitude of isolationism and a deep fear of any additional change in the status of women.

The fears of the opponents of the CEDAW have been met by the four reservations, four understandings, and two declarations offered by the State Department on behalf of the Clinton administration. These ten qualifications have made it clear that the United States will not make any concessions with regard to privacy "except as mandated by the Constitution and laws of the United States." In addition, the United States has refused to accept any obligations under the CEDAW to assign women to military positions which "may require engagement in direct conflict." The United States also has rejected any obligation to use the concept of "comparable worth" in connection with conditions for working women, and to require paid maternity leave. Nor has the United States agreed to give on a cost-free basis health care services related to family planning and pregnancy.

Even though it could be argued that the exceptions carved out by the Clinton administration nullify some of the key provisions of the CEDAW, support for the convention continues to be strong. That support was strengthened after the Equal Rights Amendment obtained the ratification of only thirty-five of the thirty-eight states required. The point was made repeatedly by advocates of women's rights that there must be some form of constitutional protection for the rights of women.

The refusal of the Senate to ratify the CEDAW derives from a wide variety of prejudices, fears, and misconceptions. The concepts set forth in that covenant are not radical or revolutionary. They represent the profound, worldwide awakening by women concerning what has been done to them for centuries. One of the main thrusts of the covenant, which remains in the mainstream of feminist aspirations, is the elimination of all customs and practices originating from the assumption that women are inferior or from stereotyped roles for women. It refers repeatedly to the exclusion of women from participation in government and the vast under-estimation of their contributions. The covenant also asserts, however, that a "change in the traditional role of men as well as the role of women in society and in the family is needed to achieve full equality between men and women."

The overall purpose of the CEDAW is to confer on women worldwide the freedom from discrimination, education, employment, and wages which is guaranteed by federal and state statutes in the United States. It is ambivalent on the need for protective legislation designed to shield women from specific harm that might come to them. But the CEDAW is very clear on the need for affirmative action, which will allow women to enter all those numerous areas of life from which they have been excluded almost from time immemorial.

Article 4 provides as follows:

> Adoption . . . of temporary special measures aimed at accelerating de facto equality between men and women shall not be considered discrimination as defined in the present convention, but shall in no way entail as a consequence the maintenance of unequal or separate standards. These measures shall be discontinued when the objectives of equality of opportunity and treatment have been achieved.

This provision echoes a similar measure in the International Convention on the Elimination of Racial Discrimination. That measure entered into force on January 4, 1969, and has been ratified with reservations by the U.S. Senate.

Article 1, 4 of the CERD reads as follows:

> Special measures taken for the sole purpose of securing adequate advancement of certain racial or ethnic groups or individuals requiring such protection as may be necessary in order to insure such groups or individuals equal enjoyment or exercise of human rights as fundamental freedoms shall not be deemed racial discrimination.

The only caveat is that "such measures do not as a consequence lead to the maintenance of separate rights for different racial groups." Such measures "shall not be continued after the objectives for which they were taken have been achieved."

These similar provisions in the CEDAW and CERD were conceived to address the situation where, as in India, a caste system had developed which excluded the untouchables from a wide variety of occupations. To correct this situation, "special measures" may be enacted with the proviso that they be eliminated as soon as they are no longer necessary.

In the heated debate over affirmative action as understood in the United States, it should be pointed out that the categories for minorities and women established by prejudice and stereotypes can be phased out with official action or "special measures" to change a pattern or conduct which the government has in essence created or permitted.

Women in America were victimized by a stereotype when a court in Illinois in the late 1800s ruled that women had no right to go to law school or enter the legal profession. The authors of the CEDAW remembered this and the fact that women could not even vote in the United States until 1920 and that some professions are still, at least de facto, closed to women.

The CERD synthesized the legitimate grievances of women worldwide and created a committee of twenty-three members which evaluates the periodic reports of the nations which have promised to implement the directives of the covenant in their own nations.

The accumulated rulings of the U.N. Committee on CEDAW constitute an ever more impressive body of legal judgment on the ways by which governments deny the rights of women. Indeed, in the near future books will bring together the accumulated wisdom of the committee and, even more important, the impact of those judgments on the way the governments of the world treat women.

There has been an astonishing awakening in the past few years to the abuse and degradation imposed on women by men and by many societies. The incidence of spousal abuse has become known as never before. News about the mistreatment of women has exploded around the world. Sophisticated ways of inhibiting or prohibiting the advancement of women have been revealed. The "glass ceiling" is only one of the less subtle ways of reinforcing a stereotype of women as limited in their abilities.

If the U.S. Senate were to ratify the CEDAW, the White House and the State Department would be required to submit periodic reports on America's compliance with the Covenant on Women's Rights. The responses of the committee on America's compliance with the CEDAW would be seen and heard by the world. The exchange between the United States and the U.N. Committee on the Rights of Women would be covered by the press. The United States would finally be required to justify American society's conduct toward women or apologize for its failure to live up to the mandates of the CEDAW.

But the United States is not the only nation in the world that is resisting a change in the status of women. On June 13, 1999, citizens of Switzerland rejected a proposal by a vote of 61–39 that would have granted fourteen weeks of maternity leave at 80 percent of a woman's salary. This sudden action kept Switzerland out of line with European standards. The vote also defied the Constitution of Switzerland, in which the concept of maternity leave was introduced in 1945. It reinforced the image of Switzerland as a chauvinistic stronghold where women did not win the right to vote until 1971. The voters also rejected the parliament of Switzerland — headed by its first female president, Ruth Dreifuss — which in 1998 had agreed on the proposed maternity benefit at a cost of some $330 million per year.

If Switzerland, a highly advanced nation, can reject a relatively basic program for women granting maternity benefits, what can be expected of some less sophisticated nations?

The unanticipated result in Switzerland undoubtedly reveals the dark fears which many men and some women have that the concept of women's rights is being pressed too aggressively and that this development is somehow weakening marriage and the family.

The machinery to carry out the CEDAW is underfunded, inadequately administered, and too feeble to meet the desperate needs women have for legal guidance and assistance. There is no optional protocol. This means that women cannot apply directly to the U.N. committee supervising their legal rights. Nor is there any legal way by which the U.N. Committee on CEDAW can force a nation to comply with its rulings. Sad to say, the half of humanity that is female has no adequate remedy to correct the oppression and discrimination they have experienced for centuries.

The international women's movement, with its international meetings every five years, offers information to the world about the centuries-old grievances of women. But legal avenues open to them are very limited. They can appeal to public opinion with the hope of mobilizing the shame which men and nations increasingly feel for the way societies dominated by men have treated women. But this grief and guilt often seems to be superficial.

Is a worldwide awakening about women's rights taking place? It surely is, but the legal aspirations of the awakening often seem peripheral. The world is still in the process of reconsidering the role assigned to women as mothers and homemakers. Are there ways of accepting and blessing that role while also opening up all the avenues for a larger life for women? That is the cosmic question with which the world is struggling. The emergence of the CEDAW is a symptom and a sign of the globe's rethinking of a very fundamental question.

That rethinking is taking form in the deliberations in the U.N. Committee on CEDAW. It is a tragedy for that group and also for the United States that America does not have a place at the table where twenty-three highly qualified women struggle to understand and articulate ways by which the human family can correct the major mistakes it has made in its treatment of women through the centuries.

The committee that supervises the implementation of the CEDAW tends to concentrate on the rights of women to vote, to hold office, to share equality in all matters with men, and, more and more, to enjoy equal opportunities in business and government. The role of rural women which is provided for in the convention does not seem to attract the same attention.

The frightening persistence of physical abuse of women has prompted the forces of feminism to promulgate a declaration (not a covenant suitable for ratification) lamenting the presence of abuse of women. It is indeed discouraging that as late as December 20, 1993, a world body felt obliged to issue a warning that the physical abuse of women continues and that in some quarters the male abuse of spouses is deemed to be a private offense not punishable by public authority.

On the subject of the elimination of violence against women, the Universal Declaration of Human Rights defines violence as any act that is "likely to result in physical, sexual or psychological harm or suffering to women . . . whether occurring in public or private life." The declaration warns that no country should "invoke any custom, tradition or religious consideration to avoid their obligations to eliminate without delay any policy or practice which assumes the inferiority or superiority of either of the sexes" or is based on "stereotype roles for men and women." Governments are furthermore urged to compile statistics on the prevalence of different forms of violence against women and on the effectiveness of measures implemented to prevent and redress violence against women.

The solemn plea in the U.N. declaration in 1993 put the U.N. General

Assembly at the heart of the struggle against violence aimed at women. It is a reaffirmation — indeed, an expansion — of the widely accepted conviction that violence against women is pervasive, endemic, and a "manifestation of historically unequal power relations between men and women." Violence against women, the declaration asserts, is "one of the crucial social mechanisms by which women are forced into a subordinate position compared with men."

The U.N. declaration on the subject of the elimination of violence against women defines violence as any act that is "likely to result in physical, sexual or psychological harm or suffering to women . . . whether occurring in public or private life." No man can be unaware of the prevalence of wife-battering, marital rape, and the sexual abuse of girls, but the spelling out of the incidence of violence has to be distressing and disturbing.

Assuming that the demands in the declaration against violence are a form of customary international law and thereby binding on governments, is there some hope that centuries-old abuses will be corrected? The basic assumption is that the globalization of the rights of women not to be subjected to violence reminds men everywhere of the shameful aspect of their violence and that the "mobilization of shame" will (at least eventually) have some impact in altering human conduct. Men must first be educated to accept the concept that their conduct in engaging in violence against women derives from their acceptance of the idea that women are inferior. If this stereotype fades away, will violence against women disappear or be sharply diminished?

That is the hope behind the urgent language of the U.N. declaration of December 1993. This statement also reflects and amplifies the strong words on violence against women that were contained in the final declaration of the World Conference on Human Rights in Vienna in June 1993.

Reports of violence against women — especially in the household — come as a shock to most men. Such reports are also appalling to human rights academics and activists. Such conduct, one likes to think, is engaged in only by men out of control or who are vicious and reckless in other areas of their life. But this correlation is not clear, because reports of sex-based domestic and other violence continue to come in from many nations and cultures. Dowry-related violence in India and elsewhere is widespread although it may be diminishing. Sexual harassment is relatively well defined in U.S. law and is presumably being deterred and inhibited, through awareness and enforcement of the law.

The anger and the anguish that instigated the 1993 U.N. declaration against violence are prevalent in the literature about the rights of women and the studies that seek to explain the centuries-old prejudice held by men that women are inferior. One story of the subordination of women by men has been retold in a 1995 study entitled "Human Rights Are Women's Rights," issued by Amnesty International. The last chapter outlines fifteen steps to protect women's human rights. The statement urges government acceptance of recommendations made by the four U.N. world conferences on women.

One of the topics discussed in the Amnesty report is female genital mutilation. An estimated 110 million women suffer serious injuries throughout their lives as a result of female genital mutilation. Approximately 2 million girls are mutilated every year. Female genital mutilation occurs in some twenty countries in Africa, parts of Asia, and the Middle East. Organized opposition to female genital mutilation seems to have surfaced in 1984 at a seminar in Dakar where participants from twenty African countries urged that female genital mutilation be abolished.

The practice has been condemned by the World Medical Association and the World Health Organization. The U.N. World Conference on Human Rights in Vienna in 1993 urged the repeal of existing laws and customs which "cause harm to the girl-child." The World Medical Association, in a statement of condemnation issued in October 1993, stated that irreversible damage is often inflicted on girls who are victimized by female genital mutilation.

But the traditional conceptions or myths continue to be believed and followed. The fear of girls and their families is that men will not marry a girl who has not submitted to female genital mutilation.

The practice seems so cruel and bizarre that its abolition would seemingly be easy and rapid. But it is by no means clear that the practice of female genital mutilation is living on borrowed time.

The actual origin of female genital mutilation can be traced to the Phoenicians and the Egyptians. But the actual purposes of the practice are hard to locate because it was done in secrecy. Mohammed, the prophet of

Islam, did not specifically denounce female genital mutilation. But the more commonly accepted view today seems to hold that the practice is neither required nor authorized by the Muslim religion.

Although it could be argued that a practice with such ancient roots could be tolerated in the name of cultural relativism, this would be difficult to justify in view of the overwhelming and mounting condemnation of female genital mutilation.

The Universal Declaration of Human Rights protects the security of a person, forbids cruel and degrading treatment, and urges protection for mothers and children. The Covenant on Civil and Political Rights and the International Covenant on Economic, Social, and Cultural Rights include similar provisions. The Convention on the Elimination of All Forms of Discrimination Against Women outlaws "practices prejudicial to the health of children."

Section 4.22 of the International Conference on Population and Development states flatly that "governments are urged to prohibit female genital mutilation whenever it exists."

The practice of female genital mutilation is now legally forbidden in Britain, Canada, France, Sweden, Switzerland, and, as of September 19, 1996, the United States. It is now banned in several African countries including Ghana, Guinea, Senegal, and Togo. On the other hand, it is estimated that 90 percent of the girls in Ethiopia, Eritrea, Somalia, and the Sudan (north) are subjected to female genital mutilation.

U.S. immigration law will now routinely grant refugee status to female immigrants if they have a well-founded fear that they or their female children will be subjected to female genital mutilation if they return to their country of origin.

The discussion of female genital mutilation offers a stark example of a practice which seems to be glaringly wrong by any acceptable modern standards. But it cannot be eliminated by any decree from a world body. Its termination can come about only through education, international pressure, and additional condemnations by world medical groups. Because the practice is not carried out by licensed physicians, it cannot be eliminated by prohibiting medical doctors from performing it. But their collaboration with the forty nations that still engage in female genital mutilation could be enormously beneficial.

Information about this topic will be discussed in the periodic reports of the 191 nations that have ratified the Convention on the Rights of the Child. But one has a right to be impatient with the continuation of a practice which the relevant agencies of the United Nations have condemned and which seems difficult to justify under anyone's conception of what is appropriate for children.

Other practices possibly as barbarous as female genital mutilation will almost certainly be discovered as the concept of the rights of women reaches remote places in China and in, for example, the fifteen newly independent nations that were born in 1990 with the collapse of the U.S.S.R.

Among all the horror stories about the degradation of women around the world, the abuse of females in Afghanistan has a special place. In 1996, the Taliban, an extremist military group that claims to follow Islamic theology, took over Kabul, the Afghan capital. The Taliban, which is not recognized by the United Nations, occupied 97 percent of Afghanistan. A special rapporteur for the U.N. Commission on Human Rights reported in September 1999 on the subjugation of women in Afghanistan. The Taliban bans girls from attending school after the age of eight, forbids most women from working outside the home, and severely restricts women's access to medical services by not allowing male physicians to treat them.

The status of women before 1945 was seemingly stable or relatively uniform in most developed countries. In retrospect, however, the status of women before the Charter of the United Nations and its cooperating agencies was in all probability thought to be unfair by many women at that time. The voices and votes of these women have in the past fifty years transformed the legal and global status of women.

The globalization of the rights of women continues to have an impact that is too profound and too long-lasting to evaluate at this time. It is possibly the most radical and revolutionary of all the changes that have occurred in the internationalization of human rights and will bring even deeper changes in the future when the United States ratifies the Convention on the Elimination of All Forms of Discrimination Against Women and joins the global dialogue on the place of women in the twenty-first century.

6

A

GLOBAL

REVOLUTION

FOR

CHILDREN

The authors of the 1945 Charter of the United Nations and the Universal Declaration of Human Rights did not refer specifically to the rights of children. From time immemorial, whatever rights children have had were subordinated to the rights of their parents or guardians. In the crudest statement of the law children "belonged" to their parents. The state was extremely reluctant to interfere with or override the almost sacred rights of parents.

In the twentieth century exceptions have been placed into the law for the delinquent child. But the broad concept of "rights" being inherent in the child was not familiar.

The emergence, therefore, of the U.N. Convention on the Rights of the Child is a breakthrough of enormous consequence. From 1945 until the 1980s virtually no one working in the field of international human rights spoke very much about the rights of those under the age of eighteen. In retrospect at least this is a curious thing because one-third or more of all the human beings in the world at any one time are minors. But the advocates of a global transformation in the way human rights are protected have not had the vision or the courage to internationalize the law regulating families. This law was the most local of all laws. Parents had almost unrestrictable discretion to discipline their children. And local and national governments had the almost total power to dictate what rights if any children should have.

But all those presumably unchangeable principles lost some of their credibility as the United Nations and its affiliated bodies internationalized the scope and enforceability of the basic human rights of all human beings.

The full thrust of the movement to globalize human rights emerged in a dramatic way when nongovernmental organizations persuaded the United Nations to approve the Convention on the Rights of the Child in 1989. The framers of the convention were careful to finesse the question of abortion by speaking only of the human rights of children already born. The drafters of the CRC also steered clear of other contentious questions. But the content and impact of the convention are strong, forthright, and in a sense revolutionary.

The promoters of the Convention on the Rights of the Child probably did not realize that it would attract more signatures in a shorter period of time than any other U.N. convention on human rights. They could not have anticipated that within a decade of approval by the United Nations, 191 nations would ratify it. In 1999, only the United States and Somalia had failed to ratify the CRC. Somalia had an excuse: there was no functional legislative body to act on the covenant.

The failure of the United States to ratify the convention is due to the existence of a handful of individuals and a few radically conservative groups that somehow think that the Convention on the Rights of the Child is anti-family. Even when these individuals are told that the Holy See, surely a pro-family organization, was the fifth nation in the world to ratify the CRC they are not persuaded that the United States should ratify this convention. Even the many reservations that would be added by the U.S. Senate do not placate the opponents of the CRC. They have demonized the treaty and are determined to prevent sixty-seven Senators from approving what they deem to be destructive of the family.

Again, the United States, as in the case of the Convention on the Elimination of All Forms of Discrimination Against Women, is not present at the table at the United Nations where a group of ten experts listen to the reports of 191 nations and prepare constructive ways to improve their treatment of children.

One likes to think that the insistent worldwide emphasis on human rights has improved the status of children throughout the world. But the evidence is mixed.

The 1999 report of UNICEF confirmed the distressing plight of children. Almost a billion people entered the twenty-first century unable to read a book or even sign their names. This means that some 855 million human beings — nearly one-fifth of humanity — are functionally illiterate as the new millennium begins.

In the year 2000, 130 million children had no access to basic education. Girls constituted 73 percent of this number. This lack of schooling for girls raises the rate of births and, hence, infant mortality. This correlation is illustrated in the southern Indian state of Kerala, where literacy is universal. There, the infant mortality rate is the lowest in the developing world. The right to education, central to the Convention on the Rights of the Child, has been heeded. In 1960 fewer than 15 percent of children ages six to eleven in developing nations were enrolled in school. By 1980 primary enrollment had more than doubled in Asia and Latin America. In Africa it had tripled.

But this progress was sharply curtailed in the 1980s. Poor countries, confronted with the interest due on the vast sums they had borrowed from lending entities in the west, allowed spending on education between 1980 and 1987 in Latin America and the Caribbean to decline by almost 40 percent. In sub-Saharan Africa it fell by 75 percent.

The forgiveness of debt for the forty poorest countries recommended by the G-7 in Cologne in 1999 may be helpful to these economically deprived nations. But they will still not be in a position to carry out completely their duties under the Convention on the Rights of the Child. But the remission of the debt that less developed nations accumulated in the 1970s and 1980s is a recognition by the world community that some of the billions borrowed were squandered by dictators or spent on projects for the rich and the well off and that in fairness, the present population should not be required to pay the interest or the capital on those mismanaged debts. The obligations these debtor nations had assumed when they ratified the CRC give present-day rulers a valid reason to ask for forgiveness of the loans so that they can carry out their duties under that convention.

The work of UNICEF and the aspirations of UNESCO continue to change the world's feelings about the rights of children. These sentiments make the task of the U.N. Convention on the Rights of the Child easier and more acceptable to the signatories which must report to the Committee on the Rights of the Child. It is not easy to evaluate the work of the committee, which began in February 1991. The information gathered by this agency and the amazing array of NGOs devoted to the improvement in the lot of children now constitutes an unprecedented resource for those under the age of eighteen.

During its first five years, the Committee on the Rights of the Child examined the records of eighty nations. Even though the committee has not yet attracted popular attention, it is developing a jurisprudence on complicated issues such as the rights of disabled children, teen pregnancy, juvenile delinquency, and corporal punishment. All the forty-one substantive provisions contained in the Convention on the Rights of the Child are being explored.

It is also astonishing to see how the signatory nations continue to include items from the Convention on the Rights of the Child in their constitutions and statutory laws. The court decisions and administrative regulations of many nations are based on the recommendations made in the CRC.

The U.N. machinery to enforce the provisions of the Convention on the Rights of the Child is only ten years old. It is, furthermore, merely a committee with no legally binding jurisdiction. Although its findings cannot be enforced, it serves as a fact-finding entity with respect to the way the signatory nations carry out their solemn promises to protect the internationally recognized rights of children. Theoretically nothing can be more repugnant to the conscience of the world than the violations of the rights of children by nations which have publicly and solemnly agreed to protect those rights.

Perhaps the next step that the United Nations and the world community can take is the protection of the rights of children by the imposition of civil sanctions and fines on the countries that defy their obligations. Such penalties and fines could be used against nations that refuse to carry out their duties under international environmental law or trade regulations.

The recent explosion of concerns over the use of child labor in the manufacturing of consumer items made in Asia and bought in America is an indication of the future direction of the U.N. Committee on the Rights of the Child. The elimination or monitoring of child labor in sweatshops and in the fields is a goal of a wide variety of groups in the developed nations. But it is a problem that is distressingly complex.

On June 15, 1999, President Clinton urged the International Labor Organization in Geneva to adopt a treaty that would bar the most abusive child labor practices. Mr. Clinton made it clear to the 174 member-nations of the ILO that his administration believes in open trade but that labor harmful to children's health, safety, and morals must be eliminated. This policy reinforces the executive order that President Clinton issued in early June 1999 requiring the federal government to buy products only after their producers certify that child labor was not included in their manufacture.

But the difficulties in protecting the rights of children are daunting. The U.N. Committee on the Rights of the Child is at present less than a fact-finding body. It is only an understaffed agency that listens to the presentations of nations which voluntarily comply with their duties under the CRC. But there is really no adversary process, nor does the committee have the resources to follow up in seeking to help various nations in carrying out their mandate under the CRC.

Again, the opportunities for nongovernmental organizations are enormous. Their believability and their voice can quite literally change the world. Advocates for the rights of children, for example, have formed a new agency for children within the structure of the Human Rights Watch. The NGOs dedicated to the rights of children have the advantage that they are not working for unappealing groups like prisoners or aliens or terrorists. But despite all the sentiment that everyone has for innocent children, the task of insisting on the fulfillment of their rights has been blocked by centuries of custom and tradition which held that children can be subordinated to their parents or their governments. The existence of thousands of child soldiers is one barbarous example of that age-old way of thinking.

But unlike the U.N. covenants on economic and political rights, the U.N. machinery to implement the rights of the child at least has been fueled by the instinctive love of children which has always been characteristic of the human race. As a result, while it is easy to think of the globalization of human rights as a utopian and unrealistic dream, it is hard to think that humanity could be entirely impervious to a repeated cry for gentleness to children.

Unfortunately, the record of the United States in its treatment of children is a poor one. The United States leads the developed world in child poverty. In 1979, the poverty rate for children was 14.7 percent; it is currently up to 20.4 percent. The incidence of poverty among children in the United States is four times that of children in western Europe. The number of children in the United States who are reportedly abused has tripled since 1980, to almost 3 million. The number of child murders doubled in the 1980s, and teenage suicide has doubled over the past twenty years. Every day in the United States 110 babies die before their first birthday. A simple analogy: if an airplane with 110 American children crashed every single day, the United States and the world would be in tears.

It is easy to be skeptical of the new energy on behalf of children that has been released by the establishment of the U.N. Committee on the Rights of the Child. This unit seems inadequate to protect the rights of almost 3 billion children in the world.

At the same time, the love of children — with their need for attention and care — is a moral bond that should transcend every local and national barrier.

The concept of the rights of children has now created an important legal mechanism to guarantee the fulfillment of those rights. It is an ancient and noble dream, first put into the world's legal aspirations in 1924 when the League of Nations in its declaration on children's rights stated, "The child that is hungry should be fed; the child that is sick should be helped . . . and the orphaned and the homeless child should be sheltered and succored."

Those moral demands have now been recognized as legally binding on the governments of 191 nations. These countries have made solemn promises and entered into binding contracts to love children by guaranteeing them their rights. The world has obtained an unprecedented level of caring and compassion. The twentieth century was probably the bloodiest and most violent 100 years in human history; perhaps the twenty-first century will be a golden age for children.

7

In addition to the already noted entities within the United Nations devoted to human rights are the committees dedicated to overseeing the compliance to the International Convention on the Elimination of All Forms of Racial Discrimination and the Convention Against Torture and Other Cruel, Inhuman, or Degrading Treatment or Punishment (also known as the Covenant Against Torture).

The United States has ratified both these treaties, but with crippling reservations. On the torture convention, for example, the Senate has accepted qualifications insisted upon by the Bush administration which in essence say that the United States agrees to restrictions on torture only if they do not go beyond existing judicial interpretations in the United States of the Fourth, Fifth, and Fourteenth Amendments.

Although torture has never been an institution, practice, or tradition in America as it is in several countries around the world, the United States looks self-centered and hypocritical when it seeks praise from the international community for ratifying the convention against torture and other cruel, inhuman, or degrading treatment while simultaneously telling the world that it will not change or expand its basic interpretation of the meaning of torture. The fact is that around the world, interpretations of the words "inhuman" and "degrading" named in the Covenant Against Torture do go beyond what American courts have determined is the intent of the "cruel and unusual punishment" forbidden in the Eighth Amendment.

The U.N. Committee on the Elimination of All Forms of Racial Discrimination (CERD) has also issued many rulings on the nature of discrimination that are more advanced than the customary definition in America. In addition, this U.N. committee, which monitors compliance with the CERD, has not directed its attention to the United States. As of late 1999 the State Department had not submitted the report that was due. Clearly the definition of discrimination based on race that the U.N. Committee on CERD has issued is more expansive than are comparable interpretations by U.S. legislatures and courts.

It is easy to criticize the caution and the mired bureaucracy of the U.N. agencies devoted to human rights. That sentiment was prominent at the U.N. World Conference on Human Rights in Vienna in 1993. The cry there, echoing a generation of similar pleas, was for the creation of the office of the U.N. High Commissioner for Human Rights. The model and even the title were taken from the U.N. High Commissioner for Refugees, an effective agency which, despite its limitations, seems to be acting where it is now needed — in Southeast Asia, Rwanda, and Kosovo.

The office of the U.N. High Commissioner on Human Rights was created in 1994 (pursuant to the 1993 World Conference on Human Rights) and is headed by Mary Robinson, the former president of Ireland. Her mandate is daunting: coordinate and intensify all U.N. efforts to improve and enhance human rights. The long-held dream of having a "czar" for human rights has been realized. But the decentralized and fragmented agencies on human rights established by the United Nations over the past fifty-five years cannot easily be integrated into a unified system.

Underlying the resistance is the seemingly ineradicable idea of national sovereignty. It would be nice to be able to think that the radical self-centeredness of individual nations has been downsized in the past fifty years. But this is not clear or at least provable.

The fact is that the victors in World War II retained their sovereignty in a basically crude way by insisting on their veto power in the U.N. Security Council. This would be tantamount to the U.S. Senate declaring that 5 of the 100 senators have the power to veto any development or vote that they disapprove. This veto power allowed—and, perhaps, helped create—the forty-five-year struggle between the United States and the U.S.S.R. If neither of these giants had the veto power, a majority of the members of the United Nations could have used all their diplomatic and even military strength to prevent the Soviet Union from invading eastern Europe and the United States from sending military forces to Vietnam.

Can the efforts of the United Nations to promote and protect those human rights guaranteed in the 1945 Charter of the United Nations and the covenants on human rights be increased as long as the veto power remains in the charter? The fact that the veto power has rarely been exercised since the collapse of Communism in 1990 is a sign of hope that the former superpowers, while they may disagree on some basic world issues, are not opponents on the question of human rights.

It should also be noted that the moral concepts underlying the protection of human rights may take time—even generations—to become embedded in the souls of governments and people around the world. The Magna Carta, it could be argued, bore fruit in the legal institutions of England and America only after hundreds of years had passed. Generations of slaves suffered and died before European nations and the United States came to the conclusion that slavery was a degrading affront to the inherent dignity of persons of color.

In evaluating the effectiveness of the United Nations on international human rights, close attention should be paid to the enormous contributions of U.N. agencies like the Food and Agriculture Organization, the World Health Organization, UNICEF, UNESCO, and the U.N. Development Fund. These agencies have quite literally transformed the world. No prior world agencies, except possibly the International Labor Organization, rival their achievements. These units, it should be pointed out, are devoted to the fulfillment of the economic rights guaranteed in the Universal Declaration of Human Rights and in the International Covenant on Economic, Social, and Cultural Rights.

These agencies have actually done extraordinarily well, considering that the population of the earth since 1945 has increased roughly from 3 billion to 6 billion.

At the Vienna World Conference on Human Rights in 1993, the issue that permeated every topic was the changes that are needed in the United Nations. The issue is complex beyond imagination. United Nations watchers who have followed this sprawling agency in the years 1948 to 1990 apparently found themselves incapable after 1990 of recommending the essential elements of a change in the U.N. structure. The Vienna meeting was not exactly devoted to that intractable topic, but the issue could not be avoided.

The Vienna conference ended without an articulated consensus on the reform of the United Nations. It did conclude that the United Nations' legacy on human rights transcends the concept of "cultural relativism." Secretary of State Warren Christopher said: "We respect the religious, social and cultural characteristics that make each country unique. But we cannot let cultural relativism become the last refuge of repression." The World Conference on Human Rights in 1993 made it clear that the end of the Cold War would not be an occasion for any group of nations to use their own long-standing practices to become, as Christopher put it, "the last refuge of repression." Child slavery or bondage and female infanticide, for example, must go the way of foot-binding in China.

What, then, are the primordial tasks facing the United Nations with regard to the promotion and protection of human rights? One is tempted to settle on massive education. If people everywhere could see and hear internationally recognized economic and political human rights exalted on CNN, on the World Wide Web, and in all the rapidly emerging avenues of communicating ideas, could there be a worldwide acceptance of those basic rights which for almost sixty years have been proclaimed as the patrimony of the human race?

No one can accurately predict what moral ideas will take hold at a particular time. This depends on the presence or absence of leadership. It also depends on the attitude of the new colonialists — the dominant industries of developed nations as they "descend" on nations like Angola, where the political scene is chaotic.

Could there be an alliance between the newer nations and the economic Goliaths of developed nations? The international mergers of the largest industrial corporations in the west and in Japan may bring an infusion of economic power to countries in Asia and Africa, which in turn could bring about a new colonialism even more savage and repressive than the worst examples of colonialism which Europe inflicted on nations in Africa and Asia.

The dream of the United Nations, as updated in the final declaration of human rights in Vienna in 1993, is that the proclamation of human rights as redefined and reasserted in 1993 will be able to direct the new economic invasions of underdeveloped countries so that the 2 or more billion people in those nations will simultaneously enjoy the benefits of capitalism and the blessings of democracy.

Although the United States — specifically, the Clinton administration — led the way in preparing for and staging the Vienna World Conference on Human Rights in 1993, the real movers were the thousands of delegates from the NGOs. These groups, stifled by the forty years of an east-west impasse, saw a way to revivify the human rights promises that had been so central to the plans underlying the very concept of the United Nations. NGOs representing the disabled, children, indigenous peoples, the tortured, and prisoners of conscience electrified the scene in Vienna. One delegate representing the disabled praised the Americans With Disabilities Act, signed by George Bush, as the best and most promising of all the laws in the world enacted to assist the mentally or physically challenged. A representative of an Asian group of battered and tortured women told me that a presidential commission on which I served to indemnify the 120,000 Japanese interned in World War II had written a report which is the model for a plan to obtain reparation for the 200,000 women forcibly taken by Japan from Korea to serve Japanese soldiers at war throughout the Pacific. She felt that the sum of $20,000 given by the U.S. government to each surviving Japanese internee was a fine model for the Korean women whose lives had been ruined by the Japanese kidnappings.

The Vienna conference sought to revive the United Nations after its long twilight in the shadow of the east-west Cold War. In the final statement, the delegates recognized that the United Nations had undergone what in essence is a rebirth, echoing that profound conviction by the pledge of 161 countries to return with vigor and enthusiasm to the original devotion to international human rights embodied in the U.N. charter, the Universal Declaration of Human Rights, and the score of covenants on human rights.

Unfortunately, the United States remains the country that neglects and defies the vision of the United Nations and the final declaration in Vienna. In addition to committing the unforgivable act of partially paralyzing the United Nations by not paying its dues, the United States failed to approve the International Criminal Court in June 1998 in Rome, has not returned to UNESCO, has declined to sign the world agreement on banning land mines, and continues to refuse to collaborate with the agreements on the law of the sea.

Is there some fatal flaw in the American character when it comes to operating as only one of 191 nations in the United Nations? Is the United States an actor in an ongoing Greek tragedy of monumental proportions? Will the United States ever return to the role of moral leadership it assumed during the first few years of the existence of the United Nations? Or is the United States irreversibly entrenched in a posture of isolationism and self-centeredness?

Everyone talks about globalization as inevitable, good for American business, and the next step somehow in the manifest destiny of America.

The discontent of the Congress and the country with America's record on human rights caused the Congress in 1976 to put into statutory law several measures to force the government to fulfill the promises it made on human rights. We now turn to that defining development in the foreign policy of the United States when the Congress acted along with President Ford in 1976.

Part II

THE
UNITED STATES
AND
HUMAN RIGHTS

8

THE UNITED STATES
INTERVENES ON BEHALF
OF INTERNATIONAL
HUMAN RIGHTS

When it came out in Senate hearings in the early 1970s that the United States had intervened in Chile and helped to bring General Augusto Pinochet to power over the popularly elected Salvador Allende, there was anger and fury in the country. The United States justified its conduct by asserting that because Allende, a professor, was a Marxist the United States had no choice. The rhetoric flowed that the Communists had planned to take over the southern cone of Latin America and that Argentina would be the next victim.

Many members of the U.S. Congress felt embarrassed that the United States in its struggle to stop Soviet aggression ended up arming dictators because they were enemies of our enemy. The pattern was familiar in America's defense of South Korea, Nicaragua's Somoza, and similar anti-Communist officials.

But the Nixon administration's part in helping General Pinochet somehow triggered a revolt. Congressman Don Fraser, the Democrat from Minnesota, was the chairman of the relevant subcommittee of the House Foreign Affairs Committee. He began a long series of hearings on the question of how the United States was carrying out its solemn pledge made in its ratification of the 1945 Charter of the United Nations to protect human rights. Congressman Fraser conducted up to a hundred hearings and heard the exiles and representatives of dozens of nations where human rights were not protected by either the United States or the United Nations.

I followed those hearings closely. I met some of the witnesses — exiles from dozens of countries like Burma, Chile, China, and the "captive nations" of eastern Europe.

Eventually Congressman Fraser prepared a bill which would remind the United States of its duties under the U.N. charter to protect and promote human rights. The actual words of the U.N. charter, and especially the pledge to advance human rights contained in Articles 55 and 56, are quoted in the preamble of the Fraser Bill. The thrust of the bill was to prevent the United States from giving aid, military or civilian, to those nations engaged in a pattern or practice of denying internationally recognized human rights. The practice must be persistent and carried out not by terrorist groups within a country but by the government itself. The State Department was designated as the agency to compile an annual report on the state of human rights in every nation that received aid from the United States. That requirement was later extended to every nation, whether or not they are the direct recipients of aid from the United States.

The first version of the Fraser Bill was vetoed by President Ford. He followed the advice of Secretary of State Henry Kissinger, who felt that the standards set by the Congress would be too mechanistic and too inflexible to be a part of the efforts of the State Department and the Department of Defense in their mission to carry out America's policy of containing Communism.

The veto was not overridden, but a second bill with some modifications was signed into law by President Ford. One of the better features of the original Fraser Bill provided for the creation of a bipartisan commission on human rights outside the State Department that, as through the highly regarded U.S. Commission on Civil Rights, would hold hearings and publish periodic reports on the state of human rights around the world. This amendment was unfortunately defeated on the floor largely by Republicans, many of whom opposed the underlying bill.

No attempt has been initiated to restore the nonpartisan commission on human rights defeated on the House floor. This way of collecting information on human rights and communicating it would have been more professional and much preferred to the present arrangement. Political and partisan positions affect the objectivity of the annual report issued by the State Department. Information in the report is gathered by U.S. ambassadors around the world aided in larger countries by their human rights officers. The reports have become less political during the twenty years of their existence. But a report issued by an agency with a reputation for objectivity would more accurately reflect the obligation the United States assumed when it agreed in Article 56 of the U.N. charter: that it would advance and enhance the human rights noted in Article 55. It should be noted that those rights are broad and inclusive. No distinction is made between economic and political rights.

Article 55 provides that all signatory nations shall promote

(a) higher standards of living, full employment and conditions of economic and social practice and development; (b) the solutions of international economic, social, health, and related problems; and international cultural and education cooperation; and (c) universal respect for and observance of human rights and fundamental freedoms for all without distinction as to race, sex, language or religion.

The Fraser Bill—which became Section 502b of the Foreign Assistance Act—begins with these words:

The United States shall, in accordance with its international obligations as set forth in the charter of the United Nations and in keeping with the constitutional heritage and traditions of the United States, promote and encourage increased respect for human rights and fundamental freedoms throughout the world without distinction as to race, sex, language or religion. Accordingly, a principal goal of the foreign policy of the United States shall be to promote increased observance of internationally recognized human rights by all countries.

The bill goes on to state that "no security assistance may be provided to any country the government of which engages in a consistent pattern of gross violations of internationally recognized human rights." It should be noted that a government must engage in a "consistent" pattern. In addition, the violations must be "gross." The president does, however, have some discretion in that he can certify that "extraordinary circumstances" exist that warrant an exception to the policy.

The basic rationale of the Fraser initiative is explained in the bill by saying that the United States should "avoid identification . . . with governments which deny to their people internationally recognized human rights and fundamental freedoms, in violation of international law or in contravention of the policy of the United States."

This policy is modified by another portion of a separate law which stipulates that the U.S. government "in connection with its voice and vote" in the international development banks must advance the humanitarian purposes and the protection for human rights implicit in the U.N. charter.

These laws have led to a cutoff of aid in fewer than ten instances — mostly in Latin America. The policy was executed by Congress itself with a specific cutoff of all aid to Chile after General Pinochet seized power. Most of the worst offenders of human rights during the years of the Cold War did not, of course, receive any U.S. aid and hence did not constitute a problem.

For a generation, there has been a great debate over the advisability, feasibility, and wisdom of Section 502b. The objectives of the measure are so laudable that hardly anyone is calling for its repeal. But U.S. ambassadors in countries with problematic human rights records (like Malaysia) are troubled about their role in collecting information on violations of human rights. Their participation in this role does not endear them to the host government.

Some of the situations on which the ambassador and his or her staff are required to report are deeply political. The most serious cases involve alleged torture, disappearances, restrictions on the press and radio, and denial of rights such as free elections. In instances like these, the facts are often disputed. Local government can always dispute the allegations of wrongdoing. Should the U.S. embassy be in a bitter dispute between contending political factions?

In the ideal scenario, some fact-finding entity related to the United Nations should be the mediator or judge. But as we have seen, the U.N. Commission on Human Rights is far less engaged in this area than would be ideal. The nongovernmental agencies, especially Amnesty International, are engaged in collecting information for their own annual reports on human rights. No ambassador would feel comfortable in contradicting findings by Amnesty International, knowing that its reputation for accuracy and credibility is very high.

The State Department report card every February now numbers over 2,000 pages. It complies with several congressional demands that the volume include all relevant information on topics such as the rights of women, the number of children who work, and the freedom of labor unions. The reports are, increasingly, the work of a professional staff in the office of the assistant secretary of state for human rights.

The annual report on human rights financed by the U.S. government is unique in the world. No other nation has even attempted to compile such a comprehensive document. Does the report alienate the governments whose human rights records are criticized? Does it ingratiate the United States with other nations?

At the very least, the report is an annual announcement that the United States is committed to the promotion of human rights. But it almost inevitably raises questions everywhere about the presumptions of America, gathering the facts and delivering the report, to the whole world.

If Japan put out an annual "shame sheet" on the United States and all the other nations of the world, it would be embarrassing for the United States and many others. All the criticized countries would challenge Japan's right to evaluate them.

The fact that nations do not openly criticize the United States for its involvement in the human rights conditions of other nations is a silent concession that the United States is deemed the world's principal leader in advancing human rights.

That is the image which politicians and some diplomats seek to project. To some extent, it is accurate. In the 1970s the Congress passed a bill named after Senator Henry Jackson (the Democrat from Washington) and Representative Charles Vanik (the Democrat from Ohio) which sought to expedite the release of Soviet Jews. Several thousand were able to migrate to Israel or to the United States. But there was and is criticism that there were better ways of accomplishing the release of some of the 3 million Jews in the Soviet Union whose religious liberty had been restricted by the Kremlin since at least 1917.

It is ironic indeed that the United States — the country which insisted on being the home of the United Nations and a nation considered the principal protector of that body — has in part abandoned its own creation on human rights by the construction of an American agency to do the work which originally the United Nations was slated to do. But the State Department's work of monitoring human rights, however valuable, cannot possibly match that which the United Nations is chartered to do. The United States disseminates its annual assessment on all the nations of the earth but does not offer consultation and guidance. Although the State Department has one remedy available to punish countries with truly egregious human rights conditions — the cutoff of funds — that remedy is seldom employed.

The enactment of Section 502b was no doubt a milestone in America's pilgrimage to carry out its pledge to comply with Article 56 of the U.N. charter. But it is an incomplete, unilateral, awkward, and problematic way of seeking to effectuate the purposes and aims of the United Nations' unprecedented efforts to focus on the fulfillment of human rights as one of the central missions of this world agency.

The new human rights program set forth in Section 502b did not become an issue in the presidential campaign in 1976. But candidate Jimmy Carter stressed human rights and promised in essence to make human rights the "soul of his foreign policy." Although Carter may have received some political support from human rights activists, there was almost no political controversy during the campaign over the Fraser-initiated novel role for the United States in advancing human rights.

But the establishment of the Bureau of Democracy, Human Rights, and Labor (previously called the Bureau of Human Rights and Humanitarian Affairs) by the State Department during the Reagan years and President Carter's appointment of Patricia Derian as its first head led to battles between the Pentagon, the State Department, and its regional bureaus. The warfare over the place of human rights in America's foreign policy waged between 1977 and 1981 has not been documented in any thorough academic way. The keepers of some of the solemn traditions of the State Department felt assaulted by the intervention of Congress. They had been trained to operate on the principle that America's interests, not its ideals, should be the predominant criterion in carrying out America's foreign policy.

In the Carter administration the highest officials spoke repeatedly and insistently that America's ideals as well as its interests should both be present in the way the United States reacts to other nations. The objectives of Section 502b were taken seriously and sometimes literally. The United States rebuked the military government of Argentina which reigned from 1976 to 1983. The threat of termination of aid to Brazil angered the ruling generals in that country. But few such threats were leveled at nations where the United States had important business or military alliances.

In the four years of the Carter administration the stress on human rights became accepted — at least on the surface. Yet, militant anti-Communists felt strongly that the policy was unfair to some U.S. allies who might have been weak on human rights but were strong in keeping the Soviets out of their area of the world.

The principal objections to the human rights program of the Carter administration were not clearly defined. The critics of the new program had to admit that Section 502b gives a great deal of discretion and flexibility to the president and to the State Department. The law does not say explicitly that the United States must sacrifice some of its important interests to avoid compromising its ideals. The law was intended to insist on a strong emphasis on human rights — but without flat command or inflexible criteria.

The speeches and rhetoric of President Carter on human rights certainly raised the decibels on that topic around the world. It gave hope and inspiration to countless dissidents and to the untold millions who longed to be free from the bondage of military dictatorships or economic penury. Indeed, it may be that the Carter administration caused the idea of human rights to enter the political and moral coinage of the nation and to some extent of the world. The concept of human rights had been everywhere since the United Nations and its agency began talking about it in the 1940s and 1950s. But seemingly overnight in the 1970s and 1980s, the United States and all the developed countries were talking about their duty to make human rights an active part of their foreign policy.

The resistance to an active role in international human rights by the United States surged as the Reagan administration took over in 1981. The Reagan White House apparently decided it was not possible to simply abolish the office of the assistant secretary of state for human rights.

Instead, it tried to do just that by indirect means: it appointed Ernest Lefever to the position of assistant secretary of state for human rights even though Lefever, the holder of a doctorate in divinity from Yale, had on several occasions opposed the very creation and perpetuation of the position of assistant secretary of state for human rights.

I recall chatting with Lefever in February 1981 in the office designated for the human rights official at the State Department. He fully expected to be confirmed by the Senate and to sit for at least four years in the chair he occupied when I and a group of human rights academics questioned him. Lefever was strong on prepossessions but short on answers to the nagging question of why he wanted the job that he said should not exist.

To the amazement of almost everyone, scores of nongovernmental organizations appeared at the Senate hearing on Lefever's appointment. Sitting in the cavernous Senate room during those hearings, I and every other participant was astonished at the number and vigor of those opposing Lefever's appointment. The new and untested NGOs dedicated to human rights seemed to discover one another and their collective strength when they gathered and lobbied against the appointment of a man who, as far as they could discern, was an enemy of any program by the United States that sought to advance human rights.

Patricia Derian had made her position into a bully pulpit for victims all over the world. The rejection of Lefever's appointment by the Republican-controlled U.S. Senate Foreign Relations Committee stunned almost everyone. To vote down a nominee for a minor position in the State Department was a rebuke to the recently elected popular President Reagan. It was also an explosive announcement that the forces behind the human rights movement had arrived in Washington and that their idealistic appeal to global standards of human decency would not fade away.

For several months the Reagan White House seemed to be in shock. No one had been appointed to the position on human rights created by the Fraser Bill and the Carter White House. Activists in the human rights movement, elated and exuberant over their victory in the Lefever matter, did not vigorously urge the appointment of another because they feared that in a second hearing they might not be able to prevail in the Republican Senate.

After months of silence and inaction, the Reagan White House appointed Elliott Abrams as assistant secretary of state for human rights. He was confirmed after making the implementation of human rights an important objective of the Reagan administration — but with the understanding that the principal objective would be to protest the intimidation of citizens in the "captive nations" of eastern Europe, in Cuba, and, of course, in China.

Abrams was confirmed because he and his colleagues had devised a plausible, if seriously curtailed, role for the office on human rights. The human rights arm of the State Department pounded away at the loss of political liberties in lands controlled by the Communists. At its annual event on December 10, Human Rights Day, the accent was always on escapees from the Soviet Union or Cuba but seldom if ever on the problems of the victims of dictatorships in Nicaragua, El Salvador, or Chile. The heroes on December 10, the day when the Universal Declaration of Human Rights was ratified in Paris in 1948, almost always supported the anti-Communist theme of Assistant Secretary of State Elliott Abrams.

But even the strong anti-Communist theme of the Reagan administration could not drown out the cries for human rights in Haiti, South Africa, and elsewhere. Under the pressure of public opinion, the Reagan administration quietly shifted to a position that embraced the violation of human rights of all kinds — whether by Communists or authoritarian regimes. The Reagan administration finally persuaded the U.S. Senate to ratify the Covenant on Genocide — which had been pending in the Senate for some forty years.

In the second Reagan administration, the fifty-year struggle of the international community against apartheid in South Africa finally reached crisis proportions. President Reagan warned everybody that he would veto tougher economic sanctions against South Africa. Despite that threat, Congress enacted Draconian sanctions against South Africa — prohibiting, in essence, U.S. banks and corporations from doing business there. To the astonishment of everyone, both the House and the Senate overrode the White House veto by the necessary two-thirds vote. It was the African-American and civil rights community in the United States that made this a decisive issue. One could probably argue that it was the international human rights movement that finally prevailed in the abolition of apartheid. And it was the boycott by the United States that prompted Pretoria to release Nelson Mandela and move toward multi-party democratic elections.

It is plausible that the negative attitude or hostility of the Reagan administration toward the promotion of human rights deepened the idealism and determination of those in the human rights movement. New NGOs were formed. The Human Rights Watch split into units to monitor conditions in Latin America, Asia, Europe, and Africa. The Lawyers Committee for Human Rights, founded in 1979, flourished. And Amnesty International, established in 1961 by a lawyer in London, continued to be the senior "guardian angel" of human rights everywhere.

At the bicentennial of Georgetown University in 1989, I chaired a series of symposia on every aspect of international human rights. The variety and vigor of the initiatives by NGOs was dazzling.

The Bush administration, like its predecessor, did not want to be aggressively proactive in its defense of human rights. The assistant secretary of human rights ambassador was Richard Schifter, whom the Reagan administration had appointed to succeed Elliott Abrams. Speaking at the Georgetown University bicentennial conference, Schifter was correct and careful, but not in any way crusading. Many of the participants were disappointed; their concept of the office of human rights at the State Department clearly differed from that of the Reagan and the Bush administrations.

Although the twelve years of the Reagan-Bush administrations did not advance human rights as many of the supporters of the Fraser bill had intended or hoped, the institutionalization of international human rights as an important component of America's foreign policy did progress. The annual reports of the State Department contained rebukes to most nondemocratic nations. NGOs, Human Rights Watch, and the Lawyers Committee for Human Rights issued annual critiques of the errors and inadequacies of these reports. The Lawyers Committee for Human Rights prepared a quadrennial report which offered constructive suggestions to the incoming president on an ever wider range of issues involving human rights. This report included recommendations on topics related to international trade, refugees, the covenants on human rights, and improvements in the way the U.S. State Department should handle issues related directly to human rights.

Proactive NGOs found the Reagan and Bush administrations seriously inadequate or even inexcusably negligent in the way they failed to promote human rights.

In fairness, those with views differing from the militant approach of groups like the Human Rights Watch are not necessarily less sensitive to human rights. The U.S. State Department, in their view, should not be compelled by Congress to "correct" or "scold" other nations. Their view of statecraft, diplomacy, and separation of powers results in a different position. Like Secretary of State Henry Kissinger in the Ford administration, they do not think that the Congress should dictate that human rights should be a crucial or paramount part of U.S. foreign policy. This body feels that the nation should weigh and balance many factors in the formulation of its foreign policy. The Congress theoretically agrees with this approach; Section 502b does not make human rights the only—or even the most crucial—factor in the making of foreign policy.

But the point of view of Kissinger and the many professionals and diplomats who agree with it has been defeated. It has succumbed to the ever-present desire of Americans to be fighting some kind of crusade for democracy, a better world, or global peace. The convictions expressed in the Declaration of Independence seem to be inherent in the psyche of Americans. Those dreams and aspirations played a significant part in America's participation in World War I and World War II as well as its support of the Cold War against the U.S.S.R. from 1948 to 1990.

Much of America's distinctive desire to protect and fight for human freedom has been the soul of the new protection offered to international human rights by the enactment of Section 502b.

The passion to enforce and expand human rights prompted President Clinton to appoint John Shattuck to the position of assistant secretary of state for human rights. Shattuck had been the director of the American Civil Liberties Union in Washington for ten years, and then became vice president and general counsel at Harvard University. He was active there in Amnesty International and was clearly identified as an enthusiast for human rights. More than any previous holder of this position, Shattuck sought to expand its role within the boundaries of the law.

Like all his predecessors, Shattuck had to take into consideration the views and interests of the White House, the Pentagon, and other relevant agencies in the formulation of what the United States should say and do about, for example, the state of human rights in China. In addition, he and his professional staff had to be sensitive to efforts being made by other branches of government in seeking to improve human rights in specific cases or in nations moving toward democracy. The mere mention of a problem in a particular nation could alienate the leaders of that country and cause them to regress on human rights initiatives.

Some day the voluminous files of the human rights office of the State Department will be opened so that humanity can see how and why the United States remained firm or became conciliatory toward abuses in a country whose leaders were sincerely moving toward compliance with their duties under the U.N. charter.

Shattuck was obligated to prepare the first American report on its compliance with the U.N. International Covenant on Civil and Political Rights. The Clinton administration had added some qualifications, understandings, and declarations that Shattuck almost certainly would oppose. But the mere filing of that report was a new milestone in America's obedience to its obligations under international law.

During Secretary Shattuck's term from 1993 to 1998 the bureau became more institutionalized and professionalized. It also acquired a new name from Congress: the Department for Democracy, Human Rights and Labor. When Shattuck was appointed as the Ambassador to the Czech Republic his position was taken by Harold Hongju Koh, a professor of human rights law at Yale who is of South Korean ancestry. The confirmation of Koh was surprisingly easy and quick. Perhaps the Republican Senate had been informed about the sincere work of Professor Koh on behalf of exiled Cubans.

Secretary Koh had some tough human rights issues facing him early in his administration. The Dayton Accords, the struggle over Kosovo, the proposed International Criminal Court all involved intricate problems at least indirectly related to the issues assigned by the Congress to the Bureau of Democracy, Human Rights, and Labor.

Koh made it clear as soon as he had been confirmed by the Senate that he, like his immediate predecessor, would reach out to nongovernmental organizations. The number, strength, and influence of the NGOs increased almost unbelievably during the Clinton administration. These organizations had been heartened by their impact at the World Conference on Human Rights in Vienna in 1993. Indeed, those who do not want the influence of the Bureau for Democracy, Human Rights and Labor to expand must be fearful of the power of the human rights lobby in Washington and in the country. These groups regularly caucus with other units and can orchestrate thousands of e-mails to the Congress and the White House. The bureau is now such a familiar part of the Washington landscape that almost everyone assumes it is a permanent part of the State Department. But even the most cursory review of this agency shows that it is an anomaly and that its role could possibly be carried out more effectively if it were part of a nonpartisan commission not inhibited by its obligation to work in harmony with the State Department, which must naturally be in political alignment with the elected officials in the White House.

The Congress that created the Bureau for Democracy, Human Rights and Labor in 1976 realized that it was fashioning an anomaly. But Congress was angry that the United States was not carrying out its promises made pursuant to the U.N. charter. The United States in 1976 had not ratified the major human rights treaties and, in addition, had polarized the world's nations according to their friendship or enmity with the Soviet Union.

Congressman Don Fraser, the prime architect of America's modern human rights policy, conducted extensive hearings on human rights and reviewed all options to the Congress. If the impeachment of President Nixon and the tumult over the Vietnam War had not been on the agenda of Congress during that period, it is conceivable that a different approach to the enforcement of international human rights might have emerged. But probably not. Beginning with the polarization of the east and the west, the invasion of eastern Europe in 1948, and the fall of Peking in 1949 to the Communists, the United States became locked into a mindset that the containment of Communism was the only objective of America's foreign policy. That objective overshadowed everything else. But the detestation of Communism was not enough to prompt the United States to invade the "captive nations" of armed Communist China or to even land in Cuba. There were a number of contradictions and incoherencies in America's approach to the U.S.S.R. and its satellites. It could be argued that containment was a policy which basically was an expansion of America's endorsement of those human rights which were made inviolable in the U.N. charter.

The members of Congress in 1976 realized all this, but they were ashamed of what their country was doing to attract authoritarian nations to join the struggle against totalitarian countries. The United States helped to create the nonaligned countries through its adamant desire to turn all nations outside the Communist sphere into the enemies of Marxism. This one myopic determination had, in the minds of a majority of Congress members, led the United States to abandon its solemn pledge in Articles 55 and 56 of the U.N. charter to work for political and economic human rights for all persons.

The months-long struggle to establish new laws protecting and promoting international human rights may well have caused an echo in Europe. The birth of the nebulous concept of detente occurred as the Congress was ending the war in Vietnam and thinking out its strategy on penalizing nations that neglected their duties under world law to observe international human rights. In the chanceries of Europe in the early 1970s a haphazard process, later called Helsinki, began to emerge. At dozens of meetings of low- and middle-level diplomats a document developed listing the rights European countries wanted their sister nations to observe. Political, economic, and cultural rights were thrown into three so-called baskets. In some cases, no one knew who had suggested these rights; they simply ended up in the 35,000-word final document signed by President Ford and the leaders of thirty-four other countries in Helsinki on August 1, 1975. Ford's coming to Helsinki on behalf of human rights was a strategy devised or at least allowed by Secretary of State Henry Kissinger. The dramatic ceremony in which the U.S.S.R. and all the satellite nations except Albania signed the document on human rights agreed to by all the European nations, Canada, and the United States was probably the greatest triumph for human rights since the U.N. General Assembly agreed to the Universal Declaration of Human Rights in 1948. Indeed, the Helsinki Accords reaffirmed most of the pledges of the Universal Declaration of Human Rights.

President Ford and Secretary Kissinger might have wanted only to deter the Congress from placing a new burden related to human rights on the State Department. But they probably strengthened the resolve of the majority in Congress to make certain that the State Department carried out the bold promises which the United States had re-ratified in Helsinki.

I happened to be in Moscow on a human rights mission on the days immediately following Moscow's dramatic signing of the Helsinki Accords. To the amazement of almost everyone, the total text of the Helsinki document was carried in the newspapers *Pravda* and *Izvestia*. My guide and translator, Anatoly Sharansky, and one of my hosts, Dr. Andre Sakharov, were amazed but jubilant. (I recall using one of the Helsinki promises in a specific way. The Accords say categorically that if a person is denied the right to leave a nation, he may not be charged a fee for a second application. I cited that clause to a sullen clerk at the Obir (immigration office). He waived the second fee!

The surge in the use of the Helsinki Accords in all the Iron Curtain countries was one of the principal reasons for the solidarity movement in Poland and comparable developments all over eastern and central Europe. This document was one of the many reasons why over 500,000 Soviets were able to immigrate to Israel.

It seems clear, therefore, that the human rights content of the U.N. charter and all its progeny came to flower in the United States and in Europe in the mid-1970s.

At a meeting of the Helsinki nations in November 1980 in Madrid, in which I participated, it seemed evident that a new era for human rights was being born. Members of the U.S. Congress like myself posed tough questions to the Soviets about specific prisoners or victims. But the smaller nations of Europe, including the Holy See, were grateful for the Helsinki process because finally they had a forum in which to raise questions about individual refugees or property taken in an east European nation or promises that had been broken concerning long festering issues of religious freedom.

The Soviets were aware in 1980 that pursuant to congressional action the State Department was now publishing an annual report on the misdeeds related to human rights in the Soviet Union and its "captive nations." The Kremlin wanted and needed trade with the United States. Soviet leaders feared the consequences of a few negative words or paragraphs in the annual report card on human rights of the State Department.

Without the protests of nongovernmental agencies in 1981 over the appointment of Ernest Lefever, the Bureau of Democracy, Human Rights, and Labor could have been eviscerated and almost extinguished. But the bureau had received such impetus and support during the Carter administration that its opponents could not destroy it or even de-fang it.

The idea, the concept, the dream of guaranteeing basic human rights to every person on the planet has entered into the human psyche and into international law. The way in which this happened was not neat or carefully planned or thoughtfully carried out. The human rights revolution occurred because certain ideas at certain times become irresistible—like the abolition of slavery or the granting of the right to vote to women.

We could go further and assert that the new support for human rights in the Helsinki Accords made the collapse of the Communist system inevitable.

The value and the beauty of the idea of a worldwide set of human rights accepted by everyone is a concept which, almost like the gospel, suddenly becomes appealing to groups or nations for reasons that are not entirely predictable or explainable. Those who advance the value of the gospel ordinarily assume that it is the grace of God which inspires believers to embrace the truths in the Bible. The proponents of international human rights do not have a superhuman source to which to appeal, but they can rely upon the firm words of the Preamble of the U.N. charter. Here all nations "reaffirm faith in fundamental human rights, in the dignity and worth of the human person, in the equal rights of men and women and of nations large and small." The term "dignity" may not be theological or metaphysical, but it is a strong, firm, clear, persuasive concept.

Theorists can speculate as to whether the secular concept of "dignity" can persuade nations to sacrifice some economic or historic gain in order to enlarge the scope of the human rights claimed by another nation, possibly even a traditional rival.

It is easy to rename "dignity" as "the rule of law" or "the democratic process," but are these ideas potentially more likely to induce a nation to comply with an intangible moral ideal which requires self-sacrifice?

It was the deep-seated self-interest of all nations—sometimes exalted to the concept of sovereignty—that led the authors of the U.N. charter to require the nations ratifying it to take on a legally binding obligation to live up to the pledges and promises therein. These nations were required for the first time in history to apply to the U.N. Security Council for permission to make war on another country. But there is no built-in mechanism in the U.N. charter to punish nations that are egregious violators of the human rights which they have agreed to safeguard. Nations which ratify the covenants on human rights are required to give an accounting of their compliance, but there are no juridical penalties for the offenders — even the worst of them.

If the development of the United Nations as an institution had not been radically and unexpectedly interrupted by the Cold War between 1948 and 1990, the idea of the inviolability of human rights even by sovereign nations might well have been at the center of a stunningly new international order.

9

THE
UNITED STATES
WALKS OUT ON THE
INTERNATIONAL
CRIMINAL COURT

The U.S. Congress was creative and persistent in establishing the machinery by which the State Department sits in judgment on the records on human rights of every member in the United Nations. That process improved during the Clinton administration.

But the Clinton White House will not be remembered as a friend of human rights; in July 1998 it declined to sign the documents of the International Criminal Court (ICC). The reasons for that decision were set forth by Ambassador at Large David J. Scheffer, who led the U.S. delegation to the Rome conference. Scheffer's ten-page exposition in the *American Journal of International Law* in January 1999 does not satisfy many persons who had been hoping for over fifty years for the establishment of a permanent Nuremberg.

Ambassador Scheffer described the six occasions on which President Clinton had endorsed the ICC prior to the diplomatic conference in Rome in June–July 1998, a meeting attended by 160 nations, 33 intergovernmental organizations, and a coalition of 236 nongovernmental organizations. The United States disappointed this impressive group when after the voice vote of 120 in favor, 7 against, and 21 abstentions, the United States elected to indicate publicly that it had voted against the statute. France, the United Kingdom, and the Russian federation supported the statute.

As often in the area of human rights, the United States voted on the basis of shortsighted reasons contrary to its obligations under world law and the expectations which the whole of humanity had for a country that, more than any other, could have put international human rights on the world agenda.

The ICC is an old and controversial entity. The United States voted against its formation after World War I. The concept of such a body received a moderate amount of attention in the years up to the establishment of the Nuremberg tribunal. According to the vast literature on the Nuremberg and Tokyo trials, the great weakness of that noble experiment was the obvious fact that it was a tribunal set up by the victors over the vanquished.

After the Nuremberg trials, Europe and especially the United States lost interest in the trials of war criminals. The hope or the illusion grew that there would never be a need for another Nuremberg. The scholars of international law probed all of the different options facing a court that seeks to develop a just process to indict, try, and punish the world's worse malefactors. The problems are baffling. Should there be an equivalent of a world's attorney general? Should the proposed tribunal be tied in with the Security Council, and, if so, should the five nations that now have the veto power be able to kill the indictment of leaders of a nation that is accused of crimes against humanity?

The questions persist. Any acceptable accommodation between the interests of the rich and powerful nations and the poor and undemocratic countries may end up in the form of a tribunal which is (or appears to be) controlled by countries that will seek the status quo if that is better for their trade routes and their economic progress.

The American Bar Association formed a task force to address these sticky issues. As a member of that task force, I gained a detailed perspective on the complexity of the problems that must be resolved before a truly independent tribunal can be born — a court that can require the leaders of sovereign nations to defend themselves against charges that they have committed or condoned crimes which for at least fifty years humanity has deemed to be inexcusable.

But the fact that 120 sovereign nations — having reviewed the matter for many years and having discussed it in Rome for seven weeks —

voted to establish the ICC means that there is substantial consensus on the topic.

Many students of the evolution of the ICC feel that its mission has been watered down in regrettable ways. The working text submitted to the Rome conference contained 116 articles, some of which were complicated with many options. The final statute is composed of a Preamble with 128 articles and 13 parts.

Possibly the most important principle is that of complementarity — that is, that the ICC may assume jurisdiction only when national legal systems are unable or unwilling to exercise jurisdiction. The ICC is clearly intended not to replace local courts but to operate only when there is no expectation that local or national courts will bring serious wrongdoers to justice.

The statute furthermore deals only with the most serious crimes that are of concern to the international community as a whole. Consequently, drug trafficking and terrorism are not included unless they somehow reach the level of crimes against humanity. The most serious crimes indictable by the ICC must be "core" offenses that are punishable as violations of customary international law.

Article 12 of the statute seems to weaken if not undermine the whole process. This provision requires the consent by the state of the nationality of the accused. The United States insisted on the inclusion of this restriction, which in the eyes of many could turn the court into a permanent invalid. The United States went further and cited the possible exclusion of Article 12 as the central reason for its opposing the entire statute. This position is apparently based on the Pentagon's fear that its military personnel could be arrested and tried for alleged crimes in nations where by treaty the United States is required to send soldiers.

The statute is weak in other ways. The traditional sovereignty of nations has scarcely been curbed by the ICC. The court can exercise its jurisdiction only if the state on whose territory the conduct in question occurred or if the state of nationality of the accused has accepted the court's jurisdiction. Iraq, consequently, is not touchable. It voted against the statute and is unlikely to join the ICC as long as Saddam Hussein is in power.

The enforceability of the Rome statute raises further questions. Article

86 imposes on state parties an obligation to "cooperate fully with the court." But the court will itself have no practical means to enforce its orders and decisions. The tribunal, moreover, is stymied in additional ways because the prosecutor does not have the authority to conduct investigations independently of national authorities. It seems disappointingly clear, therefore, that recalcitrant governments have many opportunities to defeat the letter and the spirit of the International Criminal Court.

But one positive development in the Rome statute is the explicit inclusion of crimes of sexual assault as crimes against humanity. Among the acts that can now be considered crimes against humanity and war crimes are "rape, sexual slavery, enforced prostitution, forced pregnancy, and forced sterilization or any other form of sexual violence of comparable gravity" (Article 7). The inclusion of war crimes committed in civil wars is a realistic development because most conflicts in the modern world take place within the borders of a single state.

The ICC provides for the presumption of innocence, the right to avoid self-incrimination, a prosecutor's burden of proving guilt beyond a reasonable doubt, the right of the accused to remain silent and to be questioned in the presence of counsel. No jury trial, however, is contemplated.

Jurists and academics will be debating for years on what happened in Rome and why an apparent strong consensus among nations ended up with a statute which has such serious flaws. The United States will be blamed for some of the deterioration. The fact is that the United States ends up as the only major nation in the world unwilling to contribute to the internationalization of the prosecution of offenses deemed crimes against humanity.

The United States has not ratified the U.N. covenants on economic rights, the rights of women, and the rights of the child. It has not accepted the Inter-American Convention on Human Rights (also known as the American Convention on Human Rights) or the Treaty on the Law of the Sea. Now it has boycotted the International Criminal Court. Is there something in the American psyche which favors isolationism and fears some globalization of our jurisprudence and our courts?

Clearly, the flat rejection of the ICC is unusually strong in reaction to a widely held fear of Senator Jesse Helms, the chairman of the Senate Foreign Relations Committee. The White House was inhibited, as well as the Pentagon, when Senator Helms proclaimed that the ICC would be "dead on arrival." There were other political and prudential reasons the White House and especially the Defense Department did not want to tangle with the Republican Congress over the ICC. The administration needs opportunities for collaboration and cooperation on a large number of other matters.

Ambassador David Scheffer justified the decisions the United States made in Rome in his January 1998 article in the *American Journal of International Law,* which is ultimately a lawyer's brief defending what his client requested him to do. In its most revealing sentence, he states:

> It is simply and logically untenable to expose the largest deployed military force in the world, stationed across the globe to help maintain international peace and security and to defend allies and friends, to the jurisdiction of a criminal court the United States government had not yet joined and whose authority over U.S. citizens the United States does not yet recognize. (p. 18)

The clear implication is that the Pentagon made the final decision not to sign the Rome treaty. Ambassador Scheffer concludes his remarks by stating that the "political will remains within the Clinton administration to support a treaty that is firmly and realistically constituted" (p. 21).

But the presence of American troops across the world will presumably remain. Must the proposed court give them immunity? If American military personnel engage in offenses which allegedly are crimes against humanity or crimes of war, should they not be treated like soldiers from Indonesia in East Timor? Or are American military personnel asking to be treated with special consideration?

Ambassador Scheffer concludes with the assertion that the "problems concerning the Rome treaty are solvable" (p. 21). But little has been forthcoming from the Clinton administration as to how these problems are "solvable."

The countless lawyers, human rights activists, and surviving participants in the Nuremberg process who worked for years to develop the International Criminal Court are deeply disappointed — even stunned — that the United States, the foremost proponent of the Nuremberg court and the principal architect of the ad hoc tribunal to try the perpetrators of the wars in the former Yugoslavia and in Rwanda, walked away from the creation of the ICC.

What is particularly troubling and, indeed, offensive is that no individual, no agency or group in the Clinton administration announced its responsibility for the ultimate awesome decision. The administration clearly had profound concerns, as did the thousands of advisors and participants who have been involved in the development of the ICC over the past two generations.

But who engaged in the legal or political decision-making that visibly angered the delegates from 160 nations and 236 nongovernmental organizations? The decision was not made by a public vote of the Joint Chiefs of Staff at the Pentagon or by the White House Cabinet.

Furthermore if the problems related to the ICC are "solvable," what are the White House and the Department of Defense going to do to expedite their resolution?

The process of putting the ICC into operation will go forward, but its probable success has certainly been curtailed by America's walkout. There is also the suspicion that some highly placed military officials at the Pentagon are lobbying America's allies to slow or stop the process of ratification.

The United States will continue to insist that the legal questions and the juridical process are very complicated and that the United States must be cautious and careful. No one denies that. Lawyers working on the ICC for the past several years have explored all the knotty problems and have weighed a thousand hypotheticals. But weighty decisions have to be made before any court is established; the issues involved in the establishment of the first worldwide court on human rights are complicated almost beyond comprehension.

But the impression one obtains concerning the explanation of America's walkout is that the United States has decided that while the court is a wonderful idea, it cannot be supported because it might adversely affect some American service personnel. What is brushed aside is the fact that the ICC is going to have an impact on every nation that joins and even those nations that do not. When the U.S. Constitution took effect in the United States, every single state lost some of their rights by the preemption given to Congress by the Constitution or by Congress passing laws under its constitutional right to legislate on matters affecting interstate commerce.

The ICC will have effects. The process is carefully constructed so that no nation will ever be required to accept the jurisdiction of the ICC if that nation in good faith investigates the conduct of one of its nationals charged with serious wrongdoing.

The implication of the negative vote in Rome is that the United States fears some nations will bring false charges against American personnel because these individuals have aroused suspicion or hatred within the country where they happen to reside at the moment.

Such an attitude or an assumption will almost certainly be annoying to most other nations that, following the end of the most violent century in human history, cast their votes for the world's first criminal court.

A thorough presentation of all the issues involved in the formation of the ICC was provided following the publication of Ambassador Scheffer's article in the January 1999 issue of the *American Journal of International Law*. This wonderful summary was written by Darryl Robinson, a high-level diplomat from Canada who was a member of the Canadian delegation to the Rome conference. The twenty-five-page article explores each of the major issues related to jurisdiction, potential punishment, and probable future problems with the ICC.

The rejection by the United States of the ICC still stuns activists and academics in the international human rights movement. They have been virtually forced to impute the defeat to the Pentagon and not to the White House or Secretary of State Madeleine Albright. Anger at the decision seems out of place because honest public officials sincerely devoted to human rights made the call.

The issue really involves the role of the United States in international affairs. In his journal article, Ambassador Scheffer assumes that the role of the United States must remain exactly as it is. Anything that endangers the worldwide presence of American soldiers is bad for the universe.

A great deal of ignorance or arrogance — or both — is inherent in that position. The American soldiers the Pentagon insists must be immune from the jurisdiction of the ICC were placed there during the Cold War to shore up active or potential allies of the United States in its stance against the "evil empire." Why these military personnel now remain in these faraway places is a question crying out for review. Perhaps in the not-too-distant future many or most of them will be withdrawn, as they were in West Germany. Will the ICC then be less objectionable?

The four Geneva treaties on the rules of war agreed to after World War II in 1949 are binding on U.S. military officials. The Pentagon used these treaties when it tried Lt. William Calley for alleged violations of the rules of war in the massacre at My Lai in Vietnam.

Why, then, is the United States so afraid of the International Criminal Court using these same rules — along with the Nuremberg principles — in cases when persons engaged in international or civil war are charged with crimes against humanity?

The decision of the Clinton administration in Rome not to support the ICC was particularly disappointing because it had worked so diligently and successfully to launch the tribunal for the former Yugoslavia. Key observers theorize that the 1993 court for the former Yugoslavia would facilitate the acceptance of the International Criminal Court. It may have for the vast majority of nations. But not for the United States.

10

GRADING THE STATE DEPARTMENT'S REPORTS ON HUMAN RIGHTS

It seems clear that the record of the United States on international human rights has been uneven, uncertain, and unpredictable. The moral aspirations of the United States for the world have often been laudable. But the country has been haunted by hubris, imperialism, delusions of grandeur, and just plain pride.

Yet, the United States has been consistent and persistent in its desires to enhance the ideals of democracy here and abroad. Those aspirations are spelled out in the annual report on human rights issued by the State Department pursuant to the directive of Congress. For almost twenty years the United States has annually published reports on human rights which now accumulate to some 20,000 pages. It is an astonishing achievement that has undoubtedly had enormous if unmeasurable impact on nations which for dozens of reasons want to be in the good graces of the United States.

The preface to each of the annual reports reviews the anxieties and aspirations of the U.S. government in the area of human rights. Clearly the State Department has turned around completely from the era when John Foster Dulles in one of his acts as secretary of state removed Eleanor Roosevelt from the U.N. Commission on Human Rights and claimed that the United States "would not become a party to any human rights treaty approval by the United Nations." All of Dulles's successors up to

Henry Kissinger regarded human rights as a hindrance to the pursuit of great power politics.

The State Department report on human rights for 1998 is over 2,000 pages long, including detailed accounts about every country from Angola to Zimbabwe. There does not yet exist a generally accepted formula by which to judge a nation on human rights — as there is for other criteria such as literacy, infant mortality rates, or the average age at death. But a litmus test for human rights is surely around the corner. When that becomes available nations will pay attention because corporations in developed countries are far less likely to invest in nations with human rights problems than in areas where democracy is thriving.

The facts in the annual State Department report on human rights, therefore, have consequences. What that report says can easily determine the future of a country. Take, for example, the report on Tanzania for the year 1998. The State Department reported "pervasive corruption" that had a "broad impact on human rights." There also existed, the State Department noted, "arbitrary arrest and detention" and a nation where "mob justice remains severe and widespread."

This report details the conditions of every country with respect to political and other extrajudicial killing, disappearances, torture, arbitrary arrest, denial of fair trial, the state of freedom of speech and press, freedom of religion, the right of citizens to change their government, and discrimination based on race, sex, religion, disability, and social status. Children's and workers' rights are also included.

The profile of most underdeveloped or recently decolonized countries under all these criteria leaves only a few with high grades. As one reads the very detailed reports written by American observers in struggling countries, the question repeatedly arises as to the fairness of it all. Take the fifteen pages in small print on Togo. The country they describe is not a very attractive place. One constantly wonders whether a harsh assessment would be written if the human rights criteria used in judging Togo were applied to the United States. But the State Department report does want to be fair and just. Although its five pages on Australia, for example, are necessarily positive about the highly developed democratic institutions in that country, they are blunt — even harsh — concerning the indigenous people of that country. They are imprisoned at twenty-one times the rate of nonindigenous people. The government of Australia, in the view of the human rights report, has not responded to a series of recommendations made by a 1991 royal commission.

Have such criticisms helped the indigenous people of Australia to remedy their condition? The answer of the State Department and Congress, which authorized the process of annual reports, is certainly yes. This is a way to carry out the "mobilization of shame."

Does the exposure of the neglect of its indigenous population help the government in Australia? Again, the answer has to be affirmative. This kind of exposure puts international pressure on Australia to accelerate its efforts to provide equality for the descendants of those living in Australia long before the Europeans came to colonize that vast land.

The systematic reporting of the deficiencies of all the nations of the earth is salutary in another way. The nongovernmental organizations devoted to the rights of women, the disabled, or the indigenous have a new source of information which — because that information comes from the U.S. government — is an authoritative way to demonstrate that a particular nation is violating international human rights law.

The annual report also serves as a way of reiterating world law. The first page of the report for 1998 noted that Article 21 of the Universal Declaration of Human Rights provides that "the will of the people shall be the basis of the authority of government . . . expressed in periodic and genuine elections." This gave the State Department the opportunity to boast that the U.S. government spends over $1 billion each year to defend democracies under attack. This expenditure was justified as not only "right" but also necessary, because the security of the United States as a nation "depends upon the expansion of democracy worldwide."

It is noteworthy that the State Department report includes "open and competitive economic structures" as an integral part of the respect for human rights which international law now requires. But this theme of "open and competitive" structures is muted in the State Department assessments. One could argue cogently that economic and political rights go together and that the advent of human rights depends on a healthy economy and a vigorous democratic government. That theme is suggested by State Department reports, but Congress has not mandated that the department collect and disseminate data on the state of free enterprise in individual nations. Actually, an evaluation on topics such as the tax structure for corporations and the state of antitrust law on certain economic enterprises would be helpful and meaningful to everyone. It would also illustrate the State Department's traditional position that the strength of a nation's democratic structures must include information on the freedom of operation granted to corporations. The report also includes information on the status of unions that is incomplete without data on the state of management. This would be particularly relevant for nations like the fifteen countries that since 1990 have been able to disaffiliate from the U.S.S.R.

The symbiosis between economic and political rights was noted in the final resolution of the 1993 World Conference on Human Rights in Vienna in these words: "While development facilitates the enjoyment of human rights, the lack of development may not be invoked to justify the abridgement of internationally recognized human rights."

The State Department report for 1997 stressed the interconnection between economic and political rights in this statement: "It is now well established that the ultimate economic crisis — famine and mass starvation — is not occurring . . . in those countries whose rulers bear the consequences of their decisions, whose people participate in their own government, and in which information freely circulates." The authors of the 1997 report realized that "the global movement for human rights is one of the most extraordinary political developments in modern history." But they felt constrained to recognize the slowness of progress, concluding that "the greatest works of the human spirit take a long time to come into being, and they must be constantly nurtured less they collapse, with horrific results" and that "the evolving global network of laws and institutions protecting and promoting human rights has taken a long time, but its roots lie deep in the hopes, aspirations and beliefs in human dignity of all cultures and societies."

The authors of the State Department's annual report on human rights must certainly know that their words and their accusations produce resentment, some of which might lead to long-term alienation and even violence. In 1999, a significant number of U.S. embassies felt so threatened by extremists that they closed for a period and asked Congress for vast sums of money in order to enhance security.

There is possibly no way to persuade the world's nations that the United States, lonely at the top, is really their friend and benefactor. Secretary of State Madeleine Albright called the United States "the indispensable nation." She meant it in a benign sense. But many nations want to resist the domination of one powerful country; they resent the United States for proclaiming its high political ideals and its devotion to human rights while poor countries are experiencing chronic malnutrition, AIDS epidemics, and persistent high unemployment rates. Poor countries will always resent rich countries. But today the United States simultaneously flaunts its wealth and proclaims its devotion to human rights by publicizing each year 2,000 pages of denunciations of the human rights conditions in most if not all nondemocratic poor countries in the world.

No one has publicly urged that Congress modify the law so that the United States is no longer perceived as a hypocrite that conceals its own failures on human rights but denounces similar failures in other countries.

The disparity of America's record on human rights and its blunt and sometimes brutal condemnations of countries in Latin America is especially glaring because the United States has never ratified the Inter-American Convention on Human Rights (also known as the American Convention on Human Rights). President Carter signed the treaty, but the U.S. Senate has never expressed an interest in joining in the partnership, which brings together the nations of Latin America and the Caribbean. If the United States did ratify the convention it would be a party to the Inter-American Commission and Court on Human Rights, based in San José, Costa Rica. The United States would, of course, also be subject to the jurisdiction of the commission and the court and thus could be sued by individuals and nations alleging that the United States or an entity directed or controlled by the United States had engaged in conduct in violation of the Inter-American Convention on Human Rights.

It is consequently a bit incongruous for the United States to cite the nations of Latin America for their failure to comply with internationally recognized human rights while abstaining from the elaborate process set up to offer indemnification to the people of North and South America.

The U.S. government is also open to the charge that in its reports on countries like El Salvador and Nicaragua, it is not being candid about the fact that massive U.S. involvement in these nations in the 1980s substantially altered the political structure of these countries. The Reagan administration spent over $3 billion to defeat allegedly Communist rebels in El Salvador and put in place a group closely identified with the fourteen dominant families and the strong military that has dominated El Salvador's history for generations.

There was hardly a mention of that turbulent story—in which 75,000 persons lost their lives—in the State Department Report on Human Rights in El Salvador for 1998. The report was careful and cautious, and it could easily be criticized and corrected by observers familiar with the tragedies that befell El Salvador during the twelve-year war in which the United States financed one side. The report made its own assumptions. It praised El Salvador's "market-based, mixed economy" and the "privatization and free-market reforms," although it conceded that "about 48 percent of the population lives below the poverty level."

The State Department's report was fact-filled and touched on all the topics required by Congress. But close observers of the tragedies that have occurred in El Salvador since Archbishop Oscar Romero was assassinated in March 1980 are skeptical of the report. Is the State Department required to pretend that U.S. intervention in the 1980s did not happen or did not radically change what would have happened if it had not taken up warfare against the Farabundo Marti National Liberation front (FMLN)?

We should be grateful to the staff of the U.S. Embassy in San Salvador for their comprehensive collection of facts and their meticulous reporting of them. But are there assumptions that conceal or minimize what the United States did to the poor country of El Salvador? Is the human rights report ultimately a way for the United States to exalt the U.N. human rights agenda while pretending that it is carrying out its duties to protect and promote human rights?

There is something artificial, pretentious, and hypocritical about the way in which the U.S. government through the State Department sits in judgment every year on the state of human rights in El Salvador.

The same could be said about Nicaragua. The report did not refer to the massive U.S. intervention in which it organized and deployed the

"Contras." The report said only that the civil war ended in June 1990 with the mobilization of the Nicaraguan Contras. It did concede, though, that because of a "weak judiciary" most of the "human rights abuses cited by the Tripartite Commission in well-documented reports remains un-punished."

The report on Nicaragua for 1998 reveals that the prison population rose in 1998 to 5,570, up from 3,946 in 1997. Caloric intake for the prisoners remained at 750 to 800 a day, well below the 1,800 calories per day recommended by the United Nations. The U.S. report also notes that one-third of all prisoners are jailed for six months or more without trial.

The report on Nicaragua reveals once again the tendency of the State Department to overrely on the existence of a democratically elected gov-ernment. The document opens by rejoicing in the elections of President Arnoldo Aleman in 1996 in a "free and fair election." American diplomats and elected officials regularly boast that now all the nations of Latin America except Cuba have a popularly elected government. But one must raise the question whether this new phenomenon has been used to down-play or obscure the fact that massive denials of human rights continue after a fair election. In some instances the poor have not been allowed to organize or participate in open elections where voters have a meaningful choice.

Although the State Department report on every country is probably open to criticism, the existence of a conflict of interest between the U.S. government and the nations in question needs to be explored. This is why the work of the nongovernmental organizations criticizing the depart-ment reports in the 1980s were so valuable. If the United States has had direct or indirect ideological or economic links with a nation, it is under-standable that the drafters of the report on such a nation would tend to mute the bad news and magnify the good news.

The ideological basis of the Cold War years is no longer reflected in the human rights report, except for North Korea and, of course, China. I have read and dissected every report on China since the first one appeared in 1978. The 1998 report contained harsh accusations. The human rights record "deteriorated sharply . . . with a crackdown against organized political dissent." The government, it was charged, blocked the Voice of

America broadcast, was restrictive of the press, and sought to infringe on the freedom of religion.

The charges were not new. They have horrified the world for decades. There is no suggestion that the State Department report mitigated or exaggerated the accusations against China. The issue is what the United States should do that it is not now doing to improve the status of human rights in China.

The record on this issue is extensive and contentious. Everyone wants to curb the abuses in China. For several years the United States imposed restrictions on China by denying them so-called Most Favored Nation status; this meant that the ordinary trade privileges given to America's friends and allies have not been extended to China.

In the 1990s, Congress and the White House had lengthy debates about removing the Most Favored Nation status from China. The Tiananmen massacre and the unrelenting repression of religion in China and its policy on abortion have been central to that debate. The support that China gave to the Khmer Rouge in Cambodia also played a part in the extended debate.

Members of Congress representing farm states favored the granting of the Most Favored Nation status of China lest U.S. farmers lose an opportunity to sell massive amounts of grain to that country. On the other side, the persons who want to punish China for its persistent adherence to Communism push aggressively for economic sanctions.

China has in effect now been granted the right to ship most of its exports to the United States without paying tariffs. The threat that this right could be terminated is, theoretically, an incentive to China to honor human rights. But that threat does not seem to be working.

The detente now granted to China does not really resolve the basic policy question posed by Section 502b. That law, enacted in 1976, says flatly that the United States should not extend benefits to those nations that practice gross violations of human rights. China surely falls into that category — possibly more than any other nation.

But the policy has been quietly adopted that it is better to trade with China with the hope that more frequent and better relations with that country, which counts for one-fifth to one-fourth of all humanity, will in the long run be more advantageous to the advancement of human rights than a policy of isolating and humiliating that vast country.

The best policy to follow varies with each nation and with each situation. In 1976 Congress decided that the United States must have a policy on this matter. The State Department has tried to carry out that policy. But there are intractable problems. If the U.S. government is too adamant, it might end up with more Cubas. If it is too lenient, it might be accused of being unfaithful to the objectives of Section 502b and, even worse, of being "soft" on carrying out America's basic foreign policy role as guardian of all the human rights which 160 nations re-ratified as precious and inviolable in 1993 at the Vienna conference.

In the war to protect human rights there are no quick victories or even easy problems. Crafty and evil political leaders, when combined with a poorly educated citizenry, can mislead and abuse people for a considerable period of years. Individuals in this situation can claim or reclaim their rights only if they are encouraged and supported by outside forces. Even when this support is forthcoming, it cannot succeed unless there is some deep feeling among the citizens that no government is valid without the consent of the governed.

While the State Department feels itself bound to pursue only the specific topics mandated by Congress, it does interpret the idea of human rights in a broad sense. As a result it is involved in working to bring about a satisfactory resolution of a long-hidden controversy which arose in 1997 concerning Swiss and other banks not returning money or other valuables to the descendants of Jews killed by the Nazis. The State Department report for 1998 remarks that "history's greatest genocide was almost certainly also its largest organized robbery."

In 1998, the State Department and the U.S. Holocaust Memorial Museum co-sponsored a conference in Washington attended by forty-four governments and thirteen nongovernmental organizations. The conference helped bring about the enactment of restitution laws in several European nations. The Holocaust, the report notes, more than any other event brought about the human rights movement; it is therefore necessary to move forward while the past is still a living memory.

Obviously, the promotion of elections is one of the core duties of the State Department Bureau of Human Rights. In its report it quotes the statement of Freedom House (a nongovernmental organization based in New York and Washington, devoted to the enhancement and implementation of human rights around the world) that at the end of 1998 there were 117 electoral democracies constituting 55 percent of the world's population. The number of democracies has almost doubled in the past ten years.

The State Department report also pays a good deal of attention to a new mandate on religious freedom given to it in 1997 by Congress. The directive was to place religious freedom squarely in the mainstream of U.S. foreign policy. A special representative for international religious freedom was appointed pursuant to the bill signed by President Clinton in October 1998. This measure gives the president and the State Department the right and the duty to take suitable steps to deter infringements on religious freedom around the world.

When this measure was moving through Congress, certain dissenters felt that it had been the creation of the religious right and that it exalted religious freedom over other comparably valuable human rights. It remains to be seen how the new emphasis on religious liberty will play out.

The United States speaks and acts about human rights in a wide range of forums. To some extent the government has moved to a position where, as President Carter used to say, human rights is the "soul of America's foreign policy." The unprecedented emphasis on the rights of women has certainly been heard around the world. The denunciation of female genital mutilation has helped to force a rethinking of that hitherto seldom discussed problem. The accent on the rights of millions of child workers has added a new voice to the worldwide debate on that issue. Most people still do not know that, according to the International Labor Organization, as many as 250 million children under the age of fifteen are employed full- or part-time around the world.

The report on human rights that appeared early in 1999 on the record of 1998 is deeply impressive. But, alas, probably the most critical issue on human rights in that year — the International Criminal Commission — is hardly mentioned. In June 1998 the Clinton administration voted no on the ICC in Rome. If the decision on that matter had been given to the human rights experts at the State Department, the outcome almost certainly would have been different. History books may well conclude that the abandonment of the commission by the United States was the worst mistake made by any government in the world in 1998.

The philosophical premises underlying the annual reports of the State Department are relatively clear. They reflect the 1945 Charter of the United Nations, the Universal Declaration of Human Rights, and the laws enacted by the U.S. Congress. The principles become clearer and more compelling each year. Adherence to the core moral principles that support international human rights becomes more unquestioned every year. The real problem is how to make that enforceable. The State Department cannot effectively command officials in distant lands to use their authority to enforce international human rights. Proponents of international human rights can only propose the nature and value of human rights and hope that their intrinsic value will be found attractive enough to ensure their acceptance and enforcement.

Even the mighty government of the United States must resort to the "mobilization of shame." Ultimately this is the moral power which, more than laws or economic sanctions, will induce nations to follow the less traveled road that leads to democracy and equality.

11

THE UNITED STATES PUTS THE WORLD'S TORTURERS ON TRIAL

On March 22, 1992, the United States became the first country in the world to enact legislation offering the victims of torture the right to sue their oppressors for civil damages. Under the Tort Victim Protection Act (TVPA) victims of torture now have a federal cause of action in the U.S. courts against their torturers who acted under cover of law.

The process by which this unique law came into existence began with the 1980 decision *Filartiga v. Peña Irala,* in which Judge Irving Kaufman stated that "official torture is now prohibited by the law of nations." As a result, the judge held that Dolly Filartiga could sue and recover damages from the official who tortured and killed her brother Joelito in Paraguay. The case for the plaintiff, argued creatively by lawyers from the Center for Constitutional Rights, was strengthened by the affirmative support offered by the Justice Department of the Carter administration. The decision of the Second Circuit Court of Appeals in New York eventually led to a ruling that awarded the victims a total of $10 million in compensatory and punitive damages.

The *Filartiga* decision and its progeny were obviously influenced by the adoption on December 18, 1979, of the Torture Convention by the U.N. General Assembly. Similarly, the *Filartiga* result was one of the many reasons the U.S. Senate ratified the Torture Convention on October 27, 1990, and passed the TVPA in 1992.

Judge Kaufman's opinion reminds Americans that the framers of the U.S. Constitution knew about international law and favored its inclusion in the law of the United States. The Constitution itself grants Congress the authority to "define and punish . . . offenses against the law of nations."

The power granted to Congress by the Constitution with respect to international law is the basic reason the very first Congress enacted the Alien Tort Claims Act (ATCA). The act provided that "the district courts should have original jurisdiction of any civil tort action by an alien . . . committed *in violation of the law of nations* or a treaty of the United States" [emphasis supplied]. For reasons that remain obscure, the ATCA had rarely been used until it appeared in the Filartiga decision. But U.S. courts have made it clear that international law is a part of America's legal heritage.

In 1900 the Supreme Court in *Paquete Habava* made it clear that "international law is part of our law and must be ascertained and administered by the courts of justice of appropriate jurisdiction." As a result, the Supreme Court ruled against the United States, which had captured two Spanish fishing vessels off the coast of Cuba during the Spanish-American War. The United States was not a party to any treaty or written international agreement specifying that ordinary fishing vessels were exempt from capture as a prize of war. Despite that fact, the Supreme Court ruled that the United States had violated international law as established through history. The Court determined that the capture of the vessels was unlawful and ordered the proceeds of the sale returned to the claimants with damages and costs.

The Supreme Court in *Paquete Habava* also specifically acknowledged the validity of customary international law. The words of the Court are striking: "Where there is no treaty, and no controlling executive or legislative act or judicial decision resort must be had to the customs and usages of civilized nations; and, . . . of these, to the works of jurists and commentators, who by years of labor, research and experience, have made themselves peculiarly well acquainted with the subjects of which they treat."

American jurists continue to be uneasy about utilizing norms that derive from customary international law. This resistance has been addressed by the efforts of the American Law Institute to define and clarify the precise nature of customary international law. The restatement (3rd) on the foreign relations law of the United States, a generally accepted guide to international law as applicable to the United States, names in Section 702 the following seven offenses which have achieved the status of customary international law: genocide, slavery or slave trade, murdering or causing the disappearance of individuals, torture or other cruel or inhuman or degrading treatment or punishment, prolonged arbitrary detention, systematic racial discrimination, and a consistent pattern of gross violations of internationally recognized human rights.

The list in the restatement is not meant to be exhaustive. The notes of the reporter concede that even in 1986 when the restatement was being finalized after years of discussion and debate, systematic religious discrimination, the right to own and not be arbitrarily deprived of property, and gender discrimination were already principles of customary international law or were on the verge of achieving that status.

This view was echoed in 1991 in the book *International Law in Theory and Practice,* by Oscar Schacter. He opines that the right to basic subsistence, the right to public assistance in matters of health, welfare, and basic education, and the rights of women to full equality have all gained the acceptance required to become customary international law.

The ambiguities of the content of customary international law led the Congress to codify the results of *Filartiga* and similar decisions.

When I testified before the U.S. Senate and the House on behalf of the Torture Victim Protection Act for the American Bar Association, I recognized that the issue was arcane and that it had little political appeal to the members of Congress. But the 1789 Alien Tort statute was being litigated and its ambiguities needed to be clarified by Congress.

The proposed Torture Victim Protection Act offered clarity. A ten-year statute of limitations was added to the law, which would include citizens and aliens. There really was little resistance in the Congress because all that was being attempted was the modification of law passed by the very first Congress. In addition, no immunity is granted to a foreign torturer on the basis that he or she was only following the orders of a superior. But American officials are not covered in the bill; no action can be brought against any American authority acting in his or her official capacity in the

United States or abroad. A further qualification of the law requires that all plaintiffs exhaust their remedies abroad before they can ask for relief in an American court under the Torture Victim Protection Act.

The TVPA includes "extra judicial killing" as a cause of action in addition to torture. The definition of "extra judicial killing" is taken from Article 3 of the Geneva Convention of 1949 — long since accepted by the United States. The definition of torture in the TVPA tracks the language of the Torture Convention. Under that treaty the torture must intentionally inflict "severe pain or suffering . . . whether physical or mental" in order to obtain a confession, punishment, intimidation, or coercions. The language includes mental torture as a justifiable cause of action. Other examples include intense psychological pressure, sensory deprivation, and the use of hallucinatory drugs.

My involvement in the enactment of the Tort Victim Protection Act was personalized by a meeting with a victim of torture when I was on a human rights mission in Chile just before the fall of General Pinochet. Marcella was fifteen years old when she became involved in a Catholic movement of young people. The group she headed was not political but was a unit to study Catholic social teaching. Almost inevitably the Catholic movement, which took positions on human rights, was perceived by the government to be anti-Pinochet. Marcella was questioned and tortured by the authorities, who wanted information on her colleagues. In order to intimidate Marcella and discourage her associates the government branded Marcella with a crucifix on her forehead.

A church-related clinic giving Marcella medical and psychological assistance brought her to my human rights group in Santiago. With long black hair and a frightened demeanor Marcella was reluctant to say anything. She was filled with guilt over her feeling that, under pressure and torture, she had revealed information about the other members of her Catholic group. She was also dreading her probable return to the process of torture, during which she would be required to either commit perjury or confess to alleged crimes against the dictatorship.

Marcella would now have a judicial process available to her in the United States. Would torture decrease around the world if Marcella and every victim of torture had available the remedies under the TVPA? The answer is not clear. But the remedy for the victims of torture in the TVPA is creative, constructive, and exciting.

Torture is a dark, insidious, and clandestine practice that has an astonishing presence in the world. In its annual report for 1999, Amnesty International states that the incidence of torture has increased. In 1998, 55 percent of all nations indulged in torture and other comparable abuses. In 1999, the figure rose to 66 percent.

It should be noted that the U.N. Convention Against Torture and Other Cruel, Inhuman, or Degrading Treatment or Punishment calls for no exceptions. Any exception, however useful to law enforcement, would undercut the purpose of the treaty and render it subject to uncontrollable exceptions. This means that a government may not torture someone even if such a procedure could lead to, for example, the knowledge of the identity of a kidnapper of a child. According to international law, torture for any reason is now forbidden.

The Torture Victim Protection Act did not override the Alien Tort statute of 1789. The TVPA authorizes relief only for torture and extrajudicial killing. For other wrongs the Alien Tort statute may be used.

There is a further restriction on the use of the TVPA. Visiting heads of state are immune from lawsuits under this American law. But former heads of state, like Pinochet of Chile, could conceivably be subject to suits under the TVPA. The Foreign Sovereign Immunity Act (FSIA) of 1976, however, may in some cases grant immunity to foreign visitors who were once public officials in their own nations.

An ever lengthening series of decisions based on *Filartiga* show more and more clearly that international law is becoming a source of authority for plaintiffs who seek indemnification for wrongs done to them in another country which are now compensable because they violate the law of nations.

A list of some of the cases based on the *Filartiga* decision is impressive — even though in most of the cases the petitioners have not been able to recover actual money against offending presidents or dictators. But future remedies may be forthcoming. It is noteworthy that for many years there were no remedies at law for the victims of the Holocaust whose gold or jewelry was deposited in banks in Switzerland or elsewhere. But now some settlement has been agreed to between banks in Switzerland and depositors in the United States, Germany, and elsewhere.

It is not clear that these victims could have recovered if the *Filartiga* decision had come down in 1948 instead of 1980. But surely there should have been some lawful remedy for those whose assets had been tortiously seized during the Nazi era. It could be demonstrated that the theft and / or embezzlement of the assets of the victims of Hitler were or should have been violations of international law.

In 1988, several citizens of Argentina successfully sued former General Carlos Suarez-Mason for human rights violations committed during the war years — 1976 to 1983. In 1995, a group of Guatemalan plaintiffs in Massachusetts were awarded a judgment for $47 million against General Hector Gramajo. In 1996, three women who were tortured in Ethiopia sued the perpetrators in Atlanta, Georgia. The judge awarded the plaintiffs a total of $1.5 million for torturous and arbitrary detention. The mother of a man killed in a massacre in East Timor successfully sued an Indonesian general living in Boston.

The enactment of the Torture Victim Protection Act of 1992 has not brought all the relief that many of its advocates had hoped for. But it is still a very significant piece of legislation because it is the first statute ever enacted by a country which allows aliens and its own citizens to attempt to obtain damages for violations committed in a distant land if they are contrary to international law.

The potential consequences of the TVPA are immense. As the case law and the jurisprudence engendered by the act develop, foreign leaders may hesitate to enter the United States because they could be sued for having violated international law when they were in power. The detention in England of former president of Chile Pinochet is one example of what can happen.

The impact of the *Filartiga* decision and its progeny should not be overinterpreted. The potential of this law is limited by the long tradition of deference among nations. That deference was synthesized in the 1976 law passed by Congress, the Foreign Sovereign Immunities Act. This law, which cleared Congress without difficulty, was requested by the State Department as a way of promulgating a clear statement to the world as to what the United States could or would do when a lawsuit is brought against a foreign leader in a U.S. court. The FSIA may seem to restrict the rights of plaintiffs in America to sue a foreign leader, but this is not inconsistent with the Torture Victim Protection Act. The *Filartiga* law allows victims in the United States to sue former public officials in order to acquire restitution for wrongs done in an official capacity that were a violation of world law.

Will other nations follow the progressive example of the United States and let victims sue in their courts for violations of international law committed by their political leaders in another country? As of yet, we have no concrete example. But many nations follow the legal developments in the United States and sometimes emulate them.

If most nations adopted the purposes of the TVPA, would it make an important difference in the availability of remedies for the infringement of human rights? It could, but the statute should be broadened so that it embraces not only torture but other egregious violations of international law. The various adaptations of the TVPA should also include provisions for extradition and for the collection of penalties and reparations.

The International Criminal Court is intended to implement some features of the TVPA. The ICC would take care of the indictment, trial, conviction, and punishment of the world's worst offenders. In turn, the TVPA would provide for civil penalties and compensatory damages for those who have been convicted by the ICC.

Are these scenarios too idealistic, unrealistic, and utopian? Many will think so. But the incredibly rapid movement of the globalization of commerce, communication, and democratic institutions means that almost inevitably the moral and legal principles that established the nature of international law will be accepted at the local level. That means that individuals like Dolly Filartiga will be able to obtain a remedy for the disasters that befall them.

The globalization of the law of personal injury by public officials could be closer than it now appears. The universal standards fixed by the International Labor Organization, the World Health Organization, and the new World Trade Organization will be a model for the architects of a world plan to inhibit and deter the violations of the ever enlarging group of human rights which are the legacy of all members of the human race.

The challenge underlying the struggle of American courts concerning how and when they should use international law as a source of their decisions is complex and profound. Most state judges do not want to give their opponents or critics an opportunity to challenge them on the grounds that they relied on some international document as the equivalent of sound American law. There is enormous resistance to the use of legal norms that have not been passed by Congress and signed by the president. But the fact is that American law does not always adequately extend the new protections for privacy, for example, available under international law.

If one reads the constitutions accepted by many nations in the world, it is evident that they have protections not available in the U.S. Constitution. The constitution of South Africa, for example, is the first constitution to contain guarantees against discrimination toward gays and lesbians. The constitution of Canada expresses more clearly and guarantees more expressly some of the rights not explicitly recognized in America's constitutional heritage. Some of the new constitutions have explicit guarantees for the rights of women and children not available in any constitution, federal or state, in America.

Despite the shortcomings in the constitutional protections in the United States, the courts and citizens share a profound reluctance to assert new rights not now contained in the Constitution of the United States or of the fifty states.

That is why the Torture Victim Protection Act might have surprising results. It depends on international law, but its enforcement does not require a judge to reach out to some world norm not set forth explicitly in the relevant statute.

The statute is very restrictive because it requires the defendant to be present in the United States in a manner that makes possible the services of process. This is clearly a warning to any former public official who could be subject to the act if he enters the United States. The ancient principle that the defendant must be physically present or at least reachable by legal process derives ultimately from the protections of national sovereignty. Theoretically, if a person violates international or world law he should be penalized where he is found. If the nation where the crime was committed will not try him for a violation of law that binds all nations, that country should at least be required to extradite the suspect to another nation.

This is a new jurisprudence that governs the world when a person is chargeable with a serious crime. Can this logic be extended to those who under world law have a right to damages in a civil case? That would be the next logical step if nations really desire to compensate those who have been hurt through torture or other offenses against the law of nations.

With the enactment of the Torture Victim Protection Act, the United States took a step that is unprecedented in the history of the international human rights movement. The TVPA is a timid beginning by the United States—the prime architect of the United Nations and the principal cheerleader for its efforts to promote and protect human rights. The act can be enlarged by the Congress and expanded by the courts. It is one of those laws which, like the Civil Rights Act of 1964, has the potential to transform a nation and a world.

Part III

HUMAN RIGHTS
TRANSFORM THE
WORLD

12

REGIONAL
TRIBUNALS
FOR HUMAN
RIGHTS

Events moved at lightning speed after the end of World War II in 1945. The inhabitants of Europe were stunned to learn that at least 6 million Jews had been murdered and that neither Europe nor the United States had spoken out and tried to save the Jews soon after it became clear that Hitler was determined to carry out his plan to eliminate the Jewish community. Years later the silence of the United States concerning the Jews was documented in a searing book, *The Abandonment of the Jews,* by David Wyman (Norton, 1984).

The establishment in 1953 of two separate entities, the European Convention on Human Rights (also known as the European convention) and the European Court on Human Rights, suggested the people of Europe felt shame and guilt soon after the war. Reportedly at the suggestion of Winston Churchill, all the nations of western Europe created a human rights tribunal which convened in 1953 in Strasbourg.

The history of this convention and court brings not a little glory to the nations that established it. The founding of this transnational entity is also due in part to the terror of Europeans as they saw the fall to the Kremlin of the countries of eastern and central Europe. The U.S.S.R., an ally of the United States and the United Kingdom and their partners in founding the United Nations, became the occupier of large areas of Europe after helping the allies defeat Germany's occupation of these very nations.

The preamble to the Commission and Court on Human Rights makes it clear that the victors wanted to make certain that if there ever was a dictator again in Europe, all the citizens in every country would have a place to register their protests. Such a right was theoretically granted to everyone in the world with the creation of the U.N. Commission on Human Rights. But the framers of the court in Strasbourg intended that the people living in a relatively homogeneous area with a common culture would have complaints about civil rights and civil liberties that might be too complicated and sophisticated for a worldwide commission serving the 3 billion human beings then on the planet.

The nations that formed what was probably the first transnational tribunal on human rights in the history of the human race were cautious. They made individuals prove that they had exhausted their remedies in their own country and that they could really prove a violation of one or more of the guarantees spelled out in the new European Convention on Human Rights.

Scores of pages of casuistry concerning the differing jurisdictions of the commission and the court hindered the progress of the Strasbourg tribunal. The structure of the entity in Strasbourg was greatly simplified in 1997 when the convention was folded into the court and straightforward, streamlined procedures were adopted.

It is a delight to be in England and talk to the lawyers who regularly apply to litigate in Strasbourg. England, without a written constitution and without a modernized system of judicial review, has been affected by the court in Strasbourg more than any other country. Every new decision releasing a prisoner or curbing corporal punishment of children incites again the perennial debate about the protection of civil liberties in Great Britain. That age-old quarrel has not yet been resolved, but the presence and the decisions of the court in Strasbourg have prolonged and intensified the debate.

The ever mounting number of decisions emanating from Strasbourg form a highly developed system of jurisprudence. A book entitled *Leading Cases of the European Court of Human Rights* (Gaunt, 1997), edited by R. A. Lawson and H. G. Schermers, illustrates the sweep and scope of the rapidly emerging law of human rights in Europe.

In addition, the mere existence of a complaint pending at Strasbourg frequently prompts action by a nation to change the practice complained of. Spontaneous actions by governments before actual litigation and rulings have, for example, removed the ban on Jesuits in Norway, have allowed women to vote in certain places in Switzerland, and have modified procedures against criminals. This type of reform in response to the threat of a lawsuit is now accelerating in the new nations in eastern Europe which have accepted the jurisdiction of the European Court on Human Rights.

It is significant that in 1995 the court held that the European convention "cannot be interpreted solely in accordance with the intentions of their authors as expressed more than 40 years . . . at a time when a minority of the present contracting parties adopted the convention."

There are, however, serious problems with the European court. Its docket tends to be crowded, the opinions of the majority and the dissent are sometimes prolix, and some nations comply reluctantly if at all with the decrees of Strasbourg.

But the European Court on Human Rights is without doubt the most comprehensive and efficient regional court on human rights in the world. It may be a bit premature to try to assess its overall impact on Europe and the world, but studies may be forthcoming on this topic in the relatively near future.

One of the most important features of the European Court on Human Rights is the fact that in about one-half of the states' parties the convention enjoys the status of domestic law. In these countries the convention may be invoked as law in the national courts. In these courts the Strasbourg tribunal creates rights directly enforceable by individuals. In other countries where the convention is not directly binding, courts can and do look to the European convention and the decisions interpreting it.

One of the most important changes brought about by the Strasbourg tribunal was its decision to overturn the British Parliament and the House of Lords in their decision to require the *London Times* to withhold information at the demand of the government. That ruling brought freedom of speech to England and arguably brought the country into line with the interpretations of the first amendment by the U.S. Supreme Court.

The European court has also broadened the rights of gays and lesbians, increased respect for privacy, and enhanced the rights of minorities to use their native language. The court has not yet resolved the claims of certain religious groups like the Jehovah's Witnesses nor has it taken on the question of state-sponsored religious traditions like the presence of a certain number of unelected Anglican bishops sitting in the House of Lords in London.

A conversation I had in 1999 with high officials of the European court gave me hope and confidence that the court will increasingly live up to its expectations and will continue to issue opinions that concretize and clarify the noble aspirations placed in the European Convention on Human Rights, the basic document interpreted by the European Commission and Court on Human Rights. The court will reflect the resolve of millions of people on one of the most highly developed continents in the world as they see that basic rights of their own citizens have been denied and that victims have had no place to complain.

In 1999, forty-one nations including Russia belonged to the European court. There were 9,000 applications in 1999, including 300 cases from Russia.

As one views the rapidly enlarging corpus of the decisions of the European Court on Human Rights it becomes clear that the Strasbourg tribunal is the principal constitutional court of western Europe for civil liberties. Most rights guaranteed in the convention have now been interpreted by the European Court on Human Rights. The rich case law that exists may well have a profound impact in eastern Europe as the citizens of newly liberated nations litigate in the court.

The power of the U.S. Supreme Court was not appreciated at the outset of the American republic. Even after the court clearly asserted its power to invalidate an act of Congress in *Madison v. Marbury* in 1803, the potential of the high court had not been fully recognized until many decades later. The same may be true of the European Court on Human Rights. The convention it interprets and applies is in some ways more comprehensive than the U.S. Constitution. In addition, unlike the United States, the leaders of European nations may ask for advisory opinions.

The impact of the court in Strasbourg on European entities has become increasingly clear. The court of justice of the European Common Market looks to the human rights court for fundamental principles to integrate with the legal framework of the European Community.

Similarly, the European Social Charter, which entered into force in

1965, borrows from the jurisprudence of the European Court on Human Rights in its endeavors to protect economic and social rights.

The presence of the European Social Charter, with its mission to enforce the economic guarantees of the U.N. covenants and the Universal Declaration of Human Rights, is one of the reasons the decisions of the European Court on Human Rights seem to some to concentrate on political issues that could be perceived as marginal to the vast constitutional framework present in post–World War II Europe. The conception does not minimize the monumental task of the court but only points up that the nations of Europe over the past fifty years have developed an astonishing number of interlocking entities devoted to the promotion and enforcement of that vast array of political and economic rights that came into existence as a result of the unspeakable tragedies of World War II and the foundation of the United Nations.

It should be noted that even in the highly developed machinery in Europe to enforce human rights, there is a separation of political and economic rights. Theoretically they may still be treated as equal, but they are construed and enforced by different legal bodies. Economic and social rights do not receive the same degree of constitutional protection as do civil and political rights.

Any assessment of the effectiveness of the European Court on Human Rights would be premature at this point. Its mission has hardly begun, and it is a work in progress. It is now more ready to operate than ever, having streamlined its procedures by absorbing the work of the commission into the jurisdiction of the court.

Hundreds of cases are on the docket from Poland, the Czech Republic, Hungary, and Romania. The stream of cases will overshadow what the court in Strasbourg has already achieved. These accomplishments should be remembered. No member-nation, furthermore, has ever defied a binding decision. Rulings of the court have prompted Britain and France to change their laws on telephone tapping, Germany to give non-German-speaking defendants the right to an interpreter, Austria to abolish a state monopoly on cable and satellite television, and Britain to revise its military court martial process.

It is true that the European Court on Human Rights operates on a continent where human rights are already widely respected. Nonetheless, the court at Strasbourg continues to demonstrate that the rule of law has a steady, possibly increasing appeal to nations and to individuals.

People everywhere look at the 523 volumes of decisions of the U.S. Supreme Court with awe. They recognize that Americans are people of the book.

Institutions are based on the acceptance of the law as interpreted and proclaimed by the nation's highest tribunal as the binding norm on all, whether they agree or disagree.

The European Court on Human Rights will continue to grow into that stature. It confronts an enormous challenge because Russia and seventeen other former Communist countries have now ratified the European Convention on Human Rights. The task of speaking truth to power has seldom had such a challenge.

THE INTER-AMERICAN COMMISSION AND COURT ON HUMAN RIGHTS

The attraction to human rights that surged in Europe after World War II came almost simultaneously to the thirty-two nations that formed the Organization of American States (OAS). In 1948, that focus motivated the formation of the American Convention on Human Rights — a few months before the adoption of the Universal Declaration of Human Rights on December 10, 1948.

The establishment of the Inter-American Convention on Human Rights was created in 1959 and gradually developed into the Inter-American Commission and Court on Human Rights located in Costa Rica. Its history has not been as productive or successful as the European Court on Human Rights, but it is nonetheless a very significant and promising vehicle for the advancement of international human rights.

The American convention guarantees some two dozen broad categories of civil and political rights. They track the Universal Declaration of Human Rights and the European convention. But the American convention includes a longer list of those rights which are not negotiable even in emergency situations.

Unlike the European arrangements, the American convention permits nations to file complaints against another nation if both are willing. The convention also allows all individuals to bring grievances. In Europe, nations must agree in a separate protocol to allow their citizens to file. In addition, any group of persons and some nongovernmental organizations may also become plaintiffs in Costa Rica.

Although these practices seem commonplace, it must be noted how extraordinary they are. For centuries no individual could sue the king, much less complain about the king to a tribunal outside his kingdom! In Europe and Latin America the immunity of governmental leaders from prosecution for violations of international law has now been abrogated. The right of every person to have a day in court has been elevated far beyond what was even imagined in the world prior to World War II and the Holocaust.

The nations of Latin America have yielded some of their sovereignty in agreeing to the convention, but states' rights have to some extent been maintained. Article 17 of the OAS charter provides that each state has the right to develop its cultural, political, and economic life freely and naturally. In this development, the states "shall respect the rights of the individual and the principles of universal morality."

The essential difference between these European and inter-American systems is that in the latter, the outcomes of proceedings are not necessarily legally binding decisions. This is so because very few cases reach the court where a result would be binding; the conclusions and recommendations of the commission are not legally obligatory.

This arrangement is perhaps understandable because the history of Latin America since World War II has been characterized by military dictatorships, violent repression of political opposition, and judiciaries that are not independent. As a result, the work of the tribunal in San José has been concerned with the gross violations of human rights related to formal disappearances, killings, torture, and arbitrary detention of political opponents.

Although the United States is a member of the OAS, it has never ratified the American convention. President Carter signed it in 1979 and urged the Senate to ratify it. But there has never been any serious chance that such a ratification would be possible — even with stringent reservations. The possibility of citizens from Latin American countries and citizens of the United States bringing action against the United States in a tribunal in Central America is a scenario that has never gained much acceptance among lawmakers in America. The detention of Pinochet in England has deepened the fears of American citizens against submitting to the jurisdiction of any court in Latin America or elsewhere.

Because the United States has always been juridically detached from the adjudications of human rights in Latin America, it is hard to get Americans interested — much less involved — in the commission or court. Unfortunately, the literature on the Inter-American Commission and Court on Human Rights is filled with legalistic jargon about jurisdiction, the exhaustion of remedies, and the endless difficulties in enforcing the rulings of that body.

An excellent collection of essays entitled *The Inter-American System of Human Rights* (Clarendon Press, 1998), edited by David J. Harris and Stephen Livingstone, is a comprehensive description of the difficulties and dilemmas of those who desire to make the Inter-American system of human rights more effective. The fourteen essayists are perplexed and discouraged by the ongoing, massive assault on human rights that plagues so many nations in Latin America.

Scores of questions must be resolved before the human rights court in Costa Rica can be as effective as the tribunal in Strasbourg. The central one may be whether the United States will be present or absent. If the United States ever ratified the treaty and made its citizens subject to the commission and the court, it is possible that actions for and against the United States could dominate that body in San José. Lawsuits against what the United States did in the 1980s in El Salvador and Nicaragua could be numerous. Complaints against the United States for its conduct under NAFTA are conceivable. Actions to claim damages for America's conduct in Panama, Grenada, and elsewhere are likely to be brought.

There are challenges beyond count for the Inter-American Commission and Court. One of them is the presence of 400 indigenous groups in the Americas — comprising more than 30 million people — roughly 10 percent of the population of the continent. The problems of the 4 million indigenous peoples in Guatemala is a situation well known in the United States.

A draft declaration on the rights of the indigenous has long been a project of the Organization of American States. Its implementation will not be simple or easy. It is not clear whether nations that agree to the protection of the human rights of their citizens understand that they have signed up to rectify the grievances of those groups living in large numbers in the Americas before Spain and Portugal came to conquer their ancestral lands.

Another knotty problem relates to amnesties granted by governments to officials in previous governments. The U.N. Commission on Human Rights has been inundated with petitions from victims alleging that laws giving amnesty to assailants have violated their rights to judicial protection.

One dramatic case of invalidation of an amnesty granted by a government is El Salvador. Following the murder of six Jesuit priests in that country on November 16, 1989, it became clear to all parties that neither the revolutionaries (the Farabundo Marti National Liberation front, or FMLN) nor the authoritarian government had the capacity to win militarily. Both sides asked the United Nations to negotiate a settlement. In July 1990 the parties signed an agreement which included a U.N. verification mission to oversee the human rights situation. The following year the parties agreed to the establishment of an international truth commission. That group released its report on March 15, 1993, charging senior military officers and government officials with serious wrongdoing.

President Alfredo Cristiani promptly granted a general amnesty. The Salvadoran legislative assembly passed a law that granted a "full, absolute and unconditional amnesty" to all who since January 1, 1993, had participated in political or common crimes.

The Commission on Human Rights, in its strongest response to any amnesty measure, condemned El Salvador's amnesty as incompatible with its obligations under international law. The commission insisted that El Salvador could not undermine the recommendations of the Truth Commission or erase the rights of its citizens to the guarantees under the American convention, which El Salvador had ratified. In its annual report in 1994 the commission recommended that the government in El Salvador repeal the amnesty law and punish those responsible for violating the basic rights of persons who deserve compensation.

The situation in Guatemala concerning amnesty is even more anguishing than that in El Salvador. The thirty-six-year-old civil war in Guatemala ended in comprehensive peace accords in 1996. The amnesty question, which was intentionally omitted from the final peace accords, was resolved ambiguously by the legislature in December 1996. The law enhancing national reconciliation states that amnesty does not apply to genocide, torture, forced disappearances, or acts not clearly related to a war effort. The legality of amnesties in the Americas is a question on which military and police officials have passionate views. Commissions in Argentina, Brazil, and Chile have been designed to bring about both revelations and reconciliation. Whether that has happened cannot be discerned for some time. In the interim the Commission on Human Rights will continue to search for black letter law that will spell out the duties of nations on the rights of victims. The commission has been rebuffed in its attempts to compel the nations of Latin America to fulfill their duties to their citizens before they forgive the crimes of their generals.

The Inter-American Convention on Human Rights practice of publishing country reports may be one of its most useful customs. It is not done with the regularity of the U.S. State Department, which reports every February on every nation. The commission has developed a practice of filing a report on a nation that has critical problems or where, as in the case of the new government in Nicaragua in 1980, it is asked to do so. The commission also includes relevant items in its annual report on the state of human rights in specific countries.

In addition to making periodic reports, the commission can send human rights observers to countries that need help in their efforts to becoming democracies. The commission sent observers to Argentina when a dictator took over that country in 1976. It seemed to be commonly agreed that observers who speak the same language and who share the culture of the same continent may well receive a better reception and be more effective than would visitors from foreign cultures.

Although the many efforts and several achievements of the human rights teams of the commission have not been fully documented, this function and role of the commission may be one of the most important functions assigned to it.

In one sense, the achievements of the commission and court over some twenty years have been truly remarkable. They can take some credit for the fact that all nations in Latin America except Cuba are now democracies. The continent has been transformed. The principles of human rights have, at least by implication, triumphed in the return to civilian governments in Argentina, Chile, and Brazil. Central America has also been transfigured by democratic structures.

On the other hand, the commission and court have been a part-time voice on a continent which with its resources, traditions, and culture should be doing more about the tremendous problem than it is.

Questions abound. Has the presence of a regional agency to enforce international human rights diminished the role and the importance of the U.N. Commission on Human Rights and the several U.N. units that monitor compliance with the U.N. covenants on human rights? The 1945 Charter of the United Nations neither authorizes nor forbids regional groups from supplementing its work on human rights. But if the U.N. General Assembly and Security Council were in fact fulfilling all their obligations to work on behalf of human rights under the charter and the authority of the Universal Declaration of Human Rights, would regional commissions and courts be necessary?

These questions may seem academic and remote. But the intensity of convictions and feelings about the internationalization of human rights suggests that there is more universal commitment to human rights than ever before. The desire to persuade and force nations to live up to their commitments under international law is a moral force of unprecedented magnitude.

Is this new moral consensus being fragmented by the present arrangements involving a haphazard plan for regional enforcement of human rights? No one can really say. At least it is clear that NGOs are working heroically in Europe and Latin America to stop the most egregious abuses and to develop the most promising programs.

If the global concern for international human rights continues to intensify, it may be that Latin America could in a generation become a model for the acceptance and enforcement of human rights. When the intellectual and political leaders of a country or a continent believe in and adhere to the standards included in the International Bill of Rights, dramatic transformations of public morality can occur.

The newly decolonized nations of Africa were in the 1960s understandably obsessed with apartheid in South Africa. That awful system dominated their politics and their revolutions. They longed for liberation so single-mindedly that their aspirations colored every thought about international human rights.

One would think that Africa would rally with great enthusiasm to a regime in which internationally recognized human rights would be available. But the International Bill of Rights was perceived to be a product of the European or western or, even worse, colonial powers which had done so much to destroy African culture.

An African movement for human rights did result in the establishment of legal machinery to bring the African peoples the guarantees of human rights. The African Charter on Human and Peoples' Rights was adopted in 1981 and entered into force in October 1986. This commission, inaugurated in November 1987, meets twice a year and concluded its twenty-second meeting in 1997. Made up of eleven experts, the commission has struggled to combat multiple political crises in Africa. A comprehensive report of the twenty-first and twenty-second meetings of the commission in Mauritania was published in the November 30, 1998, issue of *Human Rights Law Journal*.

The African charter is different from the European and American conventions in that it protects both civil and political rights as well as economic, social, and cultural rights. It is, moreover, specifically devoted to the preservation of the "virtues of African historical tradition and the values of African civilization." The stress is also on "peoples' rights" — which in essence is the right to development.

The African charter asserts strongly that "civil and political rights cannot be disassociated from economic, social, and cultural rights in their concept as well as universality." The charter goes further, insisting that "the satisfaction of economic, social and cultural rights is a guarantee for the enjoyment of civil and political rights."

The African charter does not stress the western concept of the supremacy of individual rights. Article 17(c) declares, "The promotion and protection of morals and traditional values recognized by the community shall be the duty of the state." Article 18 affirms the concept that "the state shall have the duty to assist the family which is the custodian of morals and traditional values recognized by the community."

The preservation of African values is central to the African charter. Article 29(7) imposes the duty "to preserve and strengthen the practice of African cultural values." As a result of this deference to African values, the charter does not provide for a court. Rather than using a judicial proceeding, disputes about human rights are to be settled by negotiation and conciliation. The absence of a court is probably unthinkable to the authorities who govern the human rights process in Europe and Latin America.

Under the African charter nations can bring complaints against other nations, but individuals can qualify only if they can bring evidence of a series of serious violations of peoples' rights.

The usual remedies for petitioners in human rights cases are not readily present in the entity created by the Organization of African Unity (OAU). Its only real sanction — publicity — can be limited by the assembly which is an essentially political body which may not always be willing to publicize violations of human rights.

At the twenty-second meeting of the African commission the participants lamented the lack of political will and compliance with its decisions on the part of its members. But the nongovernmental organizations were present and active. They raised concerns about slavery in Africa, child labor, and women's rights. Other problems were legion — in Nigeria, Kenya, Sierra Leone, Gambia, and Malawi. The International Commission of Jurists, an influential NGO in Geneva was present; the commission expressed its gratitude to the ICJ and to other NGOs for their partnership.

A reading of the tenth annual report of the commission — released in June 1997 — makes clear that the vast problems of human rights in Africa's fifty-two nations are far too complicated to be handled by the understaffed and underfunded African Charter on Human and Peoples' Rights. The question arises again as to why the United Nations and its agencies on human rights are so inactive in Africa. Indeed, the frailty of the African commission has tended to confirm the conclusion of many if not most human rights experts that Africa is the most neglected of all the continents and that this area of the world may well need enforcement of international human rights more than any other continent on the planet.

Regional tribunals for human rights will almost certainly continue and be strengthened. The long-standing desire for a human rights court for Asia may not be fulfilled soon. Would it even be conceivable that a court on human rights for China, India, and the rest of the east could function? Sad to say, this vast area — including some 2 or 3 billion human beings — can look to no agency except the U.N. Commission on Human Rights.

Must one reluctantly conclude that brave proclamations of human rights in the 1940s and 1950s brought few results in Africa? The rights in the International Bill of Rights may have become customary international law, but who can or will enforce them?

The possibility of having a human rights tribunal in Asia is an intriguing thought, but its prospects seem dubious. First, the term "Asia" is a western construct. It presumably includes China, India, Indonesia, and a dozen other less populous nations. Unlike Europe, these countries have few cultural or even geographical links.

In addition, at the Vienna World Conference on Human Rights in 1993, China protested that human rights are the invention of the west — a sentiment deeply held by influential Chinese diplomats. I recall spending three hours with twelve high-level Chinese government officials in Washington in 1996; they seemed adamant in their conviction that the United States had no right to impose allegedly western ideals of human rights on China.

India is, of course, very sensitive to human rights. Its constitution calls for a sort of affirmative action for those classes long deemed to be the "untouchables."

Human rights issues in Malaysia and Indonesia are complicated by the presence of Islamic groups, some of which aspire to make Islamic law, or Shari'ah, more controlling.

A commission on human rights in Asia or in parts of Asia should logically be the next step in the evolution of internationally recognized human rights. But the leadership or the resources to bring about such a supranational commission do not seem to be present at this time in the global human rights movement.

Could it be that the enforcement of internationally recognized human rights has actually declined since the world took up the business of making them a part of world law? Should the human family look for other ways to convey the rich treasures of its newly minted legacy? If the United States changed its attitude and became a proactive enforcer of human rights, would the world be changed? It could be, but men are not angels and crime, cruelty, and corruption will continue in government as well as in private life.

People with religious faith can have some assurance that sometimes sinners change and public officials cease to abuse their power. The U.N. documents on human rights urge such a conversion, but for secular reasons. These documents urge everyone to remember that each person has inherent dignity, possesses a conscience, and is our "brother" or "sister." When combined, the moral and philosophical content of the legal articles on human rights adds up to a moral and metaphysical teaching. This teaching is a distillation of the best thought through the ages. It embraces Asian wisdom, western teaching, and the moral precepts of the Judeo-Christian tradition. Would it be more effective if it openly embraced theistic teaching? Would the documents on which the whole human rights movement is based be more compelling if they embraced more explicitly the concept that God is the creator of humanity and ultimately the author of the moral and spiritual truths that are the basis of all international covenants on human rights?

No one can say for certain. But the nontheistic approach adopted by the authors and architects of the human rights movement is now the lynchpin of the world, the moral code which furnishes the spirituality by which the human family can avoid war and violence and bestow on everyone the basic human dignity they deserve.

13

THE
RIGHT
TO
FOOD

The framers of the documents that created the human rights movement made it clear that the right to food is fundamental. The Universal Declaration of Human Rights states, "Everyone has the right to a standard of living adequate for the health and well being of himself and his family, including food, clothing, housing, medical care and necessary social services." Article 11 of the International Covenant on Economic, Social, and Cultural Rights recognizes both a right to adequate food and the right of everyone to be free from hunger.

Signatory nations commit themselves to "take appropriate steps to insure the realization" of these rights both "individually and through international cooperation." The commitments are quite specific. Nations pledge themselves to "improve methods of production, conservation and distribution of food making full use of technical and scientific knowledge, by disseminating knowledge of the principles of nutrition and by developing or reforming agrarian systems in such a way as to achieve the most efficient development and utilization of natural resources." Economic rights, then, are not merely aspirations but definite legal commitments made by nations to their subjects and to all around the world.

A right that has become a part of customary international law empowers people. Rights are sources of power. The right to food bestowed by customary international law on every person on the planet means that people can demand action to secure their entitlements. The Food and Agriculture Organization and similar groups have performed miracles in multiplying the availability of food. The sad fact is that the fundamental right above all human rights — the right to food — has not been given the attention it deserves as a part of international law. Philip Alston, one of the world's top experts on human rights, puts it this way: "It is paradoxical, but hardly surprising, that the right to food has been endorsed more often and with greater unanimity and urgency than most other human rights while at the same time being violated more comprehensively and systematically than probably any other right."

What a shocking observation. A human right which is more compelling than most and which is more easily fulfilled than most is "violated more comprehensively and systematically than probably any other right."

The thought keeps recurring — if the international human rights movement cannot secure the primitive, fundamental right to food, then why hope that the movement can obtain the realization of other less compelling human rights?

There is no totally satisfying response to that question. The human rights movement struggles and stumbles in the face of appalling ignorance, apathy, and resistance. The only certainty is that the abuse of human rights will almost certainly increase if there are no renewed protests or more humane and humanitarian laws.

Neglect of the right to food is particularly unforgivable because today, for the first time in human history, famines can be anticipated and their effects eliminated. There is enough food for 6 billion mouths. Chronic malnutrition of some 800 million individuals and the needless deaths each day of 35,000 children are preventable. These are also offenses against international law — more clearly than any other violation of the political and economic rights guaranteed by the human race in newly emerging world law.

Constructive anger within Congress brought about the enactment of Section 502(b) in 1976, which in turn encouraged the United States to take a proactive role in defending human rights in the world. This effort led to a resolution concerning the right to food by Congress, initiated by Bread for the World Institute and other nongovernmental agencies. The resolution had been aimed at the World Conference on Hunger, which was being conducted at that time in Rome.

Congress declared:

> It is the sense of Congress that:
> The United States reaffirms the right of every person in this country and throughout the world to food and a nutritionally adequate diet; and
> The need to combat hunger shall be a fundamental point of reference in the formulation and implementation of United States policy in all areas which bear on hunger including international trade, monetary arrangements, and foreign assistance.

In response to demands from Congress, Secretary of State Henry Kissinger vowed that within a decade no child would go to bed hungry. His pledge echoed what President Kennedy said in 1961 when he declared that the 1960s would see a man on the moon and the phasing out of hunger among children.

So the question recurs: Why has the world community refused or neglected to make possible the fulfillment of the most basic of all human rights — the right to food?

There is some hope that the world scene can change so that the right to food becomes exercisable for the 1.3 billion people who live in absolute poverty — with incomes of less than a dollar a day. There is hope also for the 841 million people — almost one in seven on the planet — who are chronically malnourished. That hope derives from the death of the Cold War and the new market-oriented global economy. That economy, however, cuts in different directions. It creates great wealth for a few, and provides benefits for many, while increasing hunger and insecurity for many others.

Because the globalization of the market economy seems inevitable the countless nongovernmental agencies devoted to the alleviation and elimination of hunger must work within that framework. With that in mind the Bread for the World Institute in 1998 issued its eighth annual report on the state of world hunger. The document contains a wealth of information and exhortation. But it also makes it clear that while there has been an organized world effort to eliminate polio and other dread diseases there seems to be no one organized world movement to eliminate hunger. In fact, there is now a lull in the cries of anguish heard around the world to end hunger. The new assumption — or delusion — is that the emerging global marketplace will create a new middle class in poor countries and that somehow their wealth will trickle down. This new rationalization — or evasion — is a silent premise of conservatives and libertarians who are not asking the United States to increase its foreign aid — even to alleviate hunger.

As a result academics and activists involved in human rights who have been working for some forty years to persuade the U.S. Congress to assume a leadership role in phasing out hunger have a new and difficult barrier facing them. They are told in essence that "the magic of the marketplace" will bring food to the hungry. Any governmental interference with the "magic" will only impede the efficiency of the process by which capitalism allegedly will bring prosperity to the countries it enters.

There is, of course, some truth in this contention. But if the process is not directed and controlled, it can deny the needs and the right to food of whole populations. It is understandable that there is fierce resistance and resentment toward multinational corporations who want to establish factories or farms in underdeveloped countries.

Look at recent events in Brazil. That country is one of the major foreign investment targets in the developing world. But 32 million Brazilians are poor, and 25 million face hunger. The gap between the rich and the poor is the highest in the world, with the top 20 percent earning thirty-two times the income of the poorest 20 percent.

In Latin America I have listened to the reactions of residents who see what U.S. companies do to their countries. In one nation, for example, a huge corporation from the United States acquired 10,000 acres of formerly fertile farmland to grow orchids. Each evening, air-conditioned jets fly the flowers to the United States where on the following evening they will be worn by high school seniors at their prom in Peoria. Peasants pick the flowers but they see little of the substantial profits. In addition, a substantial number of people in that area go hungry.

The authors of the Covenant on Economic, Social, and Cultural Rights anticipated this situation and required the officials of each signatory nation to report at regular intervals to the committee that supervises compliance with the covenant. Each country must record in some detail how they are carrying out their pledge to bring the economic rights that are now a part of customary international law to the citizens of their country.

The book *The United Nations and Human Rights,* by Philip Alston, reveals some of the difficulties of accomplishing this daunting task. One of them is, of course, the fact that government officials are not able to control or even direct the economic development of their nation. Capitalistic enterprises enter and in essence are in control. Their primary purpose is not to develop energy sources in the country or to eradicate disease but to maximize profits for the stockholders of the corporation who reside in Europe or America. Public officials can tell the officials of foreign corporations that they are required to work for the fulfillment of the economic rights of their citizens. But little will happen. Many multinational corporations would respond simply by assuming or asserting that the forces of the marketplace will bring about economic justice in the country in which they have chosen to locate.

The leaders of the United Nations and related agencies in the 1950s and 1960s could see these problems coming with the massive decolonization of some 100 nations. They created the World Bank, the International Monetary Fund, and similar organizations. It is evident to everyone that the mission and mode of operation of all these agencies have to be rethought. But in the interim the world must be reminded of the unspeakable conditions that persist despite the presence of standards on human rights. No one can or should say that these standards are unenforceable. But the human right to economic equality is sometimes more difficult to enforce than political rights.

It is a truism that vast economic inequalities in developing nations bring discontent and breed dictatorships and terrorism. On the other hand, the presence of economic opportunities helps develop the adoption of democratic institutions.

There has been some progress. From 1970 to 1992 the number of people afflicted with hunger fell from 918 million to 841 million. The 1996 World Food Summit, organized by the Food and Agricultural Organization, declared that the present situation is unacceptable and pledged concerted international action to reduce the number of hungry people by half before the year 2015.

But most figures on world malnutrition are bleak — especially for children. In India 21 percent of the overall population was chronically malnourished in 1990 to 1992 but 53 percent of preschool children were underweight in 1996. Undernourishment often adversely affects children's physical and mental development.

Hunger has increased in some countries since 1970 — especially in Africa. The proportion of the population that is hungry has jumped 13 percent over the past 25 years; the absolute number of hungry Africans has more than doubled in that period. The Food and Agricultural Organization has predicted that unless recent trends change 265 million Africans will suffer from hunger in the year 2010.

But some poor countries do much better. The proportion of hungry people in China fell from 45 percent in 1969 to 1971 to 16 percent in 1990 to 1992. Despite this unusual progress some 189 million Chinese remain chronically malnourished.

Of the roughly 40,000 transnational corporations in existence, 200 account for 29 percent of global economic activity. They, more than anyone, point to trade liberalization, free markets, and private investment as the keys to solving the problem of food security.

In the next twenty-five years the world's population will grow from 6 billion to 8 billion, with more than 90 percent of that growth occurring in developing countries.

It is clear, therefore, that merely stressing the internationally recognized right to food may be an oversimplified norm to use as the most important criterion. Other human rights are intertwined along with the flexible norms set forth for nations in the U.N. Covenant on Economic, Social, and Cultural Rights.

All these problems were in play at the 1996 World Food Summit in Rome. The world scene had changed radically since the 1976 world conference also held in Rome. The summit plan of action set forth a sensible blueprint, but the passion and political will present in 1976 were not visible. It was disappointing when the Clinton administration claimed that the language in the final statement does not create an enforceable international obligation. Apparently the United States feared litigation, its own inadequate food supplies, and demands for more foreign aid.

Some 1,300 nongovernmental agencies sought to strengthen the summit plan for action at the Rome conference. They stressed "food sovereignty" and the right of each nation to maintain and develop its own capacity to produce its basic food.

In all the literature on the right to food, the persistent and pervasive theme is the need of a "political will" to alleviate hunger and starvation. The concept of "political will" is not as clear-cut as it seems. No "political will" is seemingly necessary to maintain the status quo. But it is essential — yes, indispensable — in order to change things. The assumption also is that "political will" is something that does not necessarily benefit the political actor but is something suggested by idealistic forces which have finally reached the convictions or the conscience of the political officials involved.

Massive resistance to segregation created in President Johnson the "political will" to fight to pass the Civil Rights law in 1964. Vehement opposition to the war in Vietnam impelled Congress to de-fund the war and President Nixon to acquiesce in that decision.

What kind of a worldwide movement is needed to create the "political will" to implement the right to food?

One way surely is to remind nations of their solemn pledge to carry out their commitments under the several U.N. documents that guarantee the right to food. Unfortunately the United States has never ratified the Covenant on Economic, Social, and Cultural Rights.

The other major way is to intensify the efforts of the nongovernmental agencies to insist on compliance with the right to food. The NGOs include CARE, Bread for the World, Oxfam America, Freedom From Hunger, and many more. Public agencies include UNICEF and the U.N. Development Program (UNDP).

The right to food is virtually inseparable from all the other economic and political rights which are the patrimony of all those who belong to the United Nations and are part of the human family. But the right to food is so central and crucial that its dimensions deserve very special attention. The dream of abolishing hunger is a centuries-old hope of the human race. It is not impossible that that dream can become a reality in the twenty-first century.

When President Carter was in the White House, he appointed a presidential commission on world hunger chaired by Sol Linowitz. The comprehensive report of the commission recommended that the U.S. government "make the elimination of hunger the primary focus of its relationships with the developing countries." In its report, the commission documented evidence for its conclusion that "it would be possible to eliminate the worst aspects of hunger and malnutrition by the year 2000."

The position was never adopted by the United States. Consequently, it is not now possible to predict with confidence when hunger will be phased out.

The position of the Commission on the Right to Food is an eloquent exhortation:

> Whether one speaks of human rights or basic human needs, the right to food is the most basic of all. Unless that right is first fulfilled, the protection of other human rights becomes a mockery for those who must spend all their energy merely to maintain life itself. The correct moral and ethical position on hunger is beyond debate. The world's major religions and philosophical systems share two universal values: respect for human dignity and a sense of social justice. Hunger is the ultimate affront to both.

14

DOES THE
DEATH PENALTY
VIOLATE CUSTOMARY
INTERNATIONAL
LAW?

Could the death penalty be the next thing forbidden by customary international law because that source of prohibited conduct brought about the demise of slavery and piracy? The answer increasingly seems to be in the affirmative. But it is still not entirely clear that capital punishment is living on borrowed time.

The visceral feelings which a majority of people have concerning the death penalty are not rooted entirely in reason or wisdom. They cross the spectrum from sheer vindictiveness to a deep conviction that violence may never be used for any purpose, however commendable.

The thought of the inevitability of death makes cowards of us all. It is hardly possible that anyone who is not mentally limited could conclude that he or she deserves death for mistakes or sins committed. The imposition of the death sentence somehow does not seem congruous or reasonable — at least when it applies to ourselves.

It is difficult to construct a rational case for that position. That human instinct to abhor cruelty found its first mention in Anglo-American law in the English Bill of Rights in 1689. It declared that "cruel and inhuman treatment or punishment" would not be allowed.

How could the death penalty *not* be "cruel and inhuman"? That is the question which today's international human rights movement must resolve.

During the nineteenth and twentieth centuries the norm forbidding "cruel and inhuman treatment or punishment" filtered into domestic institutions throughout the world. Despite some minor differences in the wording, the essential message is the same: cruel, unusual, inhuman, and degrading treatment or punishment violates customary international law.

Physical torture is presumably worse than cruel, inhuman, or degrading treatment or punishment. Torture is clearly outlawed by the Covenant on Torture, which most of the nations of the world, including the United States, have ratified.

In 1948 the authors of the Universal Declaration of Human Rights had to face the fact that the death penalty had been imposed by the Nuremberg and Tokyo tribunals on war criminals. In addition, the vast majority of nations employed the death penalty. It was proposed that the death penalty be noted specifically in the Universal Declaration of Human Rights as an exception to the right to life. Eleanor Roosevelt and René Cassin, the European jurist who was the principal author of the Universal Declaration of Human Rights, rejected the idea that the declaration should contain a reference to capital punishment as an exception to the right to life. Mrs. Roosevelt, who chaired the drafting committee, cited the movement under way in many countries to abolish the death penalty.

A half century later their clairvoyance must be acknowledged. That admission has allowed customary international law to develop so that today the elimination of the death penalty is more possible than ever before.

The European Convention on Human Rights, adopted two years after the Universal Declaration of Human Rights, recognized the right to life "save in the execution of a sentence of a court following his conviction of a crime for which this penalty is provided by law." But this provision was almost immediately anachronistic. In the early 1970s the Council of Europe began work on a protocol to the convention which was adopted in 1983 by which the death penalty in peacetime is abolished. In 1989, the European Court on Human Rights noted that capital punishment had been de facto abolished in Europe.

In 1976, the International Covenant on Civil and Political Rights entered into force. Article 6 of that covenant includes the death penalty as an exception to the right to life, but it lists detailed safeguards. The death penalty may be imposed only for the "most serious crimes" and with elaborate and rigorous procedural rules. Pregnant women and those under the age of eighteen are spared. Article 6, furthermore, points to the abolition of the death penalty as a human rights objective and implies that nations that have already abolished the death penalty may not reinstate it. An additional protocol adopted in 1989 proclaimed that the death penalty was abolished in Europe in time of peace and war. Many European states have signed this protocol, making the death penalty nonexistent in Europe.

The Inter-American Convention on Human Rights (also known as the American Convention on Human Rights), which entered into force in 1978, replicates the European doctrine. It forbids any nation that has abolished the death penalty to revive it. Because of this treaty and several other factors in world opinion, the death penalty has in effect been abolished in Latin America.

The African Charter of Human and Peoples' Rights, which entered into force in 1986, makes no mention of capital punishment as an exception or limitation on the right to life. Yet, the continent of Africa appears to be moving to abolish the death penalty. The countries in Africa were certainly influenced by the unanimous decision of the Supreme Court of South Africa in 1995 that declared the death penalty to be inconsistent with South Africa's new constitution.

The Arab Charter of Human Rights, adopted September 15, 1994, is somewhat different. Articles 10, 11, and 12 recognize the legitimacy of the death penalty in the case of "serious violators of general law," but it is excluded in cases involving political crimes, those under the age of eighteen, and pregnant or nursing mothers. Some Islamic nations have defended the use of the death penalty in the name of obedience to Islamic law and to strictures of the Shari'ah, which is a collection or code of laws binding those who follow the Koran.

Scholars seem to differ in their interpretation of the clarity or the binding quality of Islamic law with respect to the death penalty. Theoretically it is a question of vital importance because the forty predominantly

Muslim nations contain some 1 billion people. If the Koran and other sources of Islamic doctrine were construed as allowing or even requiring the death penalty in certain cases, this would clearly be a strong argument contrary to that of those scholars who want to reach a careful judgment as to whether customary international law now forbids the death penalty.

But the Islamic nations appear to be ambivalent on the death penalty. Those who resist the concept that the Koran is a binding source of civil law downplay the allegedly divine revelation that capital punishment is authorized by the Koran. In addition, the Islamic nations that signed the final document of the Vienna World Conference on Human Rights in 1993 agreed to re-ratify the treaties which at least clearly imply that the death penalty violates the ban on cruel and inhuman treatment and punishment.

The classic weakness of the international human rights law lies, of course, in its means of implementation. But increasingly, international human rights law is being applied in domestic courts. Courts in South Africa, Canada, Tanzania, Zimbabwe, and the United Kingdom have found international law to be helpful in the interpretation of the ban on cruel, inhuman, or degrading punishment. Several international organizations have also been skeptical of the death penalty. The United Nations leads the list. In 1968, the U.N. Commission on Human Rights initiated a resolution calling for a moratorium on the death penalty. The U.N. General Assembly agreed to this resolution with minor amendments. The vote was 94–0, with 3 abstentions. In 1972, the U.N. General Assembly passed a resolution endorsing "the desirability of abolishing the punishment in all countries."

But strong opposition to the abolition of the death penalty emerged at the U.N. Congress on Crime Prevention and Control. Meeting in Caracas in 1980, the congress drafted a resolution calling for the eventual abolition of the death penalty. The resolution was met with opposition and was withdrawn. When that same congress convened in 1990, the idea of a moratorium failed to obtain the necessary two-thirds vote.

In 1994, a resolution of the U.N. General Assembly called for a moratorium on the death penalty. It originated in a newly formed nongovernmental organization named "Hands Off Cain — the International League for Abolishing the Death Penalty." Even though the resolution had forty-nine co-sponsors, it failed to pass on a procedural gambit.

In 1997, the U.N. Commission on Human Rights passed a resolution calling for a moratorium on the death penalty. The vote was 27–11, with 14 abstentions.

The "abolitionists" are happy to see that all the nations that created the war crimes tribunal for those involved in the war in the former Yugoslavia and in Rwanda agreed to forgo capital punishment. The opponents of the death penalty also approved of the ban on the death penalty in the charter of the International Criminal Commission.

The abolitionists note that all 190 nations that have ratified the Convention on the Rights of the Child (the United States and Somalia are the only nonratifiers) have done so without a reservation to Article 37(a), which bans the death penalty for offenders who were under age eighteen at the time of the crime. In 1997, China abolished the death penalty for those under age eighteen.

Since 1990, some nineteen people in six nations are known to have been executed for crimes committed when they were under the age of eighteen. Ten of the nineteen were in the United States. In contrast, 3,670 people were on death row as of April 1, 2000; of these, 69 were juveniles who had committed crimes when they were sixteen or seventeen years old.

The worldwide picture of the use of the death penalty reveals that ninety-nine nations have abolished the punishment, whereas ninety-four retain the death penalty. This means that over 50 percent of all countries have now abolished the death penalty in law or in practice.

In 1998, at least 1,625 prisoners were reported to have been executed in 37 countries. A small number of countries accounted for most of the executions. There were, according to Amnesty International, 1,065 executions in China, over 100 in the Democratic Republic of Congo, 68 in the United States, and 66 in Iran. These four nations accounted for 80 percent of all executions. Amnesty International also received reports of hundreds of executions in Iraq but was unable to confirm most of these.

One of the most significant victories for the abolitionists occurred in 1999, when President Boris Yeltsin all but abolished capital punishment, commuting to life in prison the sentence of the last Russian prisoner on death row. Yeltsin, who had permitted the execution of 163 prisoners during his terms in office, placed a moratorium on executions in 1996 after Russia joined the Council of Europe, which bans capital punishment in peacetime. Although Yeltsin had agreed to halt any more executions, they remain legal because the parliament has been unwilling to repeal the law.

Moves to reinstitute the death penalty after it has been abolished are usually unsuccessful. Since 1985, only four abolitionist countries have reinstated the death penalty. One, Nepal, has since abolished the death penalty again. Canada and England have refused to reinstitute capital punishment even when conservative governments have come to power and urged a return to the death penalty.

To abolitionists, arguments justifying the death penalty are easy to refute. A U.N. study done in 1988 and updated in 1996 shows that crime does not increase when the death penalty is abolished. In Canada the homicide rate per 100,000 fell from a peak of 3.09 in 1975, the year before the abolition of the death penalty, to 2.41 in 1980 and has remained steady since that time. In 1993, the homicide rate was 2.19 per 100,000 people, 27 percent lower than in 1975.

The abolitionists also stress the risk of executing the innocent. A 1987 study showed that 350 persons convicted of capital crimes between 1900 and 1985 were innocent of the crimes charged, while 23 were actually executed. A report of the House Judiciary Committee in 1993 listed 48 condemned men who had been freed from death row since 1972.

The racial disparity among individuals on death row is well known. Attempts to prove that the selection of those charged with the death penalty is a process infected with racism have not been successful, as was manifest in the *McClesky* decision of the U.S. Supreme Court. That ruling made clear that the Court would not take up the sociological or statistical evidence indicating that race had played a part in the selection or prosecution of persons accused of committing a capital offense.

New efforts to seek to prevent the execution of mentally retarded or emotionally unstable individuals are also well known. In the decision *Thompson v. Oklahoma* in 1988 a plurality of the Supreme Court concluded that a death sentence for an offender who is fifteen years old at the time of his crime constituted cruel and unusual punishment under the Eighth Amendment. Justice Stevens, writing for the majority, cited views of the international community in reasoning that the death penalty would "offend civilized standards of decency." He cited decisions from western European countries as well as the Soviet Union that prohibit juvenile executions. In addition he cited the three treaties ratified or signed by the United States which explicitly prohibit juvenile death penalties. In dissent, Justice Scalia argued that international standards should never be imposed according to the U.S. Constitution. This latter view became the law of the country the following year when in *Stanford v. Kentucky* Justice Scalia in essence rejected the relevance of international law and the practices of other countries in construing the Eighth Amendment.

In 1958, the U.S. Supreme Court confirmed that the Court is entitled to look at the "evolving standards of decency that mark the progress of a maturing society" as a norm for its decisions. Judges in America are torn between the black letter law set forth in the opinion of Justice Scalia and the flexible standard of following the "evolving standards of decency." It is very clear that American judges are anxious to discover clearly defined rules that are clear rather than grope for the "evolving standards of decency." The U.S. Supreme Court in its 5–4 ruling in the *Stanford* decision tipped the scales to a norm that would preclude the use of international principles not set forth clearly in U.S. statutory law.

If the death penalty is eventually curtailed or even eliminated in the United States, will that happen because of international customary law, public opinion, or a reexamination of the concepts behind cruel, inhuman, or degrading treatment? For some — perhaps for many — the idea of detaining persons on death row for months and years, depriving them of their lives, fulfills and exceeds every standard contained in the ban on "cruel, inhuman, degrading" treatment or punishment. Even the retentionists are inclined to admit that all five current methods of execution — hanging, electrocution, shooting, lethal gas, and poisonous injection — have to be seen as cruel or inhuman or degrading. Those words are not novel in American jurisprudence. They appeared in 1689 in the English Bill of Rights. It could be hoped — indeed, expected — that over a period of 300 years the evolving standards of decency would bar ways of treating human beings which in 1689 were allowed. Anglo-American law has elevated the standards so that all forms of torture, disembowelment, amputation, and similar offenses are forbidden.

The retentionists question who decides on the "evolving standards of decency." If one nation in its legislature or courts refuses to accept or adopt a higher level, can the citizens of the nation insist that the courts be responsive to customary international law and insist that their countries are obliged to follow that form of law?

How soon will customary international law be clear and precise enough for U.S. courts to use it as a source of authority for decisions on the death penalty which do not exist in American law?

The Restatement of the Foreign Relations Law of the United States is the authoritative source for what laws are binding on U.S. courts. The latest edition, issued in 1987 by the American Law Institute, contains the black letter law which U.S. courts must follow. But the aspirations of the world community or the "emerging" norms are not codified in the restatement.

Opinions of many nations support the abolitionists' arguments. Compelling reasons are set forth in the opinion of the Supreme Court of South Africa in June 1995, which abolished the death penalty. If opinions of foreign courts are increasingly negative on the legality of the death penalty, can or should the U.S. courts follow the test and standards for the legality of capital punishment as they emerge from the courts and legislatures around the world? Not all jurists agree on the answer to this inquiry. Judges should not be excessively activist but they are nonetheless required, as the U.S. Constitution itself sets forth, to follow the law of nations.

When will the condemnations of the death penalty by the U.N. General Assembly, the committees that monitor the U.N. covenants, and comparable bodies add up to a norm which U.S. courts can use to settle disputes about the definition of concepts like cruel, inhuman, and degrading?

When will American judges take notice of the remarkable evolution of consensus of religious opinions in the United States and elsewhere against the death penalty? The Catholic Church has made the most visible and dramatic movement toward a condemnation of the death penalty. All the documents of the Second Vatican Council did not specifically disallow the death penalty but a remarkable unanimity against capital punishment has emerged in the past few years. Indeed, virtually all religious groups in the United States share in the unanimous condemnation of the death penalty which has appeared in Catholic thought. No one would say that courts should follow the opinion of one or all of the churches, but courts must employ some criteria to discern what are the "evolving standards of decency" in a democracy.

One way by which public officials in the United States could be induced to drop the death penalty is by accepting the *Soering* decision of the European Court of Human Rights. Hans Soering, a native of Germany, killed the parents of his girlfriend in Virginia. He escaped to Europe, where he fought the extradition sought by the Commonwealth of Virginia in the European Court of Human Rights in Strasbourg. It was clear that Virginia intended to execute Soering for first-degree murder. Soering's creative lawyers argued that the prospect of long years on death row in Virginia constituted a violation of international law because the experience would be cruel, inhuman, and degrading. The court spelled out with eloquence the dreadful wait and the other humiliations which Soering would be required to undergo in some seven years or more of appeals.

The officials of Virginia finally conceded and agreed to imprison Soering for life. Virginia made no admissions that the death penalty violated customary international law, but its conduct in essence admitted that.

How did the United States get itself into the trap in which it now finds itself in the struggle over the death penalty? Unlike all the major nations of the world except China, the United States keeps some 3,500 people on death row and will in due course execute most of them. Can it escape from the trap if the Supreme Court reverses its 1976 decision, which in essence said that the states could resume executions? Some kind of a mania or fixation took hold of the United States after that decision in 1976. No U.S. president since that time has taken any moral or political leadership against the death penalty. Indeed, the federal government itself enacted laws authorizing up to fifty grounds for capital punishment. Some of the twelve states without the death penalty, like New York, have restored it. A strong coalition of nongovernmental organizations lobbied vigorously at the state and federal levels, but to no avail. The Catholic bishops were energized by the vigorous opposition to the death penalty at the highest levels of the church in Rome.

In 1996, the American Bar Association voted for a moratorium on the death penalty. This surprising ruling — from an organization of 400,000 lawyers deemed to be conservative — will have an enormous impact over a period of years.

The best recent scholarly book on international law and the death penalty is *The Death Penalty as Cruel Treatment and Torture: Capital Punishment Challenged in the World's Courts,* by William A. Schavas (Northeastern University Press, 1996). The conclusions of this Canadian academic are cautious and carefully measured. He marshals evidence that the international ban on torture and cruelty may eventually grow into elimination of the death penalty. A thorough review of Schavas's flawless scholarship suggests that if the death penalty is to be ended, it will be done not by legal arguments or subtle interpretations of customary international law but by a sense of horror concerning the death penalty by the people of the world. This horror is shared and expanded by the NGOs of the world, and has been dramatized by the book entitled *Dead Man Walking,* by Sister Helen Prejean. That book portrayed the feeling in the last line of Dostoyevsky's novel *The Idiot:* "You can't treat a man like that."

Dostoyevsky's full statement explains why the death penalty is cruel, inhuman, and degrading:

"To kill for murder is an immeasurably greater evil than the crime itself. . . . Here all . . . last hope, which makes it ten times easier to die, is taken away for certain; here you have been sentenced to death, and the whole terrible agony lies in the fact that you will most certainly not escape, and there is no agony greater than that. Take a soldier and put him in front of a cannon in battle and fire at him and he will still hope, but read the same soldier his death sentence for certain, and he will go mad or burst out crying. Who says that human nature is capable of bearing this without madness? Why this cruel, hideous, unnecessary, and useless mockery? . . . It was of agony like this and of such horror that Christ spoke. No, you can't treat a man like that!"

15

THE
HUMAN RIGHTS
OF PRISONERS

It would be logical to think that the architects of the human rights movement had paid attention very early to the human rights of prisoners. Surely, hardly anyone is more vulnerable than a human being who has been deprived of his or her basic and fundamental right of freedom.

But the human rights movement cannot say that it has achieved great things for prisoners. In 1955, the United Nations adopted the Standard Minimum Rules for the Treatment of Prisoners. It was not a convention or even a declaration. Nations were not asked to ratify it as they had been for most of the documents issued by the United Nations with regard to political, economic, and social rights.

In 1988, the U.N. General Assembly issued a document entitled "Body of Principles for the Protection of All Persons Under Any Form of Detention or Imprisonment." The message sounded stern and insisted that any person under any form of detention or imprisonment should be treated "in a humane manner and with respect to the inherent dignity of the human person."

However, the U.N. document was simply a statement of thirty-nine principles that did not require member-nations to sign or ratify it.

In 1990, the United Nations issued another document entitled "Basic Principles for the Treatment of Prisoners." It advanced previous statements in that it urged the "abolition of solitary confinement as a punishment." It also recommended that favorable conditions "shall be created for the reintegration of the ex-prisoner into society under the best possible conditions."

Someday soon we may well be stating that prison inmates were the orphans in the worldwide human rights movement. To be sure, during the fifty years of the human rights movement some improvements have been made in prison life, but there has also been a decline in the quality of life and availability of opportunities in prisons during that period. One of the amazing facts in American life is that virtually no one knows anything about prisons. Wardens and jailers keep it that way. They have aggressively and systematically kept out the press and the public. In *Saxbe v. Washington Post,* prison officials won their case against the newspaper in the U.S. Supreme Court in 1974. The case was brought when prison officials kept the *Washington Post* from entering a jail where some high-level public officials in the Watergate scandal were locked up.

This state of events is even more amazing in view of the fact that the prison population in the United States has almost tripled from 1980 to 1999 — up to 1.8 million inmates — larger than any prison population in any nation on earth.

I experienced the isolation of prison life when, as a member of a subcommittee of the House Judiciary Committee with supervisory power of federal prisoners, I visited scores of prisons in every part of the country. Even in the 1970s federal prisons were overcrowded and had far too few programs to rehabilitate the inmates or to prepare them for employment when they were released.

It is, of course, easy to criticize penal officials without recognizing that many of them have to manage individuals who have committed very serious crimes and who have a history of engaging in violence.

In the 1970s federal prisons had the stated duty of seeking to rehabilitate the inmates, but that goal faded in the 1980s. Parole was abolished. Sentences became longer, and the rule of three strikes and you're out was invented.

In the 1980s and 1990s a certain amount of revenge entered into the American attitude toward criminals. It was exploited by elected officials who sought to gain attention and praise by demonstrating how "tough" they could be on law enforcement — especially toward those who sell narcotics, participate in gangs, and steal cars.

The "war on drugs," which became a mantra for politicians, led to unfortunate, unintended consequences such as the imprisonment of hundreds of thousands of persons who had not engaged in any violent conduct or even in activities that brought harm to third persons

In 1980, I participated in a conference in Caracas of penal officials from all over the world. This group, which had met every fifth year since the adoption of the Standard Minimum Rules in 1955, was perplexed and upset because while the human rights movement was gaining momentum everywhere with respect to its concern for political and economic rights, the entire human rights movement was paying little attention to the rights of prisoners.

Some eight years after the Caracas meeting, Human Rights Watch started the prison project. This NGO published reports on prisons in a score of countries including the United States. The reports are commendable and still appear. But it cannot be said that the international human rights movement has stirred up the interest in human rights for prisoners as it has for the rights of women, children, and the disabled, for example.

The neglect of prisoners by the human rights movement has not been planned or deliberate. The Convention on Civil and Political Rights, which entered into force on March 23, 1976, provided in Article 10 that "all persons deprived of their liberty shall be treated with humanity and with respect for the inherent dignity of the human person." The same article insisted that accused persons be kept apart from convicted persons and that juveniles be segregated from adults. Article 10 also made it clear that "the penitentiary shall furnish treatment of prisoners the essential aim of which shall be their reformation and social rehabilitation."

The statement is forthright — the essential aim of the institution shall be "reformation and social rehabilitation." The assumption is that this transformation is possible in a "penitentiary." The word "penitentiary" goes back to the Quaker origin of the reform of the prison system in America in the nineteenth century in Pennsylvania.

The objective of "social rehabilitation" has apparently disappeared in the contemporary jurisprudence of prisons. Yet the idea of rehabilitation was very much alive in the minds of the penal officials who gathered in Caracas in 1980. They admitted with sadness that they often did not have the resources to carry out the rehabilitation they desired, but the dominant philosophy was that incarceration is a means to a doable end and not merely for punitive purposes.

But the officials from poor nations at the Caracas conference had to admit that they were not getting the support from the United Nations which they needed to carry out the objectives that very entity had continued to endorse. This was admitted in 1993 in a report entitled "Human Rights Watch Global Report on Prisons." That document noted the concern for the human rights of prisoners in the Universal Declaration of Human Rights and in the International Covenant on Civil and Political Rights, as well as the Standard Minimum Rules. The Human Rights Watch document conceded that these "have been largely unsuccessful in improving the conditions under which prisoners live."

The human rights movement does, of course, pay more attention to political prisoners. Indeed the NGOs in the United States engage in monitoring the destiny of those who are detained for their ideological views. If these unlucky individuals are lawyers or journalists, they are more likely to obtain the attention of the international human rights community.

Amnesty International has a highly developed approach for spotting the incarceration of political prisoners and seeking to liberate them. I was very impressed at the efficacy of Amnesty International when I was on a human rights mission in Chile just before Pinochet was ousted. A medical doctor was jailed hundreds of miles from Santiago because he had correctly accused the government of employing torture. With pressure from Amnesty International, ambassadors of more than fifty countries pressured the government in Chile to release the physician. He was home within forty-eight hours.

But the human rights movement does not have the same aptitude for paying attention to prisoners who have lost their liberty because of their alleged wrongdoing. Even in South Africa after it abolished apartheid, the human rights groups of the world did not give vigorous attention to the conditions in the jails which held thousands of persons who were incarcerated partially because of their political opposition to the all-white government.

In summer 1995, I visited prisons and lectured to public officials about the international human rights of prisoners in South Africa. The human rights activists in that country understandably had many urgent priorities aside from the rights of prisoners. And, indeed, it seems true almost everywhere that the living conditions and human rights of prisoners have always seemed to be trumped by other concerns.

In the vast explosion of reports and literature on human rights, the amount of material on prisoners is relatively small. And even in reports that do address the topic of human rights and prisoners, there is little questioning of the basic assumptions of what government thinks they are doing when they take people convicted of a crime and force them to wear prison garb, live in a cell, and lose virtually every semblance of privacy.

Experts in the international human rights movement seem to leave their concerns at the door of the prison. All the norms for human rights and conduct center on what is cruel, inhuman, and degrading. How are these norms applied to the dozens of humiliations that prison guards impose on inmates?

The Standard Minimum Rules and other documents of the United Nations on the rights of those detained for any reason unfortunately function at a level of generality that does not seem to give prisoners or their attorneys anything specific to use. At least eight states in the United States have adopted the rules, but it is not certain that inmates in these states enjoy a higher level of respect for their internationally recognized human rights.

There are some provisions with "bite" in the Standard Minimum Rules. These relate to the right to be treated with dignity and respect, the right to confidentiality with one's attorney, and the right to a reasonable level of health care. But the U.N. document does not get into the harder questions of the essential fairness of, for example, taking a man away from his wife and two children for a crime related to drugs; the whole complicated question of what is condign punishment is not adequately addressed by any U.N. document that relates to crime and punishment.

One of the most helpful documents monitoring the history of human rights of prisoners is the addition to the U.S. State Department annual report on human rights. This document now by congressional mandate includes information on the state of prisons in each of the nations surveyed. In the report issued in April 1999 for the year 1998, the report on El Salvador contained three paragraphs about jails in that country. In 1998, prisons remained overcrowded, with the number of inmates at 28 percent over the designed maximum capacity; there were 7,147 men in seventeen prisons and 398 women in two facilities designed for 180 women. Gang violence—especially in the three oldest facilities—seems to be endemic in the prisons of El Salvador—as elsewhere. At least 10 deaths had occurred in the prisons as a result of violence.

A reading of the State Department reports and the extensive documents from Human Rights Watch and Amnesty International raises the basic question: Is the incarceration of prisoners—except in rare cases of persons who are dangerous—humane, effective, outdated, or just vindictive?

A book by Vivien Stern entitled *A Sin Against the Future: Imprisonment in the World* (Northeastern University Press, 1998) is an excellent summary of the history of the idea of prisons and how they are functioning today. The author clearly calls for reform, asserting that imprisonment no longer fits modern society. In many cases imprisonment "gives rise to more problems than it solves." Every prison, moreover, is a place "in which profound abuses of human rights can be carried out under the reasoning justification that this is needed to protect the public."

Stern highlights the trend in the United States with its massive number of prisoners—an example, incidentally, that appears to be attracting attention in Europe, where the minimal use of prisons has been the norm.

Stern points out forcefully that prisons do not heal or transform inmates. She concludes that after "a spell in prison the young man involved in petty crime has become a person who rejects society's values as society has rejected him" (p. 338).

The author, a British academic, makes out a powerful case for the thesis that prisons are "a sin against the future" in the same category as "polluting the environment and using up the natural resources of the globe."

Can the international human rights movement have an impact on the vast and brutal systems of prisons in the former Soviet republics, the new countries of Africa, the struggling democracies in Latin America, and the "penitentiaries" in the United States? Clearly, the academics and activists in the NGOs devoted to that objective have been working diligently with little if any recognition or reward.

It is indeed ironic that the United States, which has escalated its use of prisons beyond anyone's prediction fifteen years ago, has through its

State Department reports become the compiler of one of the most comprehensive sources of information about the state of the world's prisons.

A handful of groups in New York—especially the American Civil Liberties Union—lobby and litigate to improve the human rights of prisoners in the United States. They are confronted with almost insurmountable obstacles. One result of this work is the fact that over one-half of state prison systems are under court orders to improve the facilities or services of the nation's prisoners.

Although there have been some opportunities to take their cases to the European Court of Human Rights in Strasbourg, one must conclude that prisoners have not benefited from the international human rights movement in the way that they deserve. Prisoners under international human rights law may not be deprived of internationally recognized human rights unless such a deprivation is required by the very condition of being imprisoned. Inmates, furthermore, should not be deprived of due process by their jailers. They are already punished enough by the removal of their liberty; they cannot be further prohibited at the whim of prison guards, who have almost total control over the lives of inmates.

The depth of the desire to punish prisoners in the United States is appalling. The deprivations and humiliations inflicted in prison continue in several states where even former felons may never vote in any state election. The contempt extended to prisoners by their superiors reflects and deepens the profound feelings of alienation which the public has for prisoners. Racism is also involved, because over 50 percent of prisoners in the United States are African-Americans, although only 12 percent of the general population is black.

Compassion for prisoners is one of the virtues which Christ emphasized. Visiting those in prison is exalted in the gospels as a high virtue. It is in essence an integral part of the entire Judeo-Christian tradition. It could be argued that prison policy in the United States makes that virtue almost impossible to carry out. Prisons are erected in areas totally segregated from the communities in which they reside; this is accomplished by high walls, severe restrictions on the number of visitors, and the implicit statement that prisoners must be locked up and segregated from society because they are dangerous.

It does seem quixotic to suggest that inmates would benefit by sharing in a community beyond the walls of a prison and that this could be a very effective way to begin the reintegration of prisoners into the community to which they will inevitably be returned.

I have spoken through the years to and with prison officials. They have a difficult task, but almost automatically they tend to adopt a policy of hostility toward inmates. The guards are placed in an awkward role. They are in all probability given copies of the rules set forth by the United Nations to protect the human rights of prisoners, yet they know that these rules have no legal binding power in America's courts and that the prisoners probably have no knowledge of the existence of such rules.

Persons involved in prison reform are now deeply discouraged at the prevailing simplistic attitudes which seem to be in ascendancy at the moment.

It could be that the international human rights movement has some moral and legal principles which might inject rationality into the American obsession with the idea that more prisons and longer sentences are the solution to crime.

The ban on cruel, inhuman, and degrading treatment and punishment is one of the cornerstones of the human rights movement. If this compelling and elevating doctrine were seriously applied to the work of prisons, a global transformation could result.

16

HUMAN RIGHTS DEPEND ON AN INDEPENDENT JUDICIARY

The concept that the judge in any human rights case should be independent and impartial has always been so axiomatic that in the history of the international human rights movement there has never been any great debate about it.

The issue was seemingly settled in 1948, when Article 10 of the Universal Declaration of Human Rights proclaimed: "Everyone is entitled in full equality to a fair and public hearing by a competent, independent and impartial tribunal in the determination . . . of any charge against him."

The International Covenant on Civil and Political Rights in Article 14(1) repeats the idea that everyone's entitlement is to "a fair and public hearing by a competent, independent and impartial tribunal."

Likewise Article 8(1) of the American Convention on Human Rights insists that "every person has a right to a hearing . . . by a competent, independent and impartial tribunal." The European Convention on Human Rights also guarantees "a fair and public hearing . . . by an independent and impartial tribunal by law."

The value and importance of an independent judge are dramatically preserved in the four 1949 Geneva conventions. The 153 contracting parties to this compact, including the United States, have the right in a public emergency situation to suspend fair trial guarantees. But in Article 3 the passing of sentences and carrying out of executions cannot be done except by a regularly constituted court previously established by law.

Article 3 is not subject to derogation under any circumstances. It seems clear that jurists can argue that insisting on a regularly constituted court even in situations involving conflict should be regarded as a peremptory norm of international law.

The European Court on Human Rights and the Inter-American Commission on Human Rights have stressed the indispensability of an independent tribunal. The latter has conducted on-site investigations and has issued public reports deploring the absence of an independent judge—even in situations where a state of siege exists.

The idea and the centrality of the independence of the bench are so self-evident that one could hope there would be no sustained controversy over it. But the desire of despots to control the situation and the determination of even democratically elected governments to be completely in charge are foreign to the concept of an "independent" person or entity that makes the crucial decisions.

The idea of a judge who is "independent" and "impartial" can be seen as idealistic and even unrealistic. The Code of Judicial Conduct adopted by the American Bar Association in 1990 stresses the idea of the independence of the judge and the need to avoid all impropriety. Indeed, the code, unlike the 1983 Model Rules governing attorneys, retains and enforces the ban on even the "appearance of impropriety."

But it is still difficult to comprehend how one person can rise above all the prejudices and prepossessions that every human being inherits or develops. Justice Benjamin Cardozo said it well in his book *The Nature of the Judicial Process* (Yale University Press, 1921): "There is in each of us a stream of tendency, whether you choose to call it philosophy or not, which gives coherence and direction to thought and action. Judges cannot escape that current any more than other mortals. All their lives, forces which they do not recognize and cannot name, have been tugging at them—inherited instinct, traditional beliefs, acquired convictions; and the resultant is an outlook on life, a conception of social needs. . . . In this mental background every problem finds its setting. We may try to see things as objectively as we please. None the less, we can never see them with any eyes except our own" (pp. 12–13).

The very idea of an independent tribunal is of course foreign to the concept of majority control and to the idea that legislatures and the executive branches of government make the ultimate decisions. Judicial review is the twin of the idea that there are certain human rights which no legislature or executive branch of a government can deny. All the international and regional groups that have promulgated codes or manifestos of human rights have assumed that, even under the best of circumstances, they are not self-enforcing. The human rights that are created and guaranteed should theoretically be readily available to the persons in whom these rights inhere and who are entitled to claim them because of their inherent dignity.

But history repeats the need for a moral force to exist that thrives on moral principles and that can force the elected branches of government to carry out the promises their governments have made. No nation is being forced by a judge to do something contrary to what the elected officials or the people desire at the moment. A tribunal simply reminds a government that it has made solemn promises to carry out the mandates of a covenant on human rights, a contract which the nation has made with the international community.

It is obvious that the judge who is required to enforce such contracts can understandably be tempted to defer to the leaders whose wishes the judge must reject or at least postpone. The history of the world is filled with the sad story of judges who caved or compromised in order to retain their positions. In the dark years of Argentina from 1976 to 1983 when the military controlled the government, there were not a few judges who ruled in such a way that they retained their jobs rather than follow what was clearly required by international human rights law.

It is for all these reasons that the international human rights community has stressed and cherished the independence of the judiciary. Since 1978 the International Commission of Jurists has issued reports on the state of judicial independence throughout the world. The commission's creation, the Center for the Independence of Judges and Lawyers Code of Judicial Conduct, defines as carefully as possible the profound cluster of ideas and ideals underlining the independence of the bench and the bar. The purpose of the center is to mobilize support for judges who are being harassed or intimidated or even persecuted for their professional work in upholding the principles of the rule of law.

An ever wider group of nongovernmental organizations assists the

International Commission of Jurists. The International Bar Association in 1981, along with other legal entities, prepared a document in Siracusa, Italy, on the independence of the bench. Thirty-two principles in this document were designed to produce a properly functioning independent judiciary everywhere. They have been discussed throughout the world. There are no substantial differences on the overall purposes of the document. But difficult political questions remain, such as how judges are to be appointed and for how long.

The Siracusa Manifesto does, however, contain in Article 2 a definition on which there is a broad consensus:

> Independence of the judiciary means (1) that every judge is free to decide matters before him in accordance with his assessment of the facts and his understanding of the law without any improper influence, inducements or pressures, direct or indirect, from any quarter or for any reasons, and (2) that the judiciary is independent of the executive and legislature, and has jurisdiction, directly or by way of review, over all issues of a judicial nature.

It is questionable whether military courts of certain kinds can fulfill this definition. For generations most nations have created courts to serve exclusively military service personnel — with possibly a few exceptions. The independence of the persons who make the decisions in military courts raises thorny issues. This is especially true when martial law is declared — as in Pakistan in the 1980s where the rulings of military courts were immunized from judicial review.

The same thing happened in December 1980 in El Salvador, when the government created a military court to authorize procedures by which a civilian could remain incommunicado for 195 days. Courts of this nature constitute a major departure from the basic principles of judicial independence.

Actions that compromise the independence of lawyers are engaged in by governments who are unable or unwilling to follow the decisions of their judges. Governments seldom abolish bar associations, as was done when the government of Syria in 1980 dissolved the Damascus and Syrian bar associations for their standards opposing the prolonged emergency, arbitrary arrest, and torture of political prisoners.

Governments have tried similar tactics against lawyers in South Africa, Latin America, and especially countries where the government can appeal to the presence or threat of terrorism as a reason the defense bar should be silenced or immobilized.

The literature on the independence of the bench and the bar is extensive and growing. It is grounded in the idea of a rule of law which is rather easily knowable and which presupposes or posits the existence of international human rights which are binding on all the countries who are members of the United Nations. Enforcement of basic human rights is legally required of these countries even if they have not ratified the U.N. covenants on human rights.

The independence of the bench was one of the central ideas advanced in the Declaration of Independence and the U.S. Constitution. The Declaration of Independence enumerates a "long train of abuses," which includes the efforts of the British Crown to remove judges from their positions. Article 3 of the Constitution made the independence of judges the cornerstone of the new American government. Judges were appointed for life by the president with the consent of the Senate, and could be removed only for committing "bribery, treason or other high crimes or misdemeanors." These standards are so high that fewer than thirty federal judges have ever been impeached and removed from office by the House and the Senate.

The endemic resistance of elected officials to unelected judges surfaced early in American history when during the outbursts of Jacksonian democracy, many states outside of New England adopted the practice of electing judges. Some thirty-eight states now follow that system. The implications for the rule of law and the independence of the judiciary will continue to be debated. But the continued survival of this form of judicial review offers very relevant evidence of the worldwide tensions between the elected and the unelected officials of government.

The struggle for an independent judiciary has intensified as the international human rights movement has become more universal. The 1999 yearbook for the Center for the Independence of Judges and Lawyers listed some of the incredible attacks on judges as, for example, in Colombia, where 122 judges and jurists were murdered between 1979 and 1995.

The yearbook also noted the several international declarations promoting the independence of the judiciary. These include the U.N. General Assembly's adoption in 1985 of a set of principles on the independence of the judiciary. The United Nations has also appointed a special rapporteur who has carried out investigations and conducted missions in countries where attacks on judges have been egregious.

The academics and the activists in the international human rights movement will understandably carry forward the mobilization of shame, propaganda for the sanctity of human rights, and appeals for the rule of law. But hidden in the undertow in the struggle for human rights are subtle and silent currents through which government can undermine compliance with international human rights standards by eroding the independence of the courts. This can be done by appointing timid rather than courageous jurors or by selecting persons known to be so politically ambitious that they would be likely to make decisions based on the wishes and whims of the appointing authorities.

The thorny issue of the independence of judges clearly cannot be separated from any aspect of the human rights movement. It may be that the universal acceptance of specific human rights as international law may eventually make it difficult if not impossible for any judge anywhere, for example, to deny freedom of the press or to allow torture.

Education, in other words, is the key to a more universal acceptance of human rights. That is why the Vienna declaration in 1993 strongly urged worldwide education about the nature and universality of human rights.

The very idea of judicial independence assumes that many nations will resist the reach of the newly proclaimed internationally recognized moral and legal values which nations have agreed to accept and follow. In due course, some supranational tribunal will be established to enforce the new world standards. In the interim, judges at the national and local levels have the duty of insisting that the governments that have appointed them comply with norms set forth by the international community.

The achievement of this daunting task will require the appointment or election of judges who are competent and courageous. They can rise to this level only if they are independent and impartial.

17

IS FREEDOM OF
RELIGION THE MOST
FUNDAMENTAL OF
ALL HUMAN RIGHTS?

In writing codes and commentary about the nature of human rights all around the world, one would think that religion — as the source of the moral and spiritual values underlying the vast majority of human rights — would be referred to more than most sources of human rights. But in the fifty years of the international human rights movement, religion has not attained the level of importance that some secular ideals such as the freedom of speech have reached.

All observers and participants in the human rights movement would concede that both religious and secular activists have contributed to the development of democracy and the fulfillment of human rights. But there has been a persistent and understandable feeling over the past fifty years that religious institutions have had a checkered record of defining and legitimating the human rights of the children of God. The advocates of international human rights cannot forget that religious bodies for centuries followed the maxim that "Error has rights." The fact that the Catholic church in Vatican II in 1965 solemnly renounced this doctrine does not convince the human rights activists that religion is now the full partner of those vast official and nongovernmental organizations that have made the observance of human rights the centerpiece of a new world in which 191 nations follow the Universal Declaration of Human Rights as their national and foreign policy.

But the record of government with regard to religious freedom and other human rights has also been traumatic. The practice of many governments before 1948 and the adoption of the Universal Declaration suggests that human rights require protection from both government and religion.

Consequently, for years there has been a truce, a partnership, and a symbiosis between governments and religions with respect to the new regime in which all nations have, for the first time in history, pledged to comply with standards of human rights that are defined by the international community.

The secular advocates of human rights know that would-be friends in the religious community sometimes feel required to follow absolutes which those without religious faith do not share. Martin Luther exemplified this characteristic when in 1521 he published the words: "Dare I Stand I Can Do No Other."

This sense of being compelled by a divine intervention and driven by an irreversible demand of conscience seems antithetical to the sense of needing to accommodate to differing views — a sense which epitomizes the flexibility of those who seek to adopt universal values for the present situation. Justice Learned Hand captured this sense in his observation that "the spirit of liberty is the spirit that is not too sure it is right."

The framers of the Constitution created a situation where citizens of fundamentally different views could co-exist in peace with the separation of powers and even the right to amend the Constitution. Religious bodies, with their adherence to certain unchangeable truths, are not likely to be prepared to be flexible on certain issues. Indeed, some observers of the human rights movement claim that human rights cannot ultimately succeed unless humanity accepts and adheres to some suprahuman set of values which will assist the advocates of human rights in their struggle to resist and defeat the vigorous and vociferous defenders of nationalistic policies which defy the command of the international human rights movement. The partisans of a theological point of view do not claim that they are superior to humanists; they simply assert that persons driven by what they concede to be a call from an eternal lawgiver are more likely to be stalwart defenders of human rights than are those whose call or persuasion derives from some secular, rationalistic, or humanitarian motivation.

The sense of persons of faith that they are needed in the world struggle against barbarism is supported by what the monstrous totalitarian systems perpetuated in the twentieth century — whether those systems be Fascist, Nazi, Communist, or Maoist.

The claim of people of faith was expressed by John Paul II when he said that religious rights are the "cornerstone of all other rights."

This is the dualism which has been the underlying and often unspoken theme in the way the human rights community has treated religion.

The U.N. charter postponed the formulation of a specific bill of rights but did say that respect for "human rights and fundamental freedoms" is incompatible with any discrimination as to "race, sex, language or religion."

The Universal Declaration of Human Rights reaffirmed this in several places. Article 1 teaches that all human beings are "endowed with reason and cognizance and should act towards one another in a spirit of brotherhood." Article 18 says, "Everyone has the right to freedom of thought, conscience and religion; this right includes freedom to change his religion or belief, and freedom to live alone or in community with others and in public or private, to manifest his religion or belief in teaching, practice, worship or observance."

It is most significant that the 1993 Vienna declaration from the World Conference on Human Rights reaffirmed these sentiments. Paragraph 22 urges that all governments "take all appropriate measures to counter intolerant and related violence based on religion and belief . . . including the desecrating of religious sites, recognizing that every individual has the right to freedom of thought, conscience, expression and religion." The Vienna declaration went on to invite "all states to put into practice the provisions of the Declaration on the Elimination of all Forms of Intolerance and of Discrimination Based on Religion or Belief." The declaration gained added force by the unusual and possibly unprecedented statement that "human rights and fundamental freedoms are the birthright of all human beings; their protection and promotion is the *first* responsibility of governments" [emphasis added].

Despite the inclusion of rights based on religion in all the essential international documents on human rights, the fact is that there is no convention on religious human rights — but only a declaration issued in 1981. The history of how this happened has been traced in the book

Freedom of Religion or Belief (Kluwer, 1996), by Bahiyyih G. Tahzib. We will return to this topic.

Article 18 of the Universal Declaration makes it clear that any individual has the right to hold a "belief" instead of a "religion." There is therefore no preference in favor of believers over nonbelievers.

The Universal Declaration was adopted by a vote of forty-eight nations in favor, none against, and eight abstentions. Saudi Arabia, South Africa, and six Eastern European nations abstained from voting. All Muslim states other than Saudi Arabia voted in favor of the declaration. It seems clear, consequently, that the portions of the Universal Declaration related to religion are customary international law if not *jus cogens*.

In the early 1950s the United Nations began its efforts to formulate what ultimately became the International Covenant on Civil and Political Rights. Article 21 of this instrument includes the following protection, which does not exist in the Universal Declaration: "Any advocacy for religious hatred that constitutes incitement to discrimination, hostility or violence shall be prohibited by law." In addition, Article 24 provides that special protection shall be given to children without discrimination on account of religion.

The International Covenant on Economic, Social and Cultural Rights also supports religious freedom. Article 13 is designed to guarantee the religious freedom of parents. Article 13 proposes that parents have the right to "ensure the religious and moral education of their children in conformity with their own convictions."

Other U.N. covenants protect the right to religious freedom. Article 5 of the International Convention on the Elimination of All Forms of Racial Discrimination, which was put into force in 1965, guarantees the right to freedom of thought, conscience, and religion. The 1989 Convention on the Rights of the Child reiterates the ample protection for religious rights in other covenants. The 1990 International Convention on the Protection of the Rights of All Migrant Workers and Their Families reaffirms the provisions relating to freedom of religion or beliefs present in preexisting conventions.

The International Labor Organization has been replicating the emphasis on religious freedom found in U.N. documents. In the seventy-five years of its existence, the ILO has adopted more than 170 covenants. Since

World War II, fifteen of these ILO conventions have included provisions pertaining to freedom of religion and belief.

In 1960 following the submission by a U.N. rapporteur on religion several groups around the world felt the need for the United Nations to take a stronger position on religious freedom. A draft declaration was drawn up in 1960. Manifestations of religious intolerance had been present and across the globe. Antisemitic incidents were occurring in Europe and in the western hemisphere. The U.N. General Assembly condemned all manifestations of racial and religious hatred as violations of the U.N. charter and the Universal Declaration of Human Rights. In 1962 the U.N. General Assembly adopted a resolution calling on all members to take all necessary steps to adopt legislation to combat prejudice and intolerance. The United Nations also called for a draft convention on religious intolerance. Some nations favored the idea of a convention on religious intolerance rather than a mere declaration; a convention, unlike the declaration, would have binding power. But other observers saw great difficulties in crafting a convention on religion which would be enforceable.

Debate within the United Nations on a convention or a declaration on religious freedom went on for several years. In November 1981, the United Nations finally adopted the Declaration on the Elimination of All Forms of Intolerance and of Discrimination Based on Religion or Belief. Its paragraph preamble and its eight substantive articles are a triumph for its authors, who persisted for years in the drafting of a document on a topic which is sensitive and difficult.

The Islamic states succeeded in deleting the provision that a person has the right to change his or her religious belief. This, however, was weakened if not nullified by Article 8, which provides that nothing in the declaration concerning religious intolerance restricts or detracts from the portion of the Universal Declaration of Human Rights that specifically safeguards the right to change one's religion.

Iraq entered a collective reservation on behalf of the Organization of the Islamic Conference rejecting any provisions which would be contrary to Islamic law (Shari'ah) or to any law based on Islamic principles.

The 1981 declaration is not a convention, nor does it have a supervisory mechanism. It does not participate directly in the monitoring of the several treaty bodies within the U.N. human rights systems. But it is normative rather than exhortatory. It has, furthermore, been implemented by a series of rapporteurs who in nine reports between 1981 and 1995 pinpointed the places in the world where manifestations of religious intolerance were clear.

The question of a possibility or the need for a legally binding international instrument on freedom of religion or belief has not yet been resolved. Nongovernmental organizations continue to discuss this issue, which seems less urgent in view of the fact that at least four of the seven U.N. monitoring committees do handle petitions based on a denial of religious freedom. Controversies related to conscientious objectors, discrimination against specific religious denominations, and eligibility for public services for members of a particular religion have been some of the issues touched upon by the U.N. Commission on Human Rights, which monitors compliance with the International Covenant on Civil and Political Rights. Blasphemies, incitement to religious intolerance, compulsory religion in public schools, and the closing of places of worship are other topics touched upon by the commission.

The apparent absence of a consensus to create a legally binding mechanism within the United Nations to penalize violations of religious freedoms is clearly disappointing to many observers, whether they are religious or not. They observe the persecution of persons of faith in China, the religious controversies in India and Pakistan, and the interreligious conflicts in dozens of countries. Cannot the United Nations and its agencies do more to protect the religious beliefs and actions of millions of believers?

Material gathered by Tahzig relates to the questions and comments on reports submitted to the U.N. Commission on Human Rights, which monitors all the nations which have ratified the International Covenant on Civil and Political Rights. The commission has no specific juridical control over these countries, but it is required to raise questions and offer recommendations. Its comments on the performance of nations with regard to Article 18 are, Tahzig feels, "cautious." In the first years of the commission's existence, several cases arrived through the use of the optional protocol. Some fourteen questions about religious liberty went to the committee — eight of them on conscientious objection to war. The commission was restrictive and gave little relief to the petitioners.

The U.N. Commission on Human Rights told Costa Rica that it could not give the National Episcopal Conference of that country the power to bar Catholics from teaching religion in the public schools. The commission ruled that in Denmark, parents should not be required to obtain special permission for their children to exempt themselves from religious instruction; required religious instruction violates Article 18.

The U.N. commission interpreted Article 18 to encompass freedom of theistic, nontheistic, and atheistic beliefs. The 1981 Declaration on Religion supports that conclusion. Nevertheless, the rulings of the United Nations over the past twenty years have not conveyed the impression that the human rights watchdogs at the United Nations are aggressively broadening the parameters of religious freedom. But the relatively unknown decisions of the U.N. committees supervising the implementation of the various international covenants may be more forward-looking than they now appear. At least it is significant that for the first time in history there are units within the United Nations which observe conduct deemed to be restrictive of religious human rights and speak about it. It also seems clear that the 1981 declaration against intolerance has implications which in due course may have consequences not foreseeable at this time.

Over the past fifty years religious groups have increasingly embraced and expanded their devotion to human rights. It is fair to say that all the religions of the earth have in truly unique ways helped the dearth and growth of the international human rights movement.

Faith-based groups have wondered whether in past years they should have been proactive in seeking to obtain better juridical machinery for human rights from the United Nations. Perhaps church-based entities everywhere should have clarified their positions on human rights and annunciated them in dramatic ways.

RELIGIOUS GROUPS AND HUMAN RIGHTS

When one looks back in history, the claims of religious institutions and the claims of human rights advocates do not always reflect glory on either group. It is a consolation to be able to realize that those positions have been altered during the fifty years of the human rights revolution. The staunchest secularist has to recognize that most religious bodies have abandoned their disdain for the secularist and have embraced human rights as a direct derivative of the religious faith which they cherish. Indeed, history may reflect favorably on what religious groups have done for human rights in the decades since the formation of the United Nations. Both religion and secularism have made contributions to the human rights movement. Both have learned to rely on each other and to drop the traditional attitudes that they have competing claims. The rapprochement of secular human rights activists with traditional religious groups was dramatically realized when clerics and theologians in Vatican II and at the Episcopal conferences at Medellín and Puebla in Latin America joined in the rebirth of international human rights throughout the world.

At the same time, not all keen observers of the human rights scene think that an appeal to human rights can be simultaneously secular and religious. Louis Henkin, an emeritus professor at Columbia University and the dean of human rights experts, opines: "For our time one has to justify human rights by some contemporary universal version of natural law, whether religious or secular, by appeal to a common moral condition of human dignity." This is the sentiment of the late Catholic philosopher Jacques Maritain. When he read the charter of the United Nations he welcomed it as the embodiment of a sort of "secular faith."

On the other hand, Professor Max Stackhouse of Princeton Theological Seminary argues persuasively that "certain theological principles are indispensable to sustaining the idea of human rights." He argues that "some theological—that is some God-given and normative—insights bind all humanity together."

Stackhouse points forcefully to dreadful situations that arise when nations become "disconnected from their reasonable good." Movements that have repudiated theology, he continued, have become "the greatest violation of human rights." He points to Papa Doc in Haiti, Pol Pot in Cambodia, Marcos in the Philippines, Mao in China, and Stalin in the Soviet Union.

Does the theology of human rights matter to the revolution on human rights that started in San Francisco when the U.N. charter was adopted? By every objective norm the position of the church with regard to the evolution of human rights has to be relevant.

Robert Traer's important book, *Faith in Human Rights: The Force in Religious Tradition for a Global Struggle* (Georgetown University Press, 1991), is helpful, encouraging, and even inspiring in its examination of what has happened since 1945 among the world's great religions. In essence, religions have gone back to their roots and discovered that they are in agreement with most of the principles set forth in the U.N. documents that are foundational in the human rights revolution.

Traer, a Protestant clergyman and a lawyer, boldly proclaims that "Human rights are at the center of the global moral language that is being justified, elaborated and advocated by members of different religious traditions and cultures" (p. 10). The consensus which Traer discovered among Catholics, liberals, and conservative Protestants, as well as Christian groups around the world, is quite remarkable. Traer asserts that "faith in human rights cuts across the Christian community, uniting those that are divided by other issues of doctrine and practice" (p. 91). He concludes that "for many Christians today, human rights are as clear as God's creative and redemptive presence and as compelling as life itself. Human rights are at the heart of what they believe to be their common faith" (p. 92).

The Jewish legacy is even more supportive of human rights than are Christian traditions. Although the term "human rights" did not appear in the Bible and was invented rather recently, the entire Jewish culture can be described as one that derives directly from the sacred rights of every person. Central to Jewish and Christian belief is the certainty that every person is created as an "image of God."

THE MUSLIM APPROACH TO HUMAN RIGHTS

The attitude of the twenty-two Arab nations and the entire Islamic world concerning human rights is obviously of paramount concern to everyone involved in the struggle to promote the human rights which have been internationalized and globalized over the past five decades.

The basic beliefs of the Muslim world on human rights continue to be the subject of intense interest and extensive scholarship. When the U.N. General Assembly in 1948 approved the Universal Declaration of Human Rights, the government of Saudi Arabia abstained on the ground that the declaration did not recognize rights to be the gift of God and in addition violated the Koran by asserting the right to change one's religion. But the Muslim foreign minister of Pakistan defended his country's support for the declaration on the ground that the Koran permits one to believe or disbelieve.

The issue continues to be debated in the Islamic world. It is intertwined with the deep animosity which many in countries like Indonesia have toward the nation that colonized them. Some people in the postcolonial world feel that the European nations corrupted them, weakened their Muslim faith, and sought to impose western concepts of individualized rights not in harmony with the Muslin background of their countries.

The Muslim countries have ratified the human rights treaties and in large numbers approved the final declaration of the 1993 World Conference on Human Rights in Vienna.

It is not feasible to generalize about what the Islamic world thinks about international human rights. Each nation and each region is grappling with new problems such as the sudden massive shift to urban living in the past twenty years. In addition, there is the invasion of western popular culture and the promulgation by some countries of newly developed Islamic rules, some of which have dubious or debatable authority. All this is complicated by officials using Islamization in ways that serve their political goals.

The 1979 Constitution of the Islamic Republic of Iran adds confusion to an assessment of what the Islamic world thinks of human rights. That revolutionary constitution limits freedom of the press, the right of association, and human and cultural rights "according to Islamic standards."

All this may seem contradictory to a seminar on human rights which was organized in 1980 by the International Commission of Jurists, the University of Kuwait, and the Union of Arab Lawyers. The sixty-five participants affirmed that "Islam was the first to recognize human rights almost fourteen centuries ago." The statement continued by noting that Islam through the centuries set up guarantees and safeguards "that have only recently been incorporated in universal declarations of human rights."

In 1986, a group of Arab experts and the Arab Union of Lawyers, with a claimed membership of 100,000, reaffirmed their "faith in the principles in the charter of the United Nations and the International Bill of Rights." But they also affirmed an "Islamic interpretation of human rights that they feel is best suited to the particular needs of the modern Arab world."

There are, however, voices and authorities in the Islamic world that are less supportive of human rights. The reality is that it is virtually impossible to be certain how the nations in which over 1 billion Muslims reside are reacting to the challenges of the human rights movement. But it is clear that there is firm support in the Islamic world for international human rights. There are no major contradictions between the basic truths contained in the human rights documents and the core teachings of Islamic culture. Some observers may have problems with that generalization because of the restrictions the Islamic world places on the rights of women and some non-Islamic religions. Recognizing once again the great turmoil and the astonishing changes occurring in the world of Islam, it does seems clear that the momentum in those nations is toward democracy, freedom of speech, and fair elections.

It still is true that the Arab states are the least liberal corner of the globe. But Algeria and Egypt have granted amnesties to prisoners. Even Sudan, crippled by an interminable civil war, appears to be improving. Aging despots may be replaced by rulers who have listened to the steady drumbeat urging equality for women, freedom of the press, and suffrage for all citizens.

ASIA AND HUMAN RIGHTS

The lands of Asia with a Hindu or Buddhist background do not speak or think in terms of human rights. But the ideology underlying the notion of human rights is not incompatible with the centuries-old perspective of Chinese and Asian culture. We forget that China was one of the original sponsors of the United Nations and that it is still one of the five countries with veto power in the Security Council.

It is, however, hard to understand why China continues to be so harsh on human rights. Its record on respecting religious freedom is especially deplorable. Why did Beijing react so savagely in 1999 to the religious group Falun Gong? This group, drawing on a prayerful tradition of Buddhism and Taoism, is neither subversive nor sinister. In the eyes of the Chinese rulers, the cult constituted a challenge to their power that had to be crushed. If the entities charged with defending international human rights had been operating effectively, could swift reaction have prevented China from challenging this sect? The official suppression of Falun Gong cannot be justified by any religious tradition in China, because religious groups would clearly preach tolerance and gentleness.

U Thant, a Burmese Buddhist who served as secretary general of the United Nations (1962–1971), almost certainly reflected the Asian view of human rights. He urged: "We must all foster and encourage a climate of opinion in which human rights can flourish. We must be alive to any encroachment upon the rights and freedom of an individual. And, above all, we must practice tolerance and respect the rights and freedoms of others."

At the heart of the guarantees given to religious beliefs in all the U.N. documents is the unquestioned assumption that all individuals have the right to follow their conscience because that is their duty. The assumption is never questioned. Everyone is entitled to act "in accordance with the dictates of his own conscience" — as the Helsinki and other proclamations put it.

The major premise underlying all the U.N. provisions on religious freedom — the supremacy of conscience — also lies at the heart of the Christian religion; Martin Luther and Cardinal Newman proclaim it in almost identical phrasing. Its abiding presence in all the documents internationalizing the sovereignty of conscience has unfortunately not been adequately analyzed. This is true even in the magisterial two-volume *Religious Human Rights in Global Perspectives,* issued in 1996 by the Law and Religion Program at Emory University.

The question raised at the Vienna World Conference on Human Rights in 1993 concerning the universality of human rights did not directly attack the centrality of conscience as enshrined in international documents on human rights. The complaint, rather, focused on the alleged western orientation of the rights proclaimed in the U.N. documents.

There appears to be, then, a truth that brooks no opposition and needs no explanation: each person has the right to follow his or her conscience.

The inviolability of conscience follows as an unquestioned corollary from the basic concept affirmed in all the U.N. documents — that dignity and equality are inherent in all human beings.

At the end of the discussion on the presence and relative effectiveness of the religious and secular advocates of human rights, one would like to avoid the question and urge the participants in the struggle for human rights to battle on — whatever their ultimate motivation may be. At the same time, some human rights activists who are religious wonder whether humanists, with their nonreligious orientation, have the same depth of conviction and perseverance in the battle for human rights as those who see Christ himself in each victim and are thereby motivated to the core of their being. Although such musings may be unfair to those who identify themselves as individuals without religious faith, the onslaught of the enemies of human rights are so intense and unrelenting that surely one must need some kind of deep and abiding faith in order to persevere in the cause.

The question, however complicated and unanswerable, is nonetheless important. Among secular and religious human rights activists, there exist deep differences in the approach to certain human rights. Ideally, these differences should be discussed kindly, but at times they seem non-negotiable. This is why suspicions in both camps continue to exist, and why many people of faith — especially Catholics — are absent from the vast and growing armies who battle for improvement in human rights.

That absence is a profound abdication of militant advocacy by Catholic officials in the human rights revolution. The real question, and a troubling one, is why Catholics are significantly underrepresented among the lawyers, publicists, and workers who launched and continue the mission of the nongovernmental organizations devoted to human rights.

As the human rights movement develops, will persons of faith enter in significant numbers and will the churches make more contributions in resources and personnel? At the high official levels of the church, the endorsements and applause for human rights continue. But if America's 62 million Catholics and 100 million mainline Protestants, along with the millions of Evangelicals, the Jewish community, and all believers, really joined and participated, the difference would be dramatic.

Even if the miracle of enlightenment and grace occurred, would there be more respect for human rights in China, Africa, and elsewhere? No one can predict with much accuracy. But mass movements depend on a nearly universal consensus on some basic issues — a consensus so profound and pervasive that it simply changes the culture and the way a nation thinks and acts.

The religious bodies in the United States theoretically possess the moral and spiritual power to mobilize themselves and change the way America thinks of its role in the human rights revolution. Catholics are especially well equipped to influence the way the United States thinks about human rights. They've inherited a rich legacy from Vatican II, from the struggles of the church for human rights in Latin America, and from the compelling cry of the gospel that everyone love one another as a brother or sister.

Religion has been a formidable force throughout the fifty years of the human rights movement. Although no one should try to assess the comparative influence of secular or religious persons or institutions within that movement, the force of religion can only be described as a sleeping giant.

Another "sleeping giant" is the Declaration on Religious Freedom issued by Vatican II in 1965. For the first time in the history of the Catholic church the 2,500 bishops gathered in Rome affirmed that it is a violation of the "sacred rights of the person and the family of nations when forces are brought to bear in any way in order to destroy or repress religion."

The declaration clearly tracks the statements on the free exercise of religion which were approved in the basic documents that are the foundation of the human rights movement. The Vatican Council notes that "religious freedom has already been declared to be a civil right in most constitutions and, it is solemnly recognized in international documents." This the Vatican Council "greets with joy."

The Vatican document on religious freedom is strong. Consider these words: "In spreading religious faith and in introducing religious practices, everyone ought at all times to refrain from any manner of action which might seem to carry a hint of coercion or a kind of persuasion that would be dishonorable or unworthy, especially when dealing with poor or uneducated people." The statement bans "any form of action" which has a "hint of coercion." Such an action is a "violation of the rights of others."

The Vatican pronouncement echoed what the U.N. documents say in several ways. The Vatican asserts that "the protection and promotion of the inviolable rights of man rank among the essential duties of government." The statement of the Holy See even uses the very words of the United Nations: "the protection and promotion" of human rights.

The Vatican statement goes beyond the language of the articles of the human rights movement when it asserts that "the usages of society are to be the usage of freedom in their full range. These require that the freedom of man be respected as far as possible, and curtailed only when and insofar as necessary."

The Declaration of Religious Freedom continues to amaze the world. For centuries the Catholic church had held that if a nation is Catholic, it has some duty to prefer Catholics over non-Catholics and even to penalize those who are not believers. The history of the church's intolerance and even persecution is shameful.

The document of the Vatican in repudiating the church's long history speaks of the development of doctrine as an inherent part of the growth and sanctification of the church. The architects of the human rights movement in the past fifty years refer to a secular counterpart to the development of doctrine, called the internationalization of human rights. It is the outgrowth of the dismay of humankind at the Holocaust and the slaughters of World War II.

The parallel paths followed by the Catholic church and the human rights movement form a remarkable example of how in this age of instant communication there can be a profound interaction between institutions and movements.

Could the world regress, allowing the savage interreligious wars that have darkened history? Can the bold defense of religion which is so strong in the human rights movement and the unprecedented proclamations on behalf of religious freedom in Vatican II combine to banish the persecution of religion in dustbin of history? It has not happened yet in China, the Sudan, or North Korea. But it is plausible to think that the abolition of intolerance and persecution based on religious differences may be on the horizon.

Only the declaration, not a convention or treaty, addresses the free exercise of religion in the U.N. community. But the extraordinarily widespread respect for religious freedom and the pledge by virtually all the Christian churches and synagogues in the world to repudiate intolerance based on religion may signal the advent of an era when discrimination based on religion can go the way of slavery and piracy.

18

DO AMNESTY
AND RECONCILIATION
BRING JUSTICE?

One of the most important criteria for judging the effectiveness of a law is the manner in which it gives some type of compensation to the victims. Laws exist to punish and to deter. An element of both the punishment and the deterrence is the way the victim is treated.

The laws of many states have provisions that give monetary compensation to the victims of crime. These arrangements are not very satisfactory. The compensation is usually small, and there are no punitive damages.

At the international level, the system of giving restitution to the victims of violations of human rights is just struggling to be born. In South Africa, El Salvador, and Chile, courts and commissions are struggling to find a formula which punishes violators of human rights, deters other possible violators, and rewards victims.

The laws of every state have provisions to compensate those who have suffered unjustly by the misdeeds of others. Multiple concepts are involved: restitution, indemnification, reparations, damages, compensation, redress, rehabilitation, and reimbursement. Indeed, it seems clear that one of the major, primordial functions of the law is to return the victims of an unjust act to their previous condition.

It is clear that the framers of the intellectual human rights law intended that victims must be indemnified. The International Covenant on Civil and Political Rights in Article 9(5) and the European Convention on Human Rights in Article 5(5) referred to an "enforceable right to compensation." Similarly, the Convention Against Torture and other Cruel,

Inhuman, or Degrading Treatment or Punishment contains in Article 14(1), a measure that provides for the victims to receive redress and "an enforceable right to fair and adequate compensation" along with "means for as full a rehabilitation as possible."

The American Convention on Human Rights speaks of "compensatory damages" (Article 68), saying that "fair compensation [should] be paid to the injured party" (Article 63(i)). The African charter (Article 21(2)) guarantees the "right to an adequate compensation." The Convention on the Elimination of All Forms of Racial Discrimination appeals in Article 6 to the right to seek "just and adequate reparations or satisfaction for any damage suffered." The International Labor Organization's Convention on Indigenous Peoples refers to "fair compensation for damages" (Article 16(4)) and to full compensation "for any loss or injury" (Article 16(5)). The Convention on the Rights of the Child in Article 39 requires all nations to take all appropriate measures to "promote physical and psychological recovery."

In 1985 the U.N. General Assembly spelled out the nature of indemnification in the Declaration of Basic Principles of Justice for Victims of Crime and Abuses of Power. This declaration insists that "victims are entitled to prompt redress for the harm that they have suffered" and that offenders should "pay fair restitution to victims, their families and dependents." If such reimbursement is not available from the offender, "states should endeavor to provide financial compensation."

The four Geneva conventions of 1949 sternly provide that no contracting party shall be allowed to absolve itself from any liability incurred by itself for grave breaches, including willfully causing great suffering or serious injury.

The Geneva treaties and other documents respecting international human rights make it clear that governments have a duty to offer compensation if private persons are allowed to engage in conduct which violates internationally recognized human rights.

International juridical bodies such as the U.N. Commission on Human Rights and the Inter-American Court of Human Rights have developed a substantial body of case law in which they have defined the obligations which offending states are required to carry out. The European Court of Human Rights has awarded "just compensation" (Article 50 of the convention) in well over 100 cases. The Inter-American Court has ruled in fewer cases but the principle of the requirement of indemnification is becoming more clearly defined with each case. Punitive damages have not usually been awarded.

Reparations are, of course, not an entirely new issue. In the aftermath of World War II the new government of Germany was required to pay substantial reparations to the survivors of the Holocaust in Israel or elsewhere. In 1965, the German Federal Compensation Law became the most complete and systematic example of compensation given by any nation to the victims of its predecessor government. The overall assessment of this law is positive, but it did not reach all the victims of Nazi violence because they left Germany or were stateless or could not document their injuries.

One example of how the United States observed its duty under international law to compensate the victims of its own wrongdoing was the $20,000 indemnification it awarded to every surviving person of Japanese ancestry who was confined in camps during World War II. I served on a presidential commission that heard days of testimony from survivors and experts on the internment of up to three years of some 120,000 Japanese, half of them citizens. This action was ordered by President Roosevelt, paid for by Congress, and validated by a divided decision of the U.S. Supreme Court. After four years and a report of a presidential commission on which the late Justice Arthur Goldberg served, Congress and the president concurred in the judgment of this commission that the detention of the Japanese was not necessary and was a violation of the Constitution. The figure of $20,000 was arrived at as a result of estimates and accommodation. The amount of indemnification awarded some 75,000 survivors totaled around $1.2 billion.

In view of all these precedents why is it that the basic requirement of reparation is not receiving the attention and enforcement it deserves? This is without doubt one of the most difficult questions that confronts the international human rights movement. All around the world the victims are clearly identifiable, yet there is no precise pattern of compensation or damages.

The prospect, moreover, for adequate and systematic compensation is bleak. For example, aside from the possibility of the international criminal court entering into this field, there is little hope that malefactors in Cambodia who murdered countless thousands will be apprehended or punished. Aside from the special international tribunals set up for the former Yugoslavia and Rwanda, will the victims of Stalin's madness or China's cultural revolution ever receive a hearing or indemnification? Can the countless innocent victims of dictators and despots expect that somehow, sometime the advocates and apostles of international human rights will reward them with some compensation, however inadequate?

The questions seem overwhelming and the answers romantically unrealistic. But certain concepts and developments in international law may bring about a system of reparations for all victims analogous to the legal mechanism that made reparations to the victims of Nazi brutality.

One sign of such a development is occurring in South Africa where the Commission on Peace and Reconciliation is through its philosophy and conclusions changing the way the world thinks and acts about a government that had for a long period of time denied the basics of equality, fairness, and decency. It must be pointed out, however, that South Africa is unique. Its concept of apartheid was indefensible and had been condemned by the United Nations each year since 1945. The International Court of Justice (or the World Court) ruled that apartheid clearly violated international law. Most nations, including eventually the United States, imposed economic sanctions on South Africa. Consequently when the government in Pretoria conceded that apartheid was wrong and allowed an election the world was convinced that the all-white government of South Africa had committed many offenses which were indefensible and that some type of compensation was due.

Even the formation of the Commission on Peace and Reconciliation was creative and constructive. Headed by Archbishop Desmond Tutu, it tried to formulate a solution through which the new international human rights law could become operational. The overall philosophy of international human rights adopted by the commission has intrigued the world and has engaged the international human rights community in discussions without end. Should a government that succeeds a corrupt predecessor allow the worst malefactors in that government to escape punishment if they "confess" in public? Would this really bring about reconciliation? The establishment of the Commission on Truth and Reconciliation on July 19,

1995, has changed the entire course of thinking and action by persons involved in the international human rights movement.

Once again, the South African government is different from almost any other in the world. The 10 percent of white people who had controlled the country for generations are charged with the most serious misconduct. In a sense, all of them are guilty because they were complicit in perpetuating a system which for generations denied basic human rights to some 30 million persons of African ancestry.

The members of the African National Committee (ANC) were also guilty because for decades they participated in a series of lawless attacks on white leaders and followers. If all white people are charged with human rights violations, should the same charges be leveled at the ANC?

Is it possible or just sensible to try to punish most of the 4 million white people in South Africa? In the summer of 1995 I lectured and consulted for many weeks in South Africa. The nation — at least the blacks — were jubilant at their recent liberation. The idea of significant reconciliation was discussed everywhere. It is obviously a profoundly Christian idea, but in South Africa it was also a concept filled with utilitarian and pragmatic considerations. The country needed its white bankers and entrepreneurs; South Africa needs to be perceived as a stable country if new businesses are to be attracted. A threat to try to penalize almost every white South African would have prompted a mass migration. It could also have inhibited the nonwhite population so that a permanent anti-white class warfare would have been initiated.

For all these reasons, South Africa agreed to the creation of the Commission on Truth and Reconciliation in the 1990s. Countless assessments have been made through the years of that process. The transcripts of the hearings and conclusions of the commission are constructive. Indeed, they are awesome, challenging, and, yes, bewildering. Was this the way to try to bring some type of resolution and reconciliation to a tormented country? Frederik de Klerk, the former president and co-winner of the Nobel Peace Prize with Nelson Mandela, declined to apologize meaningfully for apartheid. He would not admit that the system he and his father had implemented was evil. It was, he conceded, a mistake because it did not work but apartheid was, he insisted, meant to benefit the interests of all South Africans.

One of the most thoughtful books on South Africa is *Between Vengeance and Forgiveness* (Beacon Press, 1998), by Martha Minow of Harvard Law School. It explores the unfathomable concept of how a society comes together after decades of deep hostility between racial groups. Many will conclude that for South Africa there was no other solution except that of allowing all sides to confess their misdeeds and thereby acquire some type of reconciliation. But others will side with the survivors of Steve Biko, the black activist who was tortured and killed by government forces. His family filed a lawsuit challenging the very existence of the Commission on Truth and Reconciliation. They claimed that the amnesty provision violated the rights of survivors to seek redress for the murders of their loved ones. The new constitutional court of South Africa rejected the claim. The justices felt that the Geneva conventions allow the government to grant amnesty in return for the truth.

The trading of a truthful confession for amnesty is, of course, the difference in the South African process. No blanket forgiveness is granted to torturers or pirates. They are required to confess their sins in public in order to receive public forgiveness.

This process in South Africa is further complicated by the use of the idea of "healing." This is a concept that is very unfamiliar in the legal language underpinning prosecution. Many psychologists and jurists feel that after a society has been polarized, there is a need for the public and the courts to promote a form of reconciliation which can be "healing." Even if "healing" is occurring in South Africa, this can hardly be satisfactory to the family of Steve Biko; they know the names of those who helped kill their son, but these individuals will go free if they confess at a hearing of the Truth and Reconciliation Commission.

What *is* the path between vengeance and forgiveness? Many years must pass before a verdict on the history of South Africa is determined. I have talked with black students in South Africa. They want to move ahead in the careers now open to them. But they are also quick to express deep anger and resentment at the former government which did such awful things to their parents and grandparents. That valid resentment may emerge in unpredictable ways. These young people — now able to go to college, to vote, and to think about participating in public affairs — dare not suggest that their "masters" have excluded them from reaping the fabulous profits enjoyed by the white majority from the gold and diamond industries. In fact, these young blacks feel strongly that they and their predecessors have been deprived of the basic education and skills required simply to obtain a decent job. The term "reconciliation" sounds peaceful and reasonable, but how do you reconcile a history in which you and everyone you know have been cheated, defeated, and dehumanized? What do you do to obtain the human rights stolen from you?

South Africa has employed a combination of techniques available in international law to balance the desire for a peaceful resolution to an awful problem. It has used the power to grant amnesty in exchange for the revelation of truth — an experiment with noble aspirations and, to date, many successes. But will it be a model applicable to future situations where a country tries to expose the truth of what dictators have done without bringing about a violent uprising or a form of anarchy where the rule of law is set aside in the name of effecting redress?

Should the idea of massive reparations — demanded of Germany, for example — be repudiated in South Africa? A nation like Germany, devastated in 1945, was able to make reparations without hindering its remarkable economic recovery. Suppose that the world community requires individuals who have benefited from the labors of those held captive by apartheid to give the downtrodden indemnification and a share of the enormous riches they helped to create?

Is it too late to initiate such a system of reparations? A comparable proposed program of giving restitution to every African American whose ancestors were slaves has never been contemplated, much less accepted, by any significant number of African American scholars or activists. Ideas along this line were proposed in the reconstruction period after the Civil War, but the majority of the white population, North and South, did not believe the program worthy of consideration.

It is clear that all the mandates to give restitution to victims outlined at the beginning of this chapter have seldom been implemented. But the plan to render justice for past wrongdoing is an essential part of the international human rights movement. When human rights have been violated, a debt is created on the part of a nation. That country should not be allowed to cancel its debt by offering amnesty — even if the amnesty requires some truth-telling.

Some consensus about the connection between the denial of human rights and the need for reconciliation is emerging. It is not yet clear on the international scene. But it is increasingly apparent that international law now requires prosecution of especially atrocious crimes. In a comprehensive article on this and related points, Professor Diane F. Orentlichter of American University Law School brought forth a persuasive argument for this new reality in international law. Writing in the *Yale Law Review* in 1991, Orentlichter argued that a successful government cannot act in accordance with international law and grant wholesale immunity to atrocious crimes committed by a previous government. This is a departure from the traditional approach of international human rights law.

How does amnesty fit into this new reality? An amnesty for the former rulers of a country could arguably violate the spirit if not the letter of recent international human rights law. It could bring about a culture of impunity which would encourage other political leaders to engage in violations of international human rights.

Latin American countries with newly elected democracies have granted amnesties but have been rebuked by the Inter-American Commission on Human Rights. For example, after six Jesuits and their housekeeper and her minor daughter were murdered on November 16, 1989, by agents of the state, the government granted amnesty to the murderers and to many others. Many felt that this was a sensible way to bring to a close the grim events outlined by a U.N. commission set up in El Salvador. There were those who were opposed to granting any amnesty until the real authorities behind the slaughter of the Jesuits were discovered. In the extensive literature on this event, the term "intellectual authors of the killings" seemed to take on a meaning of its own. It was obviously the government at its highest levels that had ordered the killings, which had been carried out by lower-level soldiers. The parties opposed to the attempts to cover up the case against the intellectual authors of the killings successfully persuaded the commission to rule that El Salvador had no right to grant amnesty because this is in contravention to the Inter-American Convention on Human Rights, which allows everyone to obtain a remedy for the violation of their rights.

Similar rulings have raised basic doubts about the amnesties granted by the legislatures in Argentina, Chile, and elsewhere. Some resolution of this complicated clash between national and international law may eventually be discovered in the resolution of the legal proceedings in Spain and England over General Augusto Pinochet. The families of victims who "disappeared" during the regime of Pinochet in Chile want information about their loved ones. The Chilean Supreme Court has raised basic questions about the amnesty laws, which have largely protected officers from prosecution. But the families of the 3,000 missing persons are not likely to be silenced.

The cries of the loved ones of the victims of human rights abuses can be heard everywhere. The families of the 1 million Cambodians killed in the Maoist regime want trials. They decry a culture which knows that dastardly crimes have been committed but watches the perpetrators go unpunished because of rampant bribery and political influence. Pol Pot, the head of the homicidal Cambodian regime, died in April 1998. It has been over twenty years since the Khmer Rouge was toppled from power in Cambodia. Discussions between officers in Phnom Penh and the United Nations about the possibility of a trial have ended in roadblocks. Democratic administrations who have succeeded regimes in which international human rights were abused are likely to theorize that if Cambodia can continue to postpone or delay trials, other governments will follow suit.

In the 1980s and 1990s, dozens of countries moved from dictatorships to democracies. The new leaders, with the possible exception of those in South Africa, fully intended to ignore their predecessors and move on to create open democracies that observed human rights. But there is now a strong international demand to hold violators of human rights to a new and ever stricter standard of accountability. The proponents of a higher standard are not an organized phalanx of militants with national or international offices. They are, among others, the citizens who lost their children in Buenos Aires, the victims of Pinochet in Chile, and the lawyers who are suing to make the murderers of the Jesuits in El Salvador accountable for their crimes.

Voices everywhere in the world echo the age-old truth that there should be no right without a remedy. These voices were present in the 1993 United Nations World Conference on Human Rights in Vienna. The final statement of the Vienna declaration recommended that "states should abrogate legislation leading to impunity for those responsible for grave violations of human rights such as torture" (II, 60).

But the process of inducing nations to try their own subjects — some of whom are their former rulers — has met with resistance. It is this resistance that led the international community to create new transnational commissions and tribunals to protect human rights. Now those international tribunals have to cope with the practice of national leaders granting amnesty to political leaders who have disgraced their nations by engaging in "ethnic cleansing" or other crimes against humanity. Even if the International Criminal Commission continues to develop and become functional, individual nations will still be authorized and even encouraged to establish courts for the prosecution of their own alleged violations of international human rights.

The tide against amnesty for political figures is strong. The Chilean Supreme Court concluded that the statute of limitations should not apply to kidnappings, because concealment of these crimes continues, making them subject to indictment and prosecution. Journalists estimated that some 3,000 people had disappeared during the Pinochet regime. The subsequent regime of President Patrice Alwyn (1991 to 1994) was able to demonstrate adequate proof that at least 1,102 persons were missing. In 1991, the Inter-American Commission on Human Rights ruled that amnesty laws are not compatible with the 1969 American Convention on Human Rights. In 1996, nongovernmental organizations fought for the exclusion of all crimes against humanity from an amnesty law in Guatemala.

Amnesties or multiple pardons are sometimes the best solution for a country that finds itself divided by factions seeking revenge or forgiveness. Virtually every national constitution has some provision allowing the chief executive to pardon criminals. Should some new international mechanism be put in place by which an international entity can set aside a decree of amnesty?

Applied to the United States, this proposal produces astonishing implications. Imagine the appropriate international body decreeing that the amnesty or pardon of former President Nixon by President Ford must be set aside. The theory would be that the pardon was a violation of the rights of those citizens who should know more about Watergate and the persons who victimized them. If this sounds impossible, then the setting aside of the amnesty decree for the murders of the six Jesuits in El Salvador sounds just as implausible to those people in El Salvador who want to "bury" everything concerning the wars in the 1990s. They do not want to remember that this war resulted in the deaths of 75,000 people, and that it produced vast numbers of refugees in and out of the country.

The intense grip which nations and patriots have on their own people is a result of centuries of political indoctrination and sincere cultural attachment. Those sentiments have been radically altered in the past fifty years—by the idea of international human rights and scores of other forces. The moves toward democratic elections and the observance of the rule of law have transformed the way citizens view their government. But intense and bitter rivalries within nations continue and even have grown more dangerous. Internationalization of the world and the globalization of human rights have doubtlessly had an irreversible impact on the options for national action.

International pressure for relief and reparation from unjust regimes has just begun. It is one of the most recent impulses in the movement for international human rights. Its impact is not yet very visible, but the widespread interest in the results of the South African Commission on Peace and Reconciliation will have an enormous influence—especially on the fifty nations of Africa.

Accountability is a priority issue in South Africa and in every country that has ousted or is in the process of getting rid of a dictator. If rulers knew that they would be held accountable for any substantial violation of international human rights law, they would, theoretically, be more law-abiding. Their aides would also be more restrained because they would know that they, too, would be held accountable.

How can accountability be inculcated in public officials? The newly established series of international guidelines could be efficacious, but their weak enforcement is the problem. Even if their enforcement is not as effective as would be desired, the fact is that some rulers—Marcos, Pol Pot, Idi Amin, Pinochet, for example—have abused their powers by not heeding the new standards of international human rights.

Curtailing the power of leaders like these individuals while they are still in power is the quintessential purpose of the United Nations. This organization was established so that a Hitler could never rise to power again. But if this goal is to be achieved, the egregious abuses of human rights must be made known and stopped. The elaborate U.N. monitoring missions and the increasing revelations of nations defying human rights are testimony to the twin, co-equal purposes of the United Nations: to stop war and enforce human rights.

Defining and guaranteeing the rights of the victims of leaders who have defied the human rights mission of the United Nations is one of the most important and solemn tasks of that body. The exaltation of human rights emerged in dramatic ways in the 1990s. Its transformation into a global moral force is, ideally, about to happen.

19

CONTEMPORARY DEVELOPMENTS IN HUMAN RIGHTS

The development of the law related to internationally recognized human rights has been uneven, sporadic, and unpredictable. Developments seem to be dependent on political movements, unexpected leadership in unusual places, or outbursts of anger and indefensible injustices.

THE WORLD AFTER PINOCHET

One such development occurred in the detention in England of General Augusto Pinochet, the dictator-president of Chile for eighteen years, whose regime began with his coup in 1973. Pinochet was charged by a prosecutor in Spain with violations of international law for government-sponsored torture in Chile. Violence led to the death of some 3,000 persons, at least 1,000 of whom disappeared without a trace.

The saga of Pinochet is particularly moving to me because in the mid-1980s I was a member of a human rights mission that traveled to Chile under the auspices of the International League for Human Rights. Chile ratified the Torture Convention and thus made a commitment to cease this unspeakable practice. Its commitment to end torture was one of the reasons Pinochet was indicted in Spain and detained in England. He and his nation had engaged in a practice which is now a crime against world law and is thus punishable in any nation where the offender is apprehended. Torture is thus a crime like piracy, which is now punishable within any nation where the pirate or slave trader is apprehended.

Whatever the ultimate outcome of the Pinochet case, it has altered world law. It has made clear that those who torture or engage in any other offenses forbidden by world law can be tried in any nation to which they travel. Will leaders who allowed atrocities in Cambodia or war crimes in Vietnam be fearful of leaving the United States?

International law is highly developed concerning nations' immunity from alleged crimes and diplomatic protection for national leaders. These issues had been unaddressed for decades, in a world where national sovereignty was sacrosanct and where nations were not accountable in any international forum for their violations of human rights. But that era is in the process of fading away. Nations and their leaders can be charged by other countries with violations of those human rights guaranteed by international law.

The ancient concept of humanitarian intervention by one nation on another in order to protect human rights needs to be rethought. The 1945 Charter of the United Nations theoretically terminated the permission to nations to engage in humanitarian intervention in order to stop abuse of human rights. The U.N. charter made it clear that no nation could make war on another country without approval by the U.N. Security Council. That arrangement has not always functioned as it was intended. Does that mean that a nation may intervene in another country to stop a massive violation of human rights? The answer is not clear, but as the preciousness of human rights is acknowledged more widely, nations or groups of nations will want to intervene in order to protect human rights.

The desire to protect international human rights was one of the many reasons NATO was extended and enlarged — even though its target, the Soviet bloc, had collapsed. But the world is still groping to discover some regional or global mechanism through which to protest the violation of those human rights acknowledged by every country and by the international order.

If the inviolability granted human rights in the U.N. charter, the Universal Declaration of Human Rights, and all the covenants were respected would there be any need for military intervention? It is not easy to predict whether legal and juridical measures will preclude the need for military force. But if there is a need for armed force, it should be centralized and controlled by the United Nations. That is the purpose of the peacekeeping forces of the United Nations — whose number has greatly increased since the end of the Cold War. America's lack of participation in these efforts has not helped the establishment of those useful ways to reestablish peace and restore human rights.

The method by which Pinochet was detained is by no means the ideal way of apprehending tyrants. A permanent investigatory body within the international criminal court — a sort of world attorney general — would be more effective, efficient, and predictable. But regardless of the final outcome of the Pinochet affair, international law has proved that it can respond positively to an unanticipated earthquake.

THE WORLD'S REFUGEES

The vast world of refugees has also developed in truly spectacular ways. The establishment of the U.N. High Commissioner on Refugees (UNHCR) in the first days of the United Nations is an accomplishment for which neither the United Nations nor the world community has received thanks. The problems of the 18 million refugees and the millions of internally displaced persons confound the mind and the heart. To be sure, there have always been refugees. But now, all nations have agreed that they will not send back a refugee who has a "well-founded fear of persecution."

In 1980, the House Judiciary Committee, of which I was a member, accepted world law on refugees and pledged the United States to follow international law and grant asylum to those who feared persecution in their country of origin. Neither the U.S. Congress nor the White House has consistently followed the implications of that pledge. But America by almost any standard must be categorized as generous in the number of immigrants and refugees it has welcomed over the past generation. In recent years the United States has probably granted residence and eventually citizenship to more persons than the rest of the world combined.

But a flood of refugees in unprecedented numbers is predictable in the United States. The absence of a functioning government in Somalia has prompted thousands of its citizens to go anyplace where they will be admitted. Other nations in Africa are experiencing the same exodus. Is it possible that countless others will move out of their countries in order to feed their children? Millions may leave their native countries — like the Vietnamese boat people, the Cubans who have fled to Miami, or Mexicans who have crossed the Rio Grande. Under international law they have a right to leave their country if they have a "well-founded fear of persecution." Should they have an equivalent right to migrate if their homeland cannot or will not give them food, medicine, and education for their children? Political rights are not superior to economic rights. All human rights are equal and indivisible.

No one at the international level — certainly not those in charge of resettling refugees — wants to consider the legal status of economic refugees. But everyone must admit that millions are being deprived of their basic economic rights. These rights are guaranteed them by world law. At the same time there is a solid consensus around the world that arrangements should be created so that most people can remain in their country of origin. Any move to another country with a different language and culture is almost always traumatic. But the experts in resettling refugees recognize more and more that millions of people, after seeing a world of freedom and plenty on television and through an ever increasing number of other media sources, will ask importunately for a better life. They will also increasingly be aware that international law guarantees them and their families the basic rights to decent housing, food, education, and medicine.

As one contemplates the predictable massive migration of hungry people, it is obvious that it behooves the prosperous nations to plan for an onslaught. The United States experienced this in a small way when thousands fled Haiti in boats bound for Florida after a military coup that deposed the democratically elected president Aristide. The U.S. government, through the Coast Guard, intercepted thousands of these refugees in international waters and returned them to Haiti. The Supreme Court held by a vote of 8–1 that international law does not impose any obligation on the United States to allow these refugees to reach the coast of Florida. The decision was legally and technically correct, but the attempted migration highlighted the pent-up anger and frustration of peoples around the world who are desperate to claim the political and economic rights promised them by their own countries and by the family of nations.

For fifty-five years the UNHCR has been virtually a model agency in the achievement of an almost impossible task. It has cared for the downtrodden and the exiles of the earth. It has carried out and enlarged international law. The heroic efforts of the commission and its noble vision of the world community struck me some time ago when I visited refugee camps in Vietnam and southeastern Asia. I cannot help but wonder whether similar camps will be necessary on a vast scale if hundreds of families leave their own countries in a desperate search for food.

The world finally agreed in 1966 to separate the U.N. political and economic covenants; each entered into force in 1976. They confer political and economic rights on the vast majority of the human race. In the near future the men, women, and children of the world will be demanding that the promises made to them be fulfilled.

THE MORAL DUTY TO PROVIDE
RESTITUTION FOR INJURY

The legal obligation to offer restitution for injury is as old as the Code of Hammurabi, the first formal set of laws in history. But this duty has been applied to nations only recently. Germany, for example, was required to offer reparations to the survivors of the 6 million people killed by the Nazis.

There are some indications that governments are recognizing or being forced to recognize that they owe indemnification to those whose rights they have violated. Various forms of such restitution are being considered in South Africa, Argentina, Chile, El Salvador, and several other countries.

Massive reparations to African Americans in the United States have occasionally been proposed. One of the most recent proposals is made in a book by Randall Robinson, an African American attorney, in his book *The Debt — What America Owes to Blacks* (Dutton/Plume, 1999). But indifference or even resistance to the idea of reparation to African Americans is predictable. The concept of affirmative action is, of course, a form of reparation because it is intended to compensate blacks for the discrimination they have suffered since the first African slaves were brought to Virginia in the early 1600s.

Affirmative action is permitted and indeed required in international law in the Convention on the Elimination of Racial Discrimination and the Convention on the Elimination of Discrimination Against Women. The call for restitution, reparation, or indemnification is implicit in the law of all countries. The United States accepted that concept when it awarded $20,000 to each person of Japanese ancestry who was interned during World War II. A commission in Oklahoma has urged reparations for the victims of a race riot in Tulsa in the 1920s. Two hundred thousand women from Korea were taken by the Japanese before and during World War II to serve Japanese soldiers all over the Pacific. Some of these victims and their survivors are making demands for reparations from the government of Japan.

American soldiers were harmed by exposure to Agent Orange in Vietnam. They successfully sued the U.S. government and the manufacturer of the defoliant for serious medical conditions caused by the chemical. Should the U.S. government similarly give restitution to the Vietnamese who were also hurt by that chemical?

If the United States admits some day that its war in Vietnam was not authorized by the United Nations or by international law, should the United States indemnify the survivors of the 2 million Vietnamese killed in that war by the American military?

The basic moral law of every society asserts that a government which wrongly injures its own citizens must make them whole insofar as this is possible. The new world order brought about by the United Nations reaffirms that obligation, although the ways to fulfill it need clarification.

Could the cry for restitution be a part of the emerging consensus that treaties and covenants are contracts between nations and that they should be enforced just as contracts between individuals can be executed by court order?

Individuals often come to a realization that they have harmed another person. Sometimes that realization comes years after the injury was inflicted. In increasing numbers, corporations are being required to make amends for products sold that were later found to be harmful. A rising number of nongovernmental organizations are now calling upon international law to remind nations of the harm that they have inflicted. The next step will be a widespread consensus that the offending governments are expected and required under the international law of human rights to make reparations to those who have been hurt.

There is strong resistance to the broad-based conviction that governments should pay money to those who have been hurt. Remnants of the old theory that the king can do no harm remain embedded in the laws of the world. There is also the myth that malingerers and troublemakers will make unfounded and exorbitant demands on the government.

But entrenched in the moral consensus everywhere is the deepening conviction that the governments should be honest with their own people, admit their mistakes, apologize to their victims, and make financial amends. Most governments, however, still try to evade and avoid any obligation to give reparation. But the emerging law of human rights will ever more insistently provide that every right must have a remedy. That powerful moral command will increasingly put moral and legal pressure on governments to ask for forgiveness for their sins and to offer relief to their victims.

Other aspirations to enforce human rights will be burgeoning — often in unpredictable ways and in unexpected places. These efforts may not necessarily be tied to any global legal initiative. Demands for justice and equality heard around the world derive from and depend on the ever more insistent cries for human rights made by the world's nongovernmental organizations and activists.

But even the most ardent supporters of human rights have to wonder whether the world would be suddenly free of tyranny if the mandates and aspirations of the 1993 Vienna Declaration on Human Rights were followed. History has been changed — even dominated — by tyrants and murderers like Stalin, Hitler, and Mao. Can laws protecting equality and demanding human rights prevent dictators from defying the decrees of world law?

For the past fifty-five years the world has for the first time proclaimed its faith in a rule of law grounded in a respect for the basic political and economic rights asserted in the Charter of the United Nations and in all its derivative covenants on human rights.

This giant experiment is in a sense another version of what the framers of the U.S. Constitution sought to do. Even the Bill of Rights, added in

1791, could not bring justice to Americans of African ancestry until 1954, when the Supreme Court decided *Brown v. Board of Education*. This disappointing record has occurred despite the fact that the U.S. Constitution — unlike the United Nations — had provided for judicial review to correct the failings of the legislative and executive branches of government.

The Code of Hammurabi, 2,500 years before Christ, declared that the purpose of law is to protect the powerless from the powerful. That is still one of the fundamental purposes of law — including the recently formulated international law.

20

THE FUTURE OF
INTERNATIONAL
HUMAN RIGHTS

Respect for others is one of the oldest moral ideas in civilization. The second commandment demands that everyone "love" their neighbor like themselves. Indeed, the love we are required to give to others must be equivalent to the love we have for ourselves and for God — as required in the First Commandment.

Injury to any child of God is wrong — indeed, it is a sacrilege.

Put in secular terms, this theory means that every individual possesses a dignity and is endowed with human rights that cannot be violated. Theoretically those who believe in a creator should be the strongest defenders of human rights. But both believers and nonbelievers are content to prescind from religious convictions when they talk about human rights. Religion has too often been used to transgress the human rights of those who are deemed to be heretics or dissidents. Religious people have, to be sure, sometimes been in the vanguard of those battling for human rights. But it is easy to think of the occasions in history when religious zealots or fanatics have trampled upon human rights in the name of a divine good.

Therefore, despite the historical similarity between the Second Commandment and the United Nations covenants on human rights, there is a worldwide consensus that the struggle for such rights is based on a nontheistic approach. Even raising this question places the focus on the problematic status of certain Muslim nations where the primacy of the Shari'ah, the basic Muslim code of law, is asserted in their adherence to the covenants on human rights. Petitioners on human rights are acutely aware of the problems in some of the nations where Muslims live. The complexity of the social and political scene in those countries is immense. In predominantly Muslim nations once colonized by European powers there resides a deep and intense feeling that the western colonial powers have destroyed some precious Islamic values and that these nations, now liberated from the west, should restore these values. Despite this deep but not unanimous feeling, Islamic countries have generally ratified the United Nations covenants on human rights. Some nations have, to be sure, insisted that the law of Shari'ah should take precedence over some of the values incorporated in the International Bill of Rights. But Islamic countries have sometimes supported the freedom of the press, the free exercise of religion, and the ever more strict, key demands of the covenants on economic and political rights. A crucial question remains for many observers: Will the Islamic countries continue to be faithful to their pledge to uphold the human rights standard in the United Nations documents?

The largest question about the future of human rights centers, of course, on China. Will this nation with 1.2 billion people — one-fifth of the global village — embrace freedom of the press, religious liberty, and the right to marry and have children without governmental interference? The horrors of China's cultural revolution still arouse the most profound anxieties about the fundamental stability of China and its adherence to the standards to which China agreed in its acceptance of the Vienna Declaration on Human Rights in 1993. It is reassuring to remember that China was one of the founders of the United Nations, is a permanent member of the U.N. Security Council, and has ratified some of the human rights covenants. But the impenetrability of China arouses the deepest anxiety among those who hope that the priority of human rights can constitute a new basis for international morality.

The fragmentation of Africa also raises the severest doubts among those who hope that the International Bill of Rights can unify the world in guaranteeing a uniform level of dignity and respect for all human beings. The horrors of Rwanda, the chaos of Zaire, and the political fragility of Nigeria are not encouraging signs that Africa is approaching an acceptable level of compliance with the standards set by the world's lawmakers over the past fifty years.

It seems self-evident that the future of human rights in the world depends upon what transpires in China and Africa. It is also clear that the United States more than any other country will shape the future of the amazing developments in international human rights that have occurred since the end of World War II. The enlightened leadership of the United States that was so dramatically effective in the late 1940s faded into twilight in the 1950s and has been sporadic since that time. The leadership of President Carter in human rights faltered during the Reagan and Bush years. It was revived to some extent during the Clinton administration, although the demise of the u.s.s.r. altered the entire history and future of international human rights.

It can be argued that the Clinton administration did not take advantage of the spectacular opportunity offered by the collapse of the Soviet bloc. Clearly, a whole new foreign policy was called for with the end of the Cold War. The foreign policy of the United States was no longer dictated by the necessity to be friendly toward less-than-democratic nations simply because they were the enemies of our enemy, the Soviet Union. But the United States in many instances did not move toward an entirely new approach. It did, however, make significant sacrifices to return Haiti to a democratic government, collaborate with others to maintain democracy in Kosovo, and use its good offices to bring democracy to Northern Ireland.

Will history look back at the United States and conclude that it squandered many opportunities in the 1990s when unprecedented occasions to advance human rights presented themselves in the nations of eastern Europe and in the other fifteen nations that separated from the former u.s.s.r.?

The United States remained firm in its policy of being prepared for war—a war that almost always resembled a conflict with the threat of nuclear weapons. Similarly, it continued to sell arms and military equipment to almost any nation—absorbing the world trade in arms previously conducted by the Soviet Union.

The United States was active in bringing together 170 nations for the 1993 World Conference on Human Rights in Vienna. It was clear then and is even clearer now that the United States has the moral and political clout to transform the nations of the earth into a world where international human rights is the coin of the realm and the starting point and centerpiece of all discussions about the future of international peace.

Still, a streak of isolationism runs deep through the United States. Surrounded by two oceans, it has never been invaded. The philosophy that prompted the U.S. Senate to refuse membership in the League of Nations is still alive. It reemerges when Congress refuses to pay its dues to the United Nations and when it fails to become a partner in the International Criminal Commission.

It is difficult to predict how enthusiastic the United States will be toward the monitoring and enforcement of international human rights. The resistance Americans routinely demonstrate to supporting world standards on the environment is echoed in its resistance to the imposition of world standards in areas such as the rights of women and the status of refugees.

At the same time, lying deep within the American soul is the desire to provide leadership and moral ideals. The United States has done that, at least in limited ways, in the field of nuclear arms control. Is there some outside event or series of events which could galvanize America's leaders to be as bold in the arena of international human rights as it was in the late 1940s?

One possible response to that question is reflected in the attitudes of the several nongovernmental organizations devoted to international human rights. The moral power of groups like Amnesty International, Human Rights Watch, and the Lawyers Committee for Human Rights is considerable. Fully engaged in the mobilization of shame, they are relentless, persuasive, and pervasive. Could they, in alliance with a broad base of NGOs, change America's policy so that the United States would become an ardent friend of international human rights around the globe? This is not impossible. Leaders and supporters of human rights were among the abolitionists who finally obtained the Emancipation Proclamation, the suffragettes who in 1920 obtained the vote for women, and those who caused the U.S. Congress to de-fund the war in Vietnam.

The level of anger of the abolitionists, the suffragettes, and the antiwar militants was high—extremely high. Could the indignation of international human rights activists rise to the level of a compelling force in American politics? It could. Yet, the worldwide violation of international human rights is not as dramatic or compelling as are daily affronts to justice and equality on American soil. But amazing things can happen when even a small group of activists come together to protest injustice. The potential is even greater when international law clearly bans the conduct in question.

The human race has been struggling for centuries to stop injustice and to offer reparations to its victims. There is no one pattern or force that prompts nations to be just. Sometimes it is the voice of the victims that accomplishes such a feat, but more often it is the conscience and moral outrage of nonvictims. Traditionally, they more than any others have championed the rights of those who have been victimized.

Solon, the ancient Athenian jurist, summed up this truth in words that have a striking relevance: "Justice will not come until those who are not hurt feel just as indignant as those who are."

VIENNA DECLARATION AND PROGRAMME OF ACTION ADOPTED AT THE WORLD CONFERENCE ON HUMAN RIGHTS, 25 JUNE 1993

The World Conference on Human Rights,

Considering that the promotion and protection of human rights is a matter of priority for the international community, and that the Conference affords a unique opportunity to carry out a comprehensive analysis of the international human rights system and of the machinery for the protection of human rights, in order to enhance and thus promote a fuller observance of those rights, in a just and balanced manner,

Recognizing and affirming that all human rights derive from the dignity and worth inherent in the human person, and that the human person is the central subject of human rights and fundamental freedoms, and consequently should be the principal beneficiary and should participate actively in the realization of these rights and freedoms,

Reaffirming their commitment to the purposes and principles contained in the Charter of the United Nations and the Universal Declaration of Human Rights,

Reaffirming the commitment contained in Article 56 of the Charter of the United Nations to take joint and separate action, placing proper emphasis on developing effective international cooperation for the realization of the purposes set out in Article 55, including universal respect for, and observance of, human rights and fundamental freedoms for all,

Emphasizing the responsibilities of all States, in conformity with the Charter of the United Nations, to develop and encourage respect for human rights and fundamental freedoms for all, without distinction as to race, sex, language or religion,

Recalling the Preamble to the Charter of the United Nations, in particular the determination to reaffirm faith in fundamental human rights, in the dignity and worth of the human person, and in the equal rights of men and women and of nations large and small,

Recalling also the determination expressed in the Preamble of the Charter of the United Nations to save succeeding generations from the scourge of war, to establish conditions under which justice and respect for obligations arising from treaties and other sources of international law can be maintained, to promote social progress and better standards of life in larger freedom, to practice tolerance and good neighbourliness, and to employ international machinery for the promotion of the economic and social advancement of all peoples,

Emphasizing that the Universal Declaration of Human Rights, which constitutes a common standard of achievement for all peoples and all nations, is the source of inspiration and has been the basis for the United Nations in making advances in standard setting as contained in the existing international human rights instruments, in particular the International Covenant on Civil and Political Rights and the International Covenant on Economic, Social and Cultural Rights,

Considering the major changes taking place on the international scene and the aspirations of all the peoples for an international order based on the principles enshrined in the Charter of the United Nations, including promoting and encouraging respect for human rights and fundamental freedoms for all and respect for the principle of equal rights and self-determination of peoples, peace, democracy, justice, equality, rule of law, pluralism, development, better standards of living and solidarity,

Deeply concerned by various forms of discrimination and violence, to which women continue to be exposed all over the world,

Recognizing that the activities of the United Nations in the field of human rights should be rationalized and enhanced in order to strengthen the United Nations machinery in this field and to further the objectives of universal respect for observance of international human rights standards,

Having taken into account the Declarations adopted by the three regional meetings at Tunis, San José and Bangkok and the contributions made by Governments, and bearing in mind the suggestions made by intergovernmental and non-governmental organizations, as well as the studies prepared by independent experts during the preparatory process leading to the World Conference on Human Rights,

Welcoming the International Year of the World's Indigenous People 1993 as a reaffirmation of the commitment of the international community to ensure their enjoyment of all human rights and fundamental freedoms and to respect the value and diversity of their cultures and identities,

Recognizing also that the international community should devise ways and means to remove the current obstacles and meet challenges to the full realization of all human rights and to prevent the continuation of human rights violations resulting thereof throughout the world,

Invoking the spirit of our age and the realities of our time which call upon the peoples of the world and all States Members of the United Nations to rededicate themselves to the global task of promoting and protecting all human rights and fundamental freedoms so as to secure full and universal enjoyment of these rights,

Determined to take new steps forward in the commitment of the international community with a view to achieving substantial progress in human rights endeavours by an increased and sustained effort of international cooperation and solidarity,

Solemnly adopts the Vienna Declaration and Programme of Action.

I

1. The World Conference on Human Rights reaffirms the solemn commitment of all States to fulfil their obligations to promote universal respect for, and observance and protection of, all human rights and fundamental freedoms for all in accordance with the Charter of the United Nations, other instruments relating to human rights, and international law. The universal nature of these rights and freedoms is beyond question.

In this framework, enhancement of international cooperation in the field of human rights is essential for the full achievement of the purposes of the United Nations.

Human rights and fundamental freedoms are the birthright of all human beings; their protection and promotion is the first responsibility of Governments.

2. All peoples have the right of self-determination. By virtue of that right they freely determine their political status, and freely pursue their economic, social and cultural development.

Taking into account the particular situation of peoples under colonial or other forms of alien domination or foreign occupation, the World Conference on Human Rights recognizes the right of peoples to take any legitimate action, in accordance with the Charter of the United Nations, to realize their inalienable right of self-determination. The World Conference on Human Rights considers the denial of the right of self-determination as a violation of human rights and underlines the importance of the effective realization of this right.

In accordance with the Declaration on Principles of International Law concerning Friendly Relations and Cooperation Among States in accordance with the Charter of the United Nations, this shall not be construed as authorizing or encouraging any action which would dismember or impair, totally or in part, the territorial integrity or political unity of sovereign and independent States conducting themselves in compliance with the principle of equal rights and self-determination of peoples and thus possessed of a Government representing the whole people belonging to the territory without distinction of any kind.

3. Effective international measures to guarantee and monitor the implementation of human rights standards should be taken in respect of people under foreign occupation, and effective legal protection against the violation of their human rights should be provided, in accordance with human rights norms and international law, particularly the Geneva Convention relative to the Protection of Civilian Persons in Time of War, of 14 August 1949, and other applicable norms of humanitarian law.

4. The promotion and protection of all human rights and fundamental freedoms must be considered as a priority objective of the United Nations in accordance with its purposes and principles, in particular the purpose of international cooperation. In the framework of these purposes and principles, the promotion and protection of all human rights is a legitimate concern of the international community. The organs and specialized

agencies related to human rights should therefore further enhance the coordination of their activities based on the consistent and objective application of international human rights instruments.

5. All human rights are universal, indivisible and interdependent and interrelated. The international community must treat human rights globally in a fair and equal manner, on the same footing, and with the same emphasis. While the significance of national and regional particularities and various historical, cultural and religious backgrounds must be borne in mind, it is the duty of States, regardless of their political, economic and cultural systems, to promote and protect all human rights and fundamental freedoms.

6. The efforts of the United Nations system towards the universal respect for, and observance of, human rights and fundamental freedoms for all, contribute to the stability and well-being necessary for peaceful and friendly relations among nations, and to improved conditions for peace and security as well as social and economic development, in conformity with the Charter of the United Nations.

7. The processes of promoting and protecting human rights should be conducted in conformity with the purposes and principles of the Charter of the United Nations, and international law.

8. Democracy, development and respect for human rights and fundamental freedoms are interdependent and mutually reinforcing. Democracy is based on the freely expressed will of the people to determine their own political, economic, social and cultural systems and their full participation in all aspects of their lives. In the context of the above, the promotion and protection of human rights and fundamental freedoms at the national and international levels should be universal and conducted without conditions attached. The international community should support the strengthening and promoting of democracy, development and respect for human rights and fundamental freedoms in the entire world.

9. The World Conference on Human Rights reaffirms that least developed countries committed to the process of democratization and economic reforms, many of which are in Africa, should be supported by the international community in order to succeed in their transition to democracy and economic development.

10. The World Conference on Human Rights reaffirms the right to

development, as established in the Declaration on the Right to Development, as a universal and inalienable right and an integral part of fundamental human rights.

As stated in the Declaration on the Right to Development, the human person is the central subject of development.

While development facilitates the enjoyment of all human rights, the lack of development may not be invoked to justify the abridgement of internationally recognized human rights.

States should cooperate with each other in ensuring development and eliminating obstacles to development. The international community should promote an effective international cooperation for the realization of the right to development and the elimination of obstacles to development.

Lasting progress towards the implementation of the right to development requires effective development policies at the national level, as well as equitable economic relations and a favourable economic environment at the international level.

11. The right to development should be fulfilled so as to meet equitably the developmental and environmental needs of present and future generations. The World Conference on Human Rights recognizes that illicit dumping of toxic and dangerous substances and waste potentially constitutes a serious threat to the human rights to life and health of everyone.

Consequently, the World Conference on Human Rights calls on all States to adopt and vigorously implement existing conventions relating to the dumping of toxic and dangerous products and waste and to cooperate in the prevention of illicit dumping.

Everyone has the right to enjoy the benefits of scientific progress and its applications. The World Conference on Human Rights notes that certain advances, notably in the biomedical and life sciences as well as in information technology, may have potentially adverse consequences for the integrity, dignity and human rights of the individual, and calls for international cooperation to ensure that human rights and dignity are fully respected in this area of universal concern.

12. The World Conference on Human Rights calls upon the international community to make all efforts to help alleviate the external debt

burden of developing countries, in order to supplement the efforts of the Governments of such countries to attain the full realization of the economic, social and cultural rights of their people.

13. There is a need for States and international organizations, in cooperation with non-governmental organizations, to create favourable conditions at the national, regional and international levels to ensure the full and effective enjoyment of human rights. States should eliminate all violations of human rights and their causes, as well as obstacles to the enjoyment of these rights.

14. The existence of widespread extreme poverty inhibits the full and effective enjoyment of human rights; its immediate alleviation and eventual elimination must remain a high priority for the international community.

15. Respect for human rights and for fundamental freedoms without distinction of any kind is a fundamental rule of international human rights law. The speedy and comprehensive elimination of all forms of racism and racial discrimination, xenophobia and related intolerance is a priority task for the international community. Governments should take effective measures to prevent and combat them. Groups, institutions, intergovernmental and non-governmental organizations and individuals are urged to intensify their efforts in cooperating and coordinating their activities against these evils.

16. The World Conference on Human Rights welcomes the progress made in dismantling apartheid and calls upon the international community and the United Nations system to assist in this process.

The World Conference on Human Rights also deplores the continuing acts of violence aimed at undermining the quest for a peaceful dismantling of apartheid.

17. The acts, methods and practices of terrorism in all its forms and manifestations as well as linkage in some countries to drug trafficking are activities aimed at the destruction of human rights, fundamental freedoms and democracy, threatening territorial integrity, security of States and destabilizing legitimately constituted Governments. The international community should take the necessary steps to enhance cooperation to prevent and combat terrorism.

18. The human rights of women and of the girl-child are an inalienable,

integral and indivisible part of universal human rights. The full and equal participation of women in political, civil, economic, social and cultural life, at the national, regional and international levels, and the eradication of all forms of discrimination on grounds of sex are priority objectives of the international community.

Gender-based violence and all forms of sexual harassment and exploitation, including those resulting from cultural prejudice and international trafficking, are incompatible with the dignity and worth of the human person, and must be eliminated. This can be achieved by legal measures and through national action and international cooperation in such fields as economic and social development, education, safe maternity and health care, and social support.

The human rights of women should form an integral part of the United Nations human rights activities, including the promotion of all human rights instruments relating to women.

The World Conference on Human Rights urges Governments, institutions, intergovernmental and non-governmental organizations to intensify their efforts for the protection and promotion of human rights of women and the girl-child.

19. Considering the importance of the promotion and protection of the rights of persons belonging to minorities and the contribution of such promotion and protection to the political and social stability of the States in which such persons live,

The World Conference on Human Rights reaffirms the obligation of States to ensure that persons belonging to minorities may exercise fully and effectively all human rights and fundamental freedoms without any discrimination and in full equality before the law in accordance with the Declaration on the Rights of Persons Belonging to National or Ethnic, Religious and Linguistic Minorities.

The persons belonging to minorities have the right to enjoy their own culture, to profess and practise their own religion and to use their own language in private and in public, freely and without interference or any form of discrimination.

20. The World Conference on Human Rights recognizes the inherent dignity and the unique contribution of indigenous people to the development and plurality of society and strongly reaffirms the commitment of

the international community to their economic, social and cultural well-being and their enjoyment of the fruits of sustainable development. States should ensure the full and free participation of indigenous people in all aspects of society, in particular in matters of concern to them. Considering the importance of the promotion and protection of the rights of indigenous people, and the contribution of such promotion and protection to the political and social stability of the States in which such people live, States should, in accordance with international law, take concerted positive steps to ensure respect for all human rights and fundamental freedoms of indigenous people, on the basis of equality and non-discrimination, and recognize the value and diversity of their distinct identities, cultures and social organization.

21. The World Conference on Human Rights, welcoming the early ratification of the Convention on the Rights of the Child by a large number of States and noting the recognition of the human rights of children in the World Declaration on the Survival, Protection and Development of Children and Plan of Action adopted by the World Summit for Children, urges universal ratification of the Convention by 1995 and its effective implementation by States parties through the adoption of all the necessary legislative, administrative and other measures and the allocation to the maximum extent of the available resources. In all actions concerning children, non-discrimination and the best interest of the child should be primary considerations and the views of the child given due weight. National and international mechanisms and programmes should be strengthened for the defence and protection of children, in particular, the girl-child, abandoned children, street children, economically and sexually exploited children, including through child pornography, child prostitution or sale of organs, children victims of diseases, including acquired immunodeficiency syndrome, refugee and displaced children, children in detention, children in armed conflict, as well as children victims of famine and drought and other emergencies. International cooperation and solidarity should be promoted to support the implementation of the Convention and the rights of the child should be a priority in the United Nations system-wide action on human rights.

The World Conference on Human Rights also stresses that the child for the full and harmonious development of his or her personality should grow up in a family environment which accordingly merits broader protection.

22. Special attention needs to be paid to ensuring non-discrimination, and the equal enjoyment of all human rights and fundamental freedoms by disabled persons, including their active participation in all aspects of society.

23. The World Conference on Human Rights reaffirms that everyone, without distinction of any kind, is entitled to the right to seek and to enjoy in other countries asylum from persecution, as well as the right to return to one's own country. In this respect it stresses the importance of the Universal Declaration of Human Rights, the 1951 Convention relating to the Status of Refugees, its 1967 Protocol and regional instruments. It expresses its appreciation to States that continue to admit and host large numbers of refugees in their territories, and to the Office of the United Nations High Commissioner for Refugees for its dedication to its task. It also expresses its appreciation to the United Nations Relief and Works Agency for Palestine Refugees in the Near East.

The World Conference on Human Rights recognizes that gross violations of human rights, including in armed conflicts, are among the multiple and complex factors leading to displacement of people.

The World Conference on Human Rights recognizes that, in view of the complexities of the global refugee crisis and in accordance with the Charter of the United Nations, relevant international instruments and international solidarity and in the spirit of burden-sharing, a comprehensive approach by the international community is needed in coordination and cooperation with the countries concerned and relevant organizations, bearing in mind the mandate of the United Nations High Commissioner for Refugees. This should include the development of strategies to address the root causes and effects of movements of refugees and other displaced persons, the strengthening of emergency preparedness and response mechanisms, the provision of effective protection and assistance, bearing in mind the special needs of women and children, as well as the achievement of durable solutions, primarily through the preferred solution of dignified and safe voluntary repatriation, including solutions such as those adopted by the international refugee conferences. The World

Conference on Human Rights underlines the responsibilities of States, particularly as they relate to the countries of origin.

In the light of the comprehensive approach, the World Conference on Human Rights emphasizes the importance of giving special attention including through intergovernmental and humanitarian organizations and finding lasting solutions to questions related to internally displaced persons including their voluntary and safe return and rehabilitation.

In accordance with the Charter of the United Nations and the principles of humanitarian law, the World Conference on Human Rights further emphasizes the importance of and the need for humanitarian assistance to victims of all natural and man-made disasters.

24. Great importance must be given to the promotion and protection of the human rights of persons belonging to groups which have been rendered vulnerable, including migrant workers, the elimination of all forms of discrimination against them, and the strengthening and more effective implementation of existing human rights instruments. States have an obligation to create and maintain adequate measures at the national level, in particular in the fields of education, health and social support, for the promotion and protection of the rights of persons in vulnerable sectors of their populations and to ensure the participation of those among them who are interested in finding a solution to their own problems.

25. The World Conference on Human Rights affirms that extreme poverty and social exclusion constitute a violation of human dignity and that urgent steps are necessary to achieve better knowledge of extreme poverty and its causes, including those related to the problem of development, in order to promote the human rights of the poorest, and to put an end to extreme poverty and social exclusion and to promote the enjoyment of the fruits of social progress. It is essential for States to foster participation by the poorest people in the decision-making process by the community in which they live, the promotion of human rights and efforts to combat extreme poverty.

26. The World Conference on Human Rights welcomes the progress made in the codification of human rights instruments, which is a dynamic and evolving process, and urges the universal ratification of human rights

treaties. All States are encouraged to accede to these international instruments; all States are encouraged to avoid, as far as possible, the resort to reservations.

27. Every State should provide an effective framework of remedies to redress human rights grievances or violations. The administration of justice, including law enforcement and prosecutorial agencies and, especially, an independent judiciary and legal profession in full conformity with applicable standards contained in international human rights instruments, are essential to the full and non-discriminatory realization of human rights and indispensable to the processes of democracy and sustainable development. In this context, institutions concerned with the administration of justice should be properly funded, and an increased level of both technical and financial assistance should be provided by the international community. It is incumbent upon the United Nations to make use of special programmes of advisory services on a priority basis for the achievement of a strong and independent administration of justice.

28. The World Conference on Human Rights expresses its dismay at massive violations of human rights especially in the form of genocide, "ethnic cleansing" and systematic rape of women in war situations, creating mass exodus of refugees and displaced persons. While strongly condemning such abhorrent practices it reiterates the call that perpetrators of such crimes be punished and such practices immediately stopped.

29. The World Conference on Human Rights expresses grave concern about continuing human rights violations in all parts of the world in disregard of standards as contained in international human rights instruments and international humanitarian law and about the lack of sufficient and effective remedies for the victims.

The World Conference on Human Rights is deeply concerned about violations of human rights during armed conflicts, affecting the civilian population, especially women, children, the elderly and the disabled. The Conference therefore calls upon States and all parties to armed conflicts strictly to observe international humanitarian law, as set forth in the Geneva Conventions of 1949 and other rules and principles of international law, as well as minimum standards for protection of human rights, as laid down in international conventions.

The World Conference on Human Rights reaffirms the right of the victims to be assisted by humanitarian organizations, as set forth in the Geneva Conventions of 1949 and other relevant instruments of international humanitarian law, and calls for the safe and timely access for such assistance.

30. The World Conference on Human Rights also expresses its dismay and condemnation that gross and systematic violations and situations that constitute serious obstacles to the full enjoyment of all human rights continue to occur in different parts of the world. Such violations and obstacles include, as well as torture and cruel, inhuman and degrading treatment or punishment, summary and arbitrary executions, disappearances, arbitrary detentions, all forms of racism, racial discrimination and apartheid, foreign occupation and alien domination, xenophobia, poverty, hunger and other denials of economic, social and cultural rights, religious intolerance, terrorism, discrimination against women and lack of the rule of law.

31. The World Conference on Human Rights calls upon States to refrain from any unilateral measure not in accordance with international law and the Charter of the United Nations that creates obstacles to trade relations among States and impedes the full realization of the human rights set forth in the Universal Declaration of Human Rights and international human rights instruments, in particular the rights of everyone to a standard of living adequate for their health and well-being, including food and medical care, housing and the necessary social services. The World Conference on Human Rights affirms that food should not be used as a tool for political pressure.

32. The World Conference on Human Rights reaffirms the importance of ensuring the universality, objectivity and non-selectivity of the consideration of human rights issues.

33. The World Conference on Human Rights reaffirms that States are duty-bound, as stipulated in the Universal Declaration of Human Rights and the International Covenant on Economic, Social and Cultural Rights and in other international human rights instruments, to ensure that education is aimed at strengthening the respect of human rights and fundamental freedoms. The World Conference on Human Rights emphasizes the importance of incorporating the subject of human rights education programmes and calls upon States to do so. Education should promote

understanding, tolerance, peace and friendly relations between the nations and all racial or religious groups and encourage the development of United Nations activities in pursuance of these objectives. Therefore, education on human rights and the dissemination of proper information, both theoretical and practical, play an important role in the promotion and respect of human rights with regard to all individuals without distinction of any kind such as race, sex, language or religion, and this should be integrated in the education policies at the national as well as international levels. The World Conference on Human Rights notes that resource constraints and institutional inadequacies may impede the immediate realization of these objectives.

34. Increased efforts should be made to assist countries which so request to create the conditions whereby each individual can enjoy universal human rights and fundamental freedoms. Governments, the United Nations system as well as other multilateral organizations are urged to increase considerably the resources allocated to programmes aiming at the establishment and strengthening of national legislation, national institutions and related infrastructures which uphold the rule of law and democracy, electoral assistance, human rights awareness through training, teaching and education, popular participation and civil society.

The programmes of advisory services and technical cooperation under the Centre for Human Rights should be strengthened as well as made more efficient and transparent and thus become a major contribution to improving respect for human rights. States are called upon to increase their contributions to these programmes, both through promoting a larger allocation from the United Nations regular budget, and through voluntary contributions.

35. The full and effective implementation of United Nations activities to promote and protect human rights must reflect the high importance accorded to human rights by the Charter of the United Nations and the demands of the United Nations human rights activities, as mandated by Member States. To this end, United Nations human rights activities should be provided with increased resources.

36. The World Conference on Human Rights reaffirms the important and constructive role played by national institutions for the promotion and protection of human rights, in particular in their advisory capacity to

the competent authorities, their role in remedying human rights violations, in the dissemination of human rights information, and education in human rights.

The World Conference on Human Rights encourages the establishment and strengthening of national institutions, having regard to the "Principles relating to the status of national institutions" and recognizing that it is the right of each State to choose the framework which is best suited to its particular needs at the national level.

37. Regional arrangements play a fundamental role in promoting and protecting human rights. They should reinforce universal human rights standards, as contained in international human rights instruments, and their protection. The World Conference on Human Rights endorses efforts under way to strengthen these arrangements and to increase their effectiveness, while at the same time stressing the importance of cooperation with the United Nations human rights activities.

The World Conference on Human Rights reiterates the need to consider the possibility of establishing regional and subregional arrangements for the promotion and protection of human rights where they do not already exist.

38. The World Conference on Human Rights recognizes the important role of non-governmental organizations in the promotion of all human rights and in humanitarian activities at national, regional and international levels. The World Conference on Human Rights appreciates their contribution to increasing public awareness of human rights issues, to the conduct of education, training and research in this field, and to the promotion and protection of all human rights and fundamental freedoms. While recognizing that the primary responsibility for standard-setting lies with States, the conference also appreciates the contribution of non-governmental organizations to this process. In this respect, the World Conference on Human Rights emphasizes the importance of continued dialogue and cooperation between Governments and non-governmental organizations. Non-governmental organizations and their members genuinely involved in the field of human rights should enjoy the rights and freedoms recognized in the Universal Declaration of Human Rights, and the protection of the national law. These rights and freedoms may not be exercised contrary to the purposes and principles of the

United Nations. Non-governmental organizations should be free to carry out their human rights activities, without interference, within the framework of national law and the Universal Declaration of Human Rights.

39. Underlining the importance of objective, responsible and impartial information about human rights and humanitarian issues, the World Conference on Human Rights encourages the increased involvement of the media, for whom freedom and protection should be guaranteed within the framework of national law.

II

A. INCREASED COORDINATION ON HUMAN RIGHTS WITHIN THE UNITED NATIONS SYSTEM

1. The World Conference on Human Rights recommends increased coordination in support of human rights and fundamental freedoms within the United Nations system. To this end, the World Conference on Human Rights urges all United Nations organs, bodies and the specialized agencies whose activities deal with human rights to cooperate in order to strengthen, rationalize and streamline their activities, taking into account the need to avoid unnecessary duplication. The World Conference on Human Rights also recommends to the Secretary-General that high-level officials of relevant United Nations bodies and specialized agencies at their annual meeting, besides coordinating their activities, also assess the impact of their strategies and policies on the enjoyment of all human rights.

2. Furthermore, the World Conference on Human Rights calls on regional organizations and prominent international and regional finance and development institutions to assess also the impact of their policies and programmes on the enjoyment of human rights.

3. The World Conference on Human Rights recognizes that relevant specialized agencies and bodies and institutions of the United Nations system as well as other relevant intergovernmental organizations whose activities deal with human rights play a vital role in the formulation, promotion and implementation of human rights standards, within their

respective mandates, and should take into account the outcome of the World Conference on Human Rights within their fields of competence.

4. The World Conference on Human Rights strongly recommends that a concerted effort be made to encourage and facilitate the ratification of and accession or succession to international human rights treaties and protocols adopted within the framework of the United Nations system with the aim of universal acceptance. The Secretary-General, in consultation with treaty bodies, should consider opening a dialogue with States not having acceded to these human rights treaties, in order to identify obstacles and to seek ways of overcoming them.

5. The World Conference on Human Rights encourages States to consider limiting the extent of any reservations they lodge to international human rights instruments, formulate any reservations as precisely and narrowly as possible, ensure that none is incompatible with the object and purpose of the relevant treaty and regularly review any reservations with a view to withdrawing them.

6. The World Conference on Human Rights, recognizing the need to maintain consistency with the high quality of existing international standards and to avoid proliferation of human rights instruments, reaffirms the guidelines relating to the elaboration of new international instruments contained in General Assembly resolution 41/120 of 4 December 1986 and calls on the United Nations human rights bodies, when considering the elaboration of new international standards, to keep those guidelines in mind, to consult with human rights treaty bodies on the necessity for drafting new standards and to request the Secretariat to carry out technical reviews of proposed new instruments.

7. The World Conference on Human Rights recommends that human rights officers be assigned if and when necessary to regional offices of the United Nations Organization with the purpose of disseminating information and offering training and other technical assistance in the field of human rights upon the request of concerned Member States. Human rights training for international civil servants who are assigned to work relating to human rights should be organized.

8. The World Conference on Human Rights welcomes the convening of emergency sessions of the Commission on Human Rights as a positive

initiative and that other ways of responding to acute violations of human rights be considered by the relevant organs of the United Nations system.

Resources

9. The World Conference on Human Rights, concerned by the growing disparity between the activities of the Centre for Human Rights and the human, financial and other resources available to carry them out, and bearing in mind the resources needed for other important United Nations programmes, requests the Secretary-General and the General Assembly to take immediate steps to increase substantially the resources for the human rights programme from within the existing and future regular budgets of the United Nations, and to take urgent steps to seek increased extrabudgetary resources.

10. Within this framework, an increased proportion of the regular budget should be allocated directly to the Centre for Human Rights to cover its costs and all other costs borne by the Centre for Human Rights, including those related to the United Nations human rights bodies. Voluntary funding of the Centre's technical cooperation activities should reinforce this enhanced budget; the World Conference on Human Rights calls for generous contributions to the existing trust funds.

11. The World Conference on Human Rights requests the Secretary-General and the General Assembly to provide sufficient human, financial and other resources to the Centre for Human Rights to enable it effectively, efficiently and expeditiously to carry out its activities.

12. The World Conference on Human Rights, noting the need to ensure that human and financial resources are available to carry out the human rights activities, as mandated by intergovernmental bodies, urges the Secretary-General, in accordance with Article 101 of the Charter of the United Nations, and Member States to adopt a coherent approach aimed at securing that resources commensurate to the increased mandates are allocated to the Secretariat. The World Conference on Human Rights invites the Secretary-General to consider whether adjustments to procedures in the programme budget cycle would be necessary or helpful to ensure the timely and effective implementation of human rights activities as mandated by Member States.

13. The World Conference on Human Rights stresses the importance of strengthening the United Nations Centre for Human Rights.

14. The Centre for Human Rights should play an important role in coordinating system-wide attention for human rights. The focal role of the Centre can best be realized if it is enabled to cooperate fully with other United Nations bodies and organs. The coordinating role of the Centre for Human Rights also implies that the office of the Centre for Human Rights in New York is strengthened.

15. The Centre for Human Rights should be assured adequate means for the system of thematic and country rapporteurs, experts, working groups and treaty bodies. Follow-up on recommendations should become a priority matter for consideration by the Commission on Human Rights.

16. The Centre for Human Rights should assume a larger role in the promotion of human rights. This role could be given shape through cooperation with Member States and by an enhanced programme of advisory services and technical assistance. The existing voluntary funds will have to be expanded substantially for these purposes and should be managed in a more efficient and coordinated way. All activities should follow strict and transparent project management rules and regular programme and project evaluations should be held periodically. To this end, the results of such evaluation exercises and other relevant information should be made available regularly. The Centre should, in particular, organize at least once a year information meetings open to all Member States and organizations directly involved in these projects and programmes.

Adaptation and strengthening of the United Nations machinery for human rights, including the question of the establishment of a United Nations High Commissioner for Human Rights

17. The World Conference on Human Rights recognizes the necessity for a continuing adaptation of the United Nations human rights machinery to the current and future needs in the promotion and protection

of human rights, as reflected in the present Declaration and within the framework of a balanced and sustainable development for all people. In particular, the United Nations human rights organs should improve their coordination, efficiency and effectiveness.

18. The World Conference on Human Rights recommends to the General Assembly that when examining the report of the Conference at its forty-eighth session, it begin, as a matter of priority, consideration of the question of the establishment of a High Commissioner for Human Rights for the promotion and protection of all human rights.

B. EQUALITY, DIGNITY AND TOLERANCE

I. RACISM, RACIAL DISCRIMINATION, XENOPHOBIA AND OTHER FORMS OF INTOLERANCE

19. The World Conference on Human Rights considers the elimination of racism and racial discrimination, in particular in their institutionalized forms such as apartheid or resulting from doctrines of racial superiority or exclusivity or contemporary forms and manifestations of racism, as a primary objective for the international community and a worldwide promotion programme in the field of human rights. United Nations organs and agencies should strengthen their efforts to implement such a programme of action related to the third decade to combat racism and racial discrimination as well as subsequent mandates to the same end. The World Conference on Human Rights strongly appeals to the international community to contribute generously to the Trust Fund for the Programme for the Decade for Action to Combat Racism and Racial Discrimination.

20. The World Conference on Human Rights urges all Governments to take immediate measures and to develop strong policies to prevent and combat all forms and manifestations of racism, xenophobia or related intolerance, where necessary by enactment of appropriate legislation, including penal measures, and by the establishment of national institutions to combat such phenomena.

21. The World Conference on Human Rights welcomes the decision of the Commission on Human Rights to appoint a Special Rapporteur

on contemporary forms of racism, racial discrimination, xenophobia and related intolerance. The World Conference on Human Rights also appeals to all States parties to the International Convention on the Elimination of All Forms of Racial Discrimination to consider making the declaration under article 14 of the Convention.

22. The World Conference on Human Rights calls upon all Governments to take all appropriate measures in compliance with their international obligations and with due regard to their respective legal systems to counter intolerance and related violence based on religion or belief, including practices of discrimination against women and including the desecration of religious sites, recognizing that every individual has the right to freedom of thought, conscience, expression and religion. The Conference also invites all States to put into practice the provisions of the Declaration on the Elimination of All Forms of Intolerance and of Discrimination Based on Religion or Belief.

23. The World Conference on Human Rights stresses that all persons who perpetrate or authorize criminal acts associated with ethnic cleansing are individually responsible and accountable for such human rights violations, and that the international community should exert every effort to bring those legally responsible for such violations to justice.

24. The World Conference on Human Rights calls on all States to take immediate measures, individually and collectively, to combat the practice of ethnic cleansing to bring it quickly to an end. Victims of the abhorrent practice of ethnic cleansing are entitled to appropriate and effective remedies.

2. PERSONS BELONGING TO NATIONAL OR ETHNIC, RELIGIOUS AND LINGUISTIC MINORITIES

25. The World Conference on Human Rights calls on the Commission on Human Rights to examine ways and means to promote and protect effectively the rights of persons belonging to minorities as set out in the Declaration on the Rights of Persons belonging to National or Ethnic, Religious and Linguistic Minorities. In this context, the World Conference on Human Rights calls upon the Centre for Human Rights to provide, at the request of Governments concerned and as part of its

programme of advisory services and technical assistance, qualified expertise on minority issues and human rights, as well as on the prevention and resolution of disputes, to assist in existing or potential situations involving minorities.

26. The World Conference on Human Rights urges States and the international community to promote and protect the rights of persons belonging to national or ethnic, religious and linguistic minorities in accordance with the Declaration on the Rights of Persons belonging to National or Ethnic, Religious and Linguistic Minorities.

27. Measures to be taken, where appropriate, should include facilitation of their full participation in all aspects of the political, economic, social, religious and cultural life of society and in the economic progress and development in their country.

Indigenous people

28. The World Conference on Human Rights calls on the Working Group on Indigenous Populations of the Sub-Commission on Prevention of Discrimination and Protection of Minorities to complete the drafting of a declaration on the rights of indigenous people at its eleventh session.

29. The World Conference on Human Rights recommends that the Commission on Human Rights consider the renewal and updating of the mandate of the Working Group on Indigenous Populations upon completion of the drafting of a declaration on the rights of indigenous people.

30. The World Conference on Human Rights also recommends that advisory services and technical assistance programmes within the United Nations system respond positively to requests by States for assistance which would be of direct benefit to indigenous people. The World Conference on Human Rights further recommends that adequate human and financial resources be made available to the Centre for Human Rights within the overall framework of strengthening the Centre's activities as envisaged by this document.

31. The World Conference on Human Rights urges States to ensure the full and free participation of indigenous people in all aspects of society, in particular in matters of concern to them.

32. The World Conference on Human Rights recommends that the

General Assembly proclaim an international decade of the world's indigenous people, to begin from January 1994, including action-orientated programmes, to be decided upon in partnership with indigenous people. An appropriate voluntary trust fund should be set up for this purpose. In the framework of such a decade, the establishment of a permanent forum for indigenous people in the United Nations system should be considered.

Migrant workers

33. The World Conference on Human Rights urges all States to guarantee the protection of the human rights of all migrant workers and their families.

34. The World Conference on Human Rights considers that the creation of conditions to foster greater harmony and tolerance between migrant workers and the rest of the society of the State in which they reside is of particular importance.

35. The World Conference on Human Rights invites States to consider the possibility of signing and ratifying, at the earliest possible time, the International Convention on the Rights of All Migrant Workers and Members of Their Families.

3. THE EQUAL STATUS AND HUMAN RIGHTS OF WOMEN

36. The World Conference on Human Rights urges the full and equal enjoyment by women of all human rights and that this be a priority for Governments and for the United Nations. The World Conference on Human Rights also underlines the importance of the integration and full participation of women as both agents and beneficiaries in the development process, and reiterates the objectives established on global action for women towards sustainable and equitable development set forth in the Rio Declaration on Environment and Development and chapter 24 of Agenda 21, adopted by the United Nations Conference on Environment and Development (Rio de Janeiro, Brazil, 3–14 June 1992).

37. The equal status of women and the human rights of women should be integrated into the mainstream of United Nations system-wide activity. These issues should be regularly and systematically addressed throughout

relevant United Nations bodies and mechanisms. In particular, steps should be taken to increase cooperation and promote further integration of objectives and goals between the Commission on the Status of Women, the Commission on Human Rights, the Committee for the Elimination of Discrimination against Women, the United Nations Development Fund for Women, the United Nations Development Programme and other United Nations agencies. In this context, cooperation and coordination should be strengthened between the Centre for Human Rights and the Division for the Advancement of Women.

38. In particular, the World Conference on Human Rights stresses the importance of working towards the elimination of violence against women in public and private life, the elimination of all forms of sexual harassment, exploitation and trafficking in women, the elimination of gender bias in the administration of justice and the eradication of any conflicts which may arise between the rights of women and the harmful effects of certain traditional or customary practices, cultural prejudices and religious extremism. The World Conference on Human Rights calls upon the General Assembly to adopt the draft declaration on violence against women and urges States to combat violence against women in accordance with its provisions. Violations of the human rights of women in situations of armed conflict are violations of the fundamental principles of international human rights and humanitarian law. All violations of this kind, including in particular murder, systematic rape, sexual slavery, and forced pregnancy, require a particularly effective response.

39. The World Conference on Human Rights urges the eradication of all forms of discrimination against women, both hidden and overt. The United Nations should encourage the goal of universal ratification by all States of the Convention on the Elimination of All Forms of Discrimination against Women by the year 2000. Ways and means of addressing the particularly large number of reservations to the Convention should be encouraged. *Inter alia,* the Committee on the Elimination of Discrimination against Women should continue its review of reservations to the Convention. States are urged to withdraw reservations that are contrary to the object and purpose of the Convention or which are otherwise incompatible with international treaty law.

40. Treaty monitoring bodies should disseminate necessary informa-

tion to enable women to make more effective use of existing implementation procedures in their pursuits of full and equal enjoyment of human rights and non-discrimination. New procedures should also be adopted to strengthen implementation of the commitment to women's equality and the human rights of women. The Commission on the Status of Women and the Committee on the Elimination of Discrimination against Women should quickly examine the possibility of introducing the right of petition through the preparation of an optional protocol to the Convention on the Elimination of All Forms of Discrimination against Women. The World Conference on Human Rights welcomes the decision of the Commission on Human Rights to consider the appointment of a special rapporteur on violence against women at its fiftieth session.

41. The World Conference on Human Rights recognizes the importance of the enjoyment by women of the highest standard of physical and mental health throughout their life span. In the context of the World Conference on Women and the Convention on the Elimination of All Forms of Discrimination against Women, as well as the Proclamation of Tehran of 1968, the World Conference on Human Rights reaffirms, on the basis of equality between women and men, a woman's right to accessible and adequate health care and the widest range of family planning services, as well as equal access to education at all levels.

42. Treaty monitoring bodies should include the status of women and the human rights of women in their deliberations and findings, making use of gender-specific data. States should be encouraged to supply information on the situation of women *de jure* and de facto in their reports to treaty monitoring bodies. The World Conference on Human Rights notes with satisfaction that the Commission on Human Rights adopted at its forty-ninth session resolution 1993/46 of 8 March 1993 stating that rapporteurs and working groups in the field of human rights should also be encouraged to do so. Steps should also be taken by the Division for the Advancement of Women in cooperation with other United Nations bodies, specifically the Centre for Human Rights, to ensure that the human rights activities of the United Nations regularly address violations of women's human rights, including gender-specific abuses. Training for United Nations human rights and humanitarian relief personnel to assist them to recognize and deal with human rights abuses particular

to women and to carry out their work without gender bias should be encouraged.

43. The World Conference on Human Rights urges Governments and regional and international organizations to facilitate the access of women to decision-making posts and their greater participation in the decision-making process. It encourages further steps within the United Nations Secretariat to appoint and promote women staff members in accordance with the Charter of the United Nations, and encourages other principal and subsidiary organs of the United Nations to guarantee the participation of women under conditions of equality.

44. The World Conference on Human Rights welcomes the World Conference on Women to be held in Beijing in 1995 and urges that human rights of women should play an important role in its deliberations, in accordance with the priority themes of the World Conference on Women of equality, development and peace.

4. THE RIGHTS OF THE CHILD

45. The World Conference on Human Rights reiterates the principle of "First Call for Children" and, in this respect, underlines the importance of major national and international efforts, especially those of the United Nations Children's Fund, for promoting respect for the rights of the child to survival, protection, development and participation.

46. Measures should be taken to achieve universal ratification of the Convention on the Rights of the Child by 1995 and the universal signing of the World Declaration on the Survival, Protection and Development of Children and Plan of Action adopted by the World Summit for Children, as well as their effective implementation. The World Conference on Human Rights urges States to withdraw reservations to the Convention on the Rights of the Child contrary to the object and purpose of the Convention or otherwise contrary to international treaty law.

47. The World Conference on Human Rights urges all nations to undertake measures to the maximum extent of their available resources, with the support of international cooperation, to achieve the goals in the World Summit Plan of Action. The Conference calls on States to integrate the Convention on the Rights of the Child into their national action

plans. By means of these national action plans and through international efforts, particular priority should be placed on reducing infant and maternal mortality rates, reducing malnutrition and illiteracy rates and providing access to safe drinking water and to basic education. Whenever so called for, national plans of action should be devised to combat devastating emergencies resulting from natural disasters and armed conflicts and the equally grave problem of children in extreme poverty.

48. The World Conference on Human Rights urges all States, with the support of international cooperation, to address the acute problem of children under especially difficult circumstances. Exploitation and abuse of children should be actively combated, including by addressing their root causes. Effective measures are required against female infanticide, harmful child labour, sale of children and organs, child prostitution, child pornography, as well as other forms of sexual abuse.

49. The World Conference on Human Rights supports all measures by the United Nations and its specialized agencies to ensure the effective protection and promotion of human rights of the girl child. The World Conference on Human Rights urges States to repeal existing laws and regulations and remove customs and practices which discriminate against and cause harm to the girl child.

50. The World Conference on Human Rights strongly supports the proposal that the Secretary-General initiate a study into means of improving the protection of children in armed conflicts. Humanitarian norms should be implemented and measures taken in order to protect and facilitate assistance to children in war zones. Measures should include protection for children against indiscriminate use of all weapons of war, especially anti-personnel mines. The need for aftercare and rehabilitation of children traumatized by war must be addressed urgently. The Conference calls on the Committee on the Rights of the Child to study the question of raising the minimum age of recruitment into armed forces.

51. The World Conference on Human Rights recommends that matters relating to human rights and the situation of children be regularly reviewed and monitored by all relevant organs and mechanisms of the United Nations system and by the supervisory bodies of the specialized agencies in accordance with their mandates.

52. The World Conference on Human Rights recognizes the important

role played by non-governmental organizations in the effective implementation of all human rights instruments and, in particular, the Convention on the Rights of the Child.

53. The World Conference on Human Rights recommends that the Committee on the Rights of the Child, with the assistance of the Centre for Human Rights, be enabled expeditiously and effectively to meet its mandate, especially in view of the unprecedented extent of ratification and subsequent submission of country reports.

5. FREEDOM FROM TORTURE

54. The World Conference of Human Rights welcomes the ratification by many Member States of the Convention against Torture and Other Cruel, Inhuman or Degrading Treatment or Punishment and encourages its speedy ratification by all other Member States.

55. The World Conference on Human Rights emphasizes that one of the most atrocious violations against human dignity is the act of torture, the result of which destroys the dignity and impairs the capability of victims to continue their lives and their activities.

56. The World Conference on Human Rights reaffirms that under human rights law and international humanitarian law, freedom from torture is a right which must be protected under all circumstances, including in times of internal or international disturbance or armed conflicts.

57. The World Conference on Human Rights therefore urges all States to put an immediate end to the practice of torture and eradicate this evil forever through full implementation of the Universal Declaration of Human Rights as well as the relevant conventions and, where necessary, strengthening of existing mechanisms. The World Conference on Human Rights calls on all States to cooperate fully with the Special Rapporteur on the question of torture in the fulfilment of his mandate.

58. Special attention should be given to ensure universal respect for, and effective implementation of, the Principles of Medical Ethics relevant to the Role of Health Personnel, particularly Physicians, in the Protection of Prisoners and Detainees against Torture and other Cruel, Inhuman or Degrading Treatment or Punishment adopted by the General Assembly of the United Nations.

59. The World Conference on Human Rights stresses the importance of further concrete action within the framework of the United Nations with the view to providing assistance to victims of torture and ensure more effective remedies for their physical, psychological and social rehabilitation. Providing the necessary resources for this purpose should be given high priority, *inter alia,* by additional contributions to the United Nations Voluntary Fund for the Victims of Torture.

60. States should abrogate legislation leading to impunity for those responsible for grave violations of human rights such as torture and prosecute such violations, thereby providing a firm basis for the rule of law.

61. The World Conference on Human Rights reaffirms that efforts to eradicate torture should, first and foremost, be concentrated on prevention and, therefore, calls for the early adoption of an optional protocol to the Convention against Torture and Other Cruel, Inhuman and Degrading Treatment or Punishment, which is intended to establish a preventive system of regular visits to places of detention.

Enforced disappearances

62. The World Conference on Human Rights, welcoming the adoption by the General Assembly of the Declaration on the Protection of All Persons from Enforced Disappearance, calls upon all States to take effective legislative, administrative, judicial or other measures to prevent, terminate and punish acts of enforced disappearances. The World Conference on Human Rights reaffirms that it is the duty of all States, under any circumstances, to make investigations whenever there is reason to believe that an enforced disappearance has taken place on a territory under their jurisdiction and, if allegations are confirmed, to prosecute its perpetrators.

6. THE RIGHTS OF THE DISABLED PERSON

63. The World Conference on Human Rights reaffirms that all human rights and fundamental freedoms are universal and thus unreservedly include persons with disabilities. Every person is born equal and has the same rights to life and welfare, education and work, living independently and active participation in all aspects of society. Any direct discrimination or other negative discriminatory treatment of a disabled person is

therefore a violation of his or her rights. The World Conference on Human Rights calls on Governments, where necessary, to adopt or adjust legislation to assure access to these and other rights for disabled persons.

64. The place of disabled persons is everywhere. Persons with disabilities should be guaranteed equal opportunity through the elimination of all socially determined barriers, be they physical, financial, social or psychological, which exclude or restrict full participation in society.

65. Recalling the World Programme of Action concerning Disabled Persons, adopted by the General Assembly at its thirty-seventh session, the World Conference on Human Rights calls upon the General Assembly and the Economic and Social Council to adopt the draft standard rules on the equalization of opportunities for persons with disabilities, at their meetings in 1993.

C. COOPERATION, DEVELOPMENT AND STRENGTHENING OF HUMAN RIGHTS

66. The World Conference on Human Rights recommends that priority be given to national and international action to promote democracy, development and human rights.

67. Special emphasis should be given to measures to assist in the strengthening and building of institutions relating to human rights, strengthening of a pluralistic civil society and the protection of groups which have been rendered vulnerable. In this context, assistance provided upon the request of Governments for the conduct of free and fair elections, including assistance in the human rights aspects of elections and public information about elections, is of particular importance. Equally important is the assistance to be given to the strengthening of the rule of law, the promotion of freedom of expression and the administration of justice, and to the real and effective participation of the people in the decision-making processes.

68. The World Conference on Human Rights stresses the need for the implementation of strengthened advisory services and technical assistance activities by the Centre for Human Rights. The Centre should make available to States upon request assistance on specific human rights issues, including the preparation of reports under human rights treaties as well as

for the implementation of coherent and comprehensive plans of action for the promotion and protection of human rights. Strengthening the institutions of human rights and democracy, the legal protection of human rights, training of officials and others, broad-based education and public information aimed at promoting respect for human rights should all be available as components of these programmes.

69. The World Conference on Human Rights strongly recommends that a comprehensive programme be established within the United Nations in order to help States in the task of building and strengthening adequate national structures which have a direct impact on the overall observance of human rights and the maintenance of the rule of law. Such a programme, to be coordinated by the Centre for Human Rights, should be able to provide, upon the request of the interested Government, technical and financial assistance to national projects in reforming penal and correctional establishments, education and training of lawyers, judges and security forces in human rights, and any other sphere of activity relevant to the good functioning of the rule of law. That programme should make available to States assistance for the implementation of plans of action for the promotion and protection of human rights.

70. The World Conference on Human Rights requests the Secretary-General of the United Nations to submit proposals to the United Nations General Assembly, containing alternatives for the establishment, structure, operational modalities and funding of the proposed programme.

71. The World Conference on Human Rights recommends that each State consider the desirability of drawing up a national action plan identifying steps whereby that State would improve the promotion and protection of human rights.

72. The World Conference on Human Rights reaffirms that the universal and inalienable right to development, as established in the Declaration on the Right to Development, must be implemented and realized. In this context, the World Conference on Human Rights welcomes the appointment by the Commission on Human Rights of a thematic working group on the right to development and urges that the Working Group, in consultation and cooperation with other organs and agencies of the United Nations system, promptly formulate, for early consideration by the United Nations General Assembly, comprehensive and effective

measures to eliminate obstacles to the implementation and realization of the Declaration on the Right to Development and recommending ways and means towards the realization of the right to development by all States.

73. The World Conference on Human Rights recommends that non-governmental and other grass-roots organizations active in development and/or human rights should be enabled to play a major role on the national and international levels in the debate, activities and implementation relating to the right to development and, in cooperation with Governments, in all relevant aspects of development cooperation.

74. The World Conference on Human Rights appeals to Governments, competent agencies and institutions to increase considerably the resources devoted to building well-functioning legal systems able to protect human rights, and to national institutions working in this area. Actors in the field of development cooperation should bear in mind the mutually reinforcing interrelationship between development, democracy and human rights. Cooperation should be based on dialogue and transparency. The World Conference on Human Rights also calls for the establishment of comprehensive programmes, including resource banks of information and personnel with expertise relating to the strengthening of the rule of law and of democratic institutions.

75. The World Conference on Human Rights encourages the Commission on Human Rights, in cooperation with the Committee on Economic, Social and Cultural Rights, to continue the examination of optional protocols to the International Covenant on Economic, Social and Cultural Rights.

76. The World Conference on Human Rights recommends that more resources be made available for the strengthening or the establishment of regional arrangements for the promotion and protection of human rights under the programmes of advisory services and technical assistance of the Centre for Human Rights. States are encouraged to request assistance for such purposes as regional and subregional workshops, seminars and information exchanges designed to strengthen regional arrangements for the promotion and protection of human rights in accord with universal human rights standards as contained in international human rights instruments.

77. The World Conference on Human Rights supports all measures by the United Nations and its relevant specialized agencies to ensure the effective promotion and protection of trade union rights, as stipulated in the International Covenant on Economic, Social and Cultural Rights and other relevant international instruments. It calls on all States to abide fully by their obligations in this regard contained in international instruments.

D. HUMAN RIGHTS EDUCATION

78. The World Conference on Human Rights considers human rights education, training and public information essential for the promotion and achievement of stable and harmonious relations among communities and for fostering mutual understanding, tolerance and peace.

79. States should strive to eradicate illiteracy and should direct education towards the full development of the human personality and to the strengthening of respect for human rights and fundamental freedoms. The World Conference on Human Rights calls on all States and institutions to include human rights, humanitarian law, democracy and rule of law as subjects in the curricula of all learning institutions in formal and non-formal settings.

80. Human rights education should include peace, democracy, development and social justice, as set forth in international and regional human rights instruments, in order to achieve common understanding and awareness with a view to strengthening universal commitment to human rights.

81. Taking into account the World Plan of Action on Education for Human Rights and Democracy, adopted in March 1993 by the International Congress on Education for Human Rights and Democracy of the United Nations Educational, Scientific and Cultural Organization, and other human rights instruments, the World Conference on Human Rights recommends that States develop specific programmes and strategies for ensuring the widest human rights education and the dissemination of public information, taking particular account of the human rights needs of women.

82. Governments, with the assistance of intergovernmental organizations, national institutions and non-governmental organizations, should

promote an increased awareness of human rights and mutual tolerance. The World Conference on Human Rights underlines the importance of strengthening the World Public Information Campaign for Human Rights carried out by the United Nations. They should initiate and support education in human rights and undertake effective dissemination of public information in this field. The advisory services and technical assistance programmes of the United Nations system should be able to respond immediately to requests from States for educational and training activities in the field of human rights as well as for special education concerning standards as contained in international human rights instruments and in humanitarian law and their application to special groups such as military forces, law enforcement personnel, policy and the health profession. The proclamation of a United Nations decade for human rights education in order to promote, encourage and focus these educational activities should be considered.

E. IMPLEMENTATION AND MONITORING METHODS

83. The World Conference on Human Rights urges Governments to incorporate standards as contained in international human rights instruments in domestic legislation and to strengthen national structures, institutions and organs of society which play a role in promoting and safeguarding human rights.

84. The World Conference on Human Rights recommends the strengthening of United Nations activities and programmes to meet requests for assistance by States which want to establish or strengthen their own national institutions for the promotion and protection of human rights.

85. The World Conference on Human Rights also encourages the strengthening of cooperation between national institutions for the promotion and protection of human rights, particularly through exchanges of information and experience, as well as cooperation with regional organizations and the United Nations.

86. The World Conference on Human Rights strongly recommends in this regard that representatives of national institutions for the promotion

and protection of human rights convene periodic meetings under the auspices of the Centre for Human Rights to examine ways and means of improving their mechanisms and sharing experiences.

87. The World Conference on Human Rights recommends to the human rights treaty bodies, to the meetings of chairpersons of the treaty bodies and to the meetings of States parties that they continue to take steps aimed at coordinating the multiple reporting requirements and guidelines for preparing State reports under the respective human rights conventions and study the suggestion that the submission of one overall report on treaty obligations undertaken by each State would make these procedures more effective and increase their impact.

88. The World Conference on Human Rights recommends that the States parties to international human rights instruments, the General Assembly and the Economic and Social Council should consider studying the existing human rights treaty bodies and the various thematic mechanisms and procedures with a view to promoting greater efficiency and effectiveness through better coordination of the various bodies, mechanisms and procedures, taking into account the need to avoid unnecessary duplication and overlapping of their mandates and tasks.

89. The World Conference on Human Rights recommends continued work on the improvement of the functioning, including the monitoring tasks, of the treaty bodies, taking into account multiple proposals made in this respect, in particular those made by the treaty bodies themselves and by the meetings of the chairpersons of the treaty bodies. The comprehensive national approach taken by the Committee on the Rights of the Child should also be encouraged.

90. The World Conference on Human Rights recommends that States parties to human rights treaties consider accepting all the available optional communication procedures.

91. The World Conference on Human Rights views with concern the issue of impunity of perpetrators of human rights violations, and supports the efforts of the Commission on Human Rights and the Sub-Commission on Prevention of Discrimination and Protection of Minorities to examine all aspects of the issue.

92. The World Conference on Human Rights recommends that the

Commission on Human Rights examine the possibility for better implementation of existing human rights instruments at the international and regional levels and encourages the International Law Commission to continue its work on an international criminal court.

93. The World Conference on Human Rights appeals to States which have not yet done so to accede to the Geneva Conventions of 12 August 1949 and the Protocols thereto, and to take all appropriate national measures, including legislative ones, for their full implementation.

94. The World Conference on Human Rights recommends the speedy completion and adoption of the draft declaration on the right and responsibility of individuals, groups and organs of society to promote and protect universally recognized human rights and fundamental freedoms.

95. The World Conference on Human Rights underlines the importance of preserving and strengthening the system of special procedures, rapporteurs, representatives, experts and working groups of the Commission on Human Rights and the Sub-Commission on the Prevention of Discrimination and Protection of Minorities, in order to enable them to carry out their mandates in all countries throughout the world, providing them with the necessary human and financial resources. The procedures and mechanisms should be enabled to harmonize and rationalize their work through periodic meetings. All States are asked to cooperate fully with these procedures and mechanisms.

96. The World Conference on Human Rights recommends that the United Nations assume a more active role in the promotion and protection of human rights in ensuring full respect for international humanitarian law in all situations of armed conflict, in accordance with the purposes and principles of the Charter of the United Nations.

97. The World Conference on Human Rights, recognizing the important role of human rights components in specific arrangements concerning some peace-keeping operations by the United Nations, recommends that the Secretary-General take into account the reporting, experience and capabilities of the Centre for Human Rights and human rights mechanisms, in conformity with the Charter of the United Nations.

98. To strengthen the enjoyment of economic, social and cultural rights, additional approaches should be examined, such as a system of indicators to measure progress in the realization of the rights set forth in

the International Covenant on Economic, Social and Cultural Rights. There must be a concerted effort to ensure recognition of economic, social and cultural rights at the national, regional and international levels.

F. FOLLOW-UP TO THE WORLD CONFERENCE ON HUMAN RIGHTS

99. The World Conference on Human Rights recommends that the General Assembly, the Commission on Human Rights and other organs and agencies of the United Nations system related to human rights consider ways and means for the full implementation, without delay, of the recommendations contained in the present Declaration, including the possibility of proclaiming a United Nations decade for human rights. The World Conference on Human Rights further recommends that the Commission on Human Rights annually review the progress towards this end.

100. The World Conference on Human Rights requests the Secretary-General of the United Nations to invite on the occasion of the fiftieth anniversary of the Universal Declaration of Human Rights all States, all organs and agencies of the United Nations system related to human rights, to report to him on the progress made in the implementation of the present Declaration and to submit a report to the General Assembly at its fifty-third session, through the Commission on Human Rights and the Economic and Social Council. Likewise, regional and, as appropriate, national human rights institutions, as well as non-governmental organizations, may present their views to the Secretary-General on the progress made in the implementation of the present Declaration. Special attention should be paid to assessing the progress towards the goal of universal ratification of international human rights treaties and protocols adopted within the framework of the United Nations system.

SOURCES OF INFORMATION ON INTERNATIONAL HUMAN RIGHTS

The proliferation of reports and literature on international human rights has been so immense that one hesitates to point to any one source as being more important than another. The fact is that the cascading information about human rights forms a seamless web. All human rights are universal, interrelated, and indivisible. Some of the most important information on human rights can be found in the following ten sources:

1. When Congress in 1976 mandated the U.S. Department of State to issue an annual report on the state of human rights around the world, the initial annual review was small, hesitant, and incomplete. But the report for 1999 runs to some 2,000 pages in two volumes. It is comprehensive and covers virtually every major aspect of the struggle for human rights in 191 nations. Leaders and followers in the scores of nations that are less than fully free use the annual State Department country reports on human rights practices as their guide. As a result, the United States has set the bar for compliance with internationally recognized human rights standards.

Those who want to learn about the status of human rights anywhere in the world could profitably begin with the current annual *U.S. Department of State's Country Reports on Human Rights Practices*.

2. Any biases or inaccuracies that may exist in the State Department's reports on human rights do not exist in the annual reports on human

rights issued by Amnesty International and Human Rights Watch. These candid documents can be supplemented by the copious reports issued by the Lawyers Committee for Human Rights and the International League for Human Rights. A more academic approach can be found in the twenty volumes of the *Human Rights Quarterly* and in a dozen law reviews devoted to a discussion of international human rights.

3. The amazing but little-known work of the United Nations on human rights is reported in a magisterial work edited by Philip Alston, *The United Nations and Human Rights: A Critical Appraisal* (Oxford University Press, 1995). Here are essays by several experts on the work of the United Nations Commission on Human Rights and the several U.N. committees that monitor compliance with the covenants on human rights. For several years, committees at the United Nations have been assessing the compliance of nations on treaties related to race, torture, and the rights of women and children. The backup material of these several committees constitutes a gold mine for those who desire to learn how highly developed nations and less developed countries try to carry out their commitments to the covenants on human rights that they have ratified.

4. One of the least known but very important nongovernmental organizations is Article 19, based in London. It keeps the world's mind on compliance with Article 19 of the Universal Declaration of Human Rights, which guarantees freedom of the press. Article 19 issues authoritative material on the status of freedom of expression and the press around the world. It is probably no exaggeration to say that freedom of the press is the matrix and the guarantor of all human rights.

5. It is evident that the right to religious freedom is central to everyone who cherishes human rights. The right to worship according to one's conscience is central to every declaration on human rights. For complicated reasons, no covenant on religious freedom has emerged from the United Nations. But declarations and resolutions do exist that are morally binding on nations.

The present status of religious freedom in the world is expressed in a very important work. The main title of the twin volumes on the legal and religious perspectives on human rights is *Religious Human Rights in Global Perspective* (Scholars Press and Kluwer Academie, 1996). The two volumes were produced by an ongoing project of the Carter Center and Emory University.

6. The final statement of the 1993 U.N. World Conference on Human Rights in Vienna makes it clear that economic and political rights are equal and indivisible. But economic rights have always been deemed — at least by the United States — to be less important, or at least less enforceable, than political rights. This "heresy" has been refuted in an excellent book entitled *Basic Rights: Subsistence, Affluence, and U.S. Foreign Policy*, second edition, by Henry Shue (Princeton University Press, 1996). This outstanding explanation of the right to food and basic subsistence has made clear that the nations by ratifying the 1945 Charter of the United Nations and the Universal Declaration of Human Rights along with similar treaties have solemnly pledged to guarantee the right of every individual to adequate nutrition and basic economic equality.

7. On one issue, international law seems to be evolving into a consensus that the death penalty violates customary international law. The classic — even definitive — study on this issue is entitled *The Death Penalty as Cruel Treatment and Torture*, by William A. Schabas, a Canadian academic (Northeastern University Press, 1996).

Schabas is careful and cautious but demonstrates how international law can evolve from the growth of a moral consensus among nations.

A related volume is *The Killing State: Capital Punishment in Law, Politics and Culture*, edited by Austin Sarat (Oxford University Press, 1998).

8. Literature and court rulings on the rights of women have appeared in abundance everywhere in the recent past. It is hard to think of any area of human rights where the development of legal and moral doctrine has been more spectacular. There are a score of legal periodicals on gender and the law, while feminist nongovernmental organizations can claim an escalating influence. Most instructive are the rulings and advisories of the U.N. committee that monitors compliance with the U.N. Convention on the Elimination of All Forms of Discrimination Against Women.

9. The rapid acceptance of the U.N. Covenant on the Rights of the Child illustrates the sensitivity of the conscience of nations to the rights of its most vulnerable citizens. The recent application of the moral principle of equality to children has produced watchdog agencies with increasing

influence. The moral indignation they are proclaiming today may well become the binding law of tomorrow.

10. The philosophical basis of human rights may be the most important aspect of the human rights movement. Many participants in the human rights revolution tend to feel that the presence and preciousness of human rights is a truth that is self-evident.

One thoughtful presentation of the philosophy underlying human rights appeared in a 1983 issue of *Daedalus* (a quarterly published by the American Academy of Arts and Sciences). It discusses the philosophical and religious background of human rights. NOMOS XXIII, the yearbook for the American Society for Political and Legal Philosophy, titled *Human Rights* (New York University Press, 1981), also pays a good deal of thoughtful attention to the future of rights.

INDEX